Descendants of Roger de Coigniers I

First Generation

1. DE COIGNIERS I:Roger (b. 1075) England:Durham **Roger de Coigniers I** was born in 1075 in Durham, England.England:Durham:Darlington:Sockburn He died after 1144 at the age of 69 in Sockburn, Darlington, Durham, England. Roger de Coigneries, to whom the ancestry of the American family has been traced, was born in France, about 1075. To him the Bishop of Durham gave the constableship of Durham.

In 1143, Roger de Conyers (Rogerde Coignieres; Coniers) was supposedly granted, by Bishop William de Sancta Barbara, (In year 1 of his pontificate) a Durham licence to crenellate (Bishopton Castle Hill)

"The family of Coigniers was denominated from their ancient place of residence in the Duchy of Normandy; and one of them having attended the Norman Duke in his victorious expeditions into Eng. was rewarded by the Conqueror with grants and divers lands in Yorkshire, whereupon he settled in this kingdom and became the common ancestor of the several branches of the families of Coigniers, Coniers, Conyers, etc. The Bishop of Durham (who d. 1095) gave to Roger de Coigniers the Constable-ship of the city of Durham. His descendant, Roger de Coigniers was Lord of Howton Coignier and of Sokebourne. Roger de Coigneries emigrated from Navarre, France, to England with William the Conquerer in the eleventh century. The Bishop of Durham gave him the constableship of Durham.

The de Coigneries family was in France with William of Normandy (1028-1087) and was active in its political history.

The original seat of the Conyers family was in Navarre, France, whence was Roger de Coigneries, who immigrated to England and became Constable of Durham about 1087, at the time of the death of William the Conqueror. One of the residences, in Navarre, France, is known as the Chateau de Coigniers. It was occupied in the 16th century. It is also written as Chateuax de Coigniers.

Convers of Horden, Durham, was created Baronet. Sir Humphrey, 8th General, wrote the name Coigners and Sir Christopher, 20th General, wrote the name Conyers. They were Huguenots (followers of John Calvin). In the Massacre on St.Bartholomew's Day, 1572, many Conyers fell victim to the Papist's rape and Pierre Coigniers, attached to the Court of Henry IV, witnessed the assassination of his kingsman, Admiral Coligny, and left with his wife and two infants for Essus County, England. His son married a wealthy lady and their son was created a Baronet by Charles II.

The family motto was: In Deo Solo Confido ("In God Alone I Trust").

Roger de Coigneries, who was born 1075, was a Chieftainin the army of William the Conqueror at the battle of Hastings or Senlac, England. He would fare well after the conquest and receive large estates that formerly belonged to the Saxons who escaped to the lowlands of Scotland as opponents of William of Normandy, who became King of England.

Sources:

1. 'Parishes: Sockburn', A History of the County of York North Riding:
Volume 1 (1914), pp. 449-454
2. Harleian Society, Vol 80, Knights of Edward I , Vol I (London:
1929) p 234
3. Calendar of Fine Rolls, Vol 1, p 403
4. Calendar of Fine Rolls, Vol 1, p 424
5. Chancery: Certificates of Statute Merchant and Statute Staple, C
241/68/74
6. Calendar of Fine Rolls, Vol 1, p 432
7. 'Parishes: Long Newton', A History of the County of Durham: Volume
3 (1928), pp. 299-304
8. Archaeologica Aeliana, Third Series, Vol 6 (Newcastle:1910) p 45

9. John Hodgson, A History of Northumberland, Vol V (Vol 3, Part 1)
(London: 1820) p 53 & 104
10. Archaeologica Aeliana, Third Series, Vol 6(Newcastle: 1910) p 48
11. 45th Annual Report of the Deputy Keeper of the Public Records
(London: 1885) p 175
12. 'Parishes: Ormesby', A History of the County of York North Riding:
Volume 2 (1923), pp. 276-283
13. 45th Annual Report of the Deputy Keeper of the Public Records
(London: 1885) p 183
14. Archaeologica Aeliana, Third Series, Vol 7(Newcastle: 1910) p 59
15. Surtees Society, Vol 30, Testamenta Eboracensia, Part II (Durham:
1855) p 64n
16. Calendar of Patent Rolls, Henry 6, Vol 1, p 28
17. Complete Peerage, Vol 5, p 277
18. Lincolnshire Archives, Yarborough [YARB 16/1/1]

Title: VCH-Yorkshire North Riding, available inwww.british-history.ac.uk
Repository:
Media: Book
Page: see notes under Robert Conyers, d. 1431

Roger de Coigniers I had the following child:

DE COIGNIERS II:Roger (b. 1110)   +2   i.   **Roger de Coigniers II**, born 1110, Sockburn, Darlington,
Durham, EnglandEngland:Durham:Darlington:Sockburn ; died 1166, Hutton Conyers, North Riding
Yorkshire, EnglandEngland:North Riding Yorkshire:Hutton Conyers .

Second Generation

2. DE COIGNIERS II:Roger (b. 1110) England:Durham:Darlington:Sockburn **Roger de Coigniers II** (Roger-1) was born in
1110 in Sockburn, Darlington, Durham, England.England:North Riding Yorkshire:Hutton Conyers He died in 1166 at the
age of 56 in Hutton Conyers, North Riding Yorkshire, England. Roger de Coigniers was Lord Howton Coignier and of
Sokebourn, by the gift of Ranulph de Durham.

Sources:

1. 'Parishes: Sockburn', A History of the County of York North Riding:
Volume 1 (1914), pp. 449-454
2. Harleian Society, Vol 80, Knights of Edward I , Vol I (London:
1929) p 234
3. Calendar of Fine Rolls, Vol 1, p 403
4. Calendar of Fine Rolls, Vol 1, p 424
5. Chancery: Certificates of Statute Merchant and Statute Staple, C
241/68/74
6. Calendar of Fine Rolls, Vol 1, p 432
7. 'Parishes: Long Newton', A History of the County of Durham: Volume

3 (1928), pp. 299-304

8. Archaeologica Aeliana, Third Series, Vol 6 (Newcastle:1910) p 45

9. John Hodgson, A History of Northumberland, Vol V (Vol 3, Part 1) (London: 1820) p 53 & 104

10. Archaeologica Aeliana, Third Series, Vol 6(Newcastle: 1910) p 48

11. 45th Annual Report of the Deputy Keeper of the Public Records (London: 1885) p 175

12. 'Parishes: Ormesby', A History of the County of York North Riding: Volume 2 (1923), pp. 276-283

13. 45th Annual Report of the Deputy Keeper of the Public Records (London: 1885) p 183

14. Archaeologica Aeliana, Third Series, Vol 7(Newcastle: 1910) p 59

15. Surtees Society, Vol 30, Testamenta Eboracensia, Part II (Durham: 1855) p 64n

16. Calendar of Patent Rolls, Henry 6, Vol 1, p 28

17. Complete Peerage, Vol 5, p 277

18. Lincolnshire Archives, Yarborough [YARB 16/1/1]

Title: VCH-Yorkshire North Riding, available inwww.british-history.ac.uk
Repository:
Media: Book
Page: see notes under Robert Conyers, d. 1431

<NO SURNAME>:Maud (b. 1120)
England:Durham:Sockburn **Maud** was born in 1120 in Sockburn, Durham, England.England:Durham:Sockburn She died in 1168 at the age of 48 in Sockburn, Durham, England. Sources:

1. 'Parishes: Sockburn', A History of the County of York North Riding: Volume 1 (1914), pp. 449-454

2. Harleian Society, Vol 80, Knights of Edward I , Vol I(London: 1929) p 234

3. Calendar of Fine Rolls, Vol 1, p 403

4. Calendar of Fine Rolls, Vol 1, p 424

5. Chancery: Certificates of Statute Merchant and Statute Staple, C 241/68/74

6. Calendar of Fine Rolls, Vol 1, p 432

7. 'Parishes: Long Newton', A History of the County of Durham: Volume 3 (1928), pp. 299-304

8. Archaeologica Aeliana, Third Series, Vol 6 (Newcastle:1910) p 45

9. John Hodgson, A History of Northumberland, Vol V (Vol 3, Part 1) (London: 1820) p 53 & 104

10. Archaeologica Aeliana, Third Series, Vol 6(Newcastle: 1910) p 48

11. 45th Annual Report of the Deputy Keeper of the Public Records (London: 1885) p 175

12. 'Parishes: Ormesby', A History of the County of York North Riding: Volume 2 (1923), pp. 276-283

13. 45th Annual Report of the Deputy Keeper of the Public Records (London: 1885) p 183

14. Archaeologica Aeliana, Third Series, Vol 7(Newcastle: 1910) p 59

15. Surtees Society, Vol 30, Testamenta Eboracensia, Part II (Durham: 1855) p 64n

16. Calendar of Patent Rolls, Henry 6, Vol 1, p 28

17. Complete Peerage, Vol 5, p 277

18. Lincolnshire Archives, Yarborough [YARB 16/1/1]

Title: VCH-Yorkshire North Riding, available inwww.british-history.ac.uk
Repository:
Media: Book
Page: see notes under Robert Conyers, d. 1431

Roger de Coigniers II and Maud had the following child:

DE COIGNIERS III:Roger (b. 1140)　　　+3　　i.　　**Roger de Coigniers III**, born 1140, Hutton Conyers, North Riding Yorkshire, EnglandEngland:North Riding Yorkshire:Hutton Conyers ; died 1195, Sockburn, Darlington, Durham, EnglandEngland:Durham:Darlington:Sockburn .

Third Generation

3. DE COIGNIERS III:Roger (b. 1140) England:North Riding Yorkshire:Hutton Conyers **Roger de Coigniers III** (Roger-2, Roger-1) was born in 1140 in Hutton Conyers, North Riding Yorkshire, England.England:Durham:Darlington:Sockburn He died in 1195 at the age of 55 in Sockburn, Darlington, Durham, England. Roger de Coiners, 1134-1174, appears to have spelled the name Conyers and was from Horden, Durham County, in the north of England. He was created Baronet and was probably known as Lord of Bishopton.

Roger de Coniers, 3rd of the name possessed of Howton Coigniers in com. Ebor and of Sokebourne in the County of Durham, said to be one of the Barons of Bishopric. He was Constable of Durham castle.

Sources:

1. 'Parishes: Sockburn', A History of the County of York North Riding:
Volume 1 (1914), pp. 449-454
2. Harleian Society, Vol 80, Knights of Edward I , Vol I (London:
1929) p 234
3. Calendar of Fine Rolls, Vol 1, p 403
4. Calendar of Fine Rolls, Vol 1, p 424
5. Chancery: Certificates of Statute Merchant and Statute Staple, C
241/68/74
6. Calendar of Fine Rolls, Vol 1, p 432
7. 'Parishes: Long Newton', A History of the County of Durham: Volume
3 (1928), pp. 299-304
8. Archaeologica Aeliana, Third Series, Vol 6 (Newcastle:1910) p 45
9. John Hodgson, A History of Northumberland, Vol V (Vol 3, Part 1)
(London: 1820) p 53 & 104
10. Archaeologica Aeliana, Third Series, Vol 6(Newcastle: 1910) p 48
11. 45th Annual Report of the Deputy Keeper of the Public Records
(London: 1885) p 175
12. 'Parishes: Ormesby', A History of the County of York North Riding:
Volume 2 (1923), pp. 276-283
13. 45th Annual Report of the Deputy Keeper of the Public Records
(London: 1885) p 183
14. Archaeologica Aeliana, Third Series, Vol 7(Newcastle: 1910) p 59
15. Surtees Society, Vol 30, Testamenta Eboracensia, Part II (Durham:

1855) p 64n
16. Calendar of Patent Rolls, Henry 6, Vol 1, p 28
17. Complete Peerage, Vol 5, p 277
18. Lincolnshire Archives, Yarborough [YARB 16/1/1]

Title: VCH-Yorkshire North Riding, available inwww.british-history.ac.uk
Repository:
Media: Book
Page: see notes under Robert Conyers, d. 1431

<NO SURNAME>:Basilia (b. 1145)
England:Durham:Darlington:Sockburn **Basilia** was born in 1145 in Sockburn, Darlington, Durham,
England.England:Durham:Darlington:Sockburn She died in 1195 at the age of 50 in Sockburn, Darlington, Durham,
England. Sources:

1. 'Parishes: Sockburn', A History of the County of York North Riding:
Volume 1 (1914), pp. 449-454
2. Harleian Society, Vol 80, Knights of Edward I , Vol I (London:
1929) p 234
3. Calendar of Fine Rolls, Vol 1, p 403
4. Calendar of Fine Rolls, Vol 1, p 424
5. Chancery: Certificates of Statute Merchant and Statute Staple, C
241/68/74
6. Calendar of Fine Rolls, Vol 1, p 432
7. 'Parishes: Long Newton', A History of the County of Durham: Volume
3 (1928), pp. 299-304
8. Archaeologica Aeliana, Third Series, Vol 6 (Newcastle:1910) p 45
9. John Hodgson, A History of Northumberland, Vol V (Vol 3, Part 1)
(London: 1820) p 53 & 104
10. Archaeologica Aeliana, Third Series, Vol 6(Newcastle: 1910) p 48
11. 45th Annual Report of the Deputy Keeper of the Public Records
(London: 1885) p 175
12. 'Parishes: Ormesby', A History of the County of York North Riding:
Volume 2 (1923), pp. 276-283
13. 45th Annual Report of the Deputy Keeper of the Public Records
(London: 1885) p 183
14. Archaeologica Aeliana, Third Series, Vol 7(Newcastle: 1910) p 59
15. Surtees Society, Vol 30, Testamenta Eboracensia, Part II (Durham:
1855) p 64n
16. Calendar of Patent Rolls, Henry 6, Vol 1, p 28
17. Complete Peerage, Vol 5, p 277
18. Lincolnshire Archives, Yarborough [YARB 16/1/1]

Title: VCH-Yorkshire North Riding, available inwww.british-history.ac.uk
Repository:
Media: Book
Page: see notes under Robert Conyers, d. 1431

Roger de Coigniers III and Basilia had the following child:

CONYERS I:Sir Geoffery (b. 1178)　　　+4　　i.　　**Sir Geoffery Conyers I**, born 1178, Sockburn, Darlington, Durham, EnglandEngland:Durham:Darlington:Sockburn ; died 1225, Sockburn, Darlington, Durham, EnglandEngland:Durham:Darlington:Sockburn .

Fourth Generation

4. CONYERS I:Sir Geoffery (b. 1178) England:Durham:Darlington:Sockburn **Sir Geoffery Conyers I** (Roger-3, Roger-2, Roger-1) was born in 1178 in Sockburn, Darlington, Durham, England.England:Durham:Darlington:Sockburn He died in 1225 at the age of 47 in Sockburn, Darlington, Durham, England. The following is reprinted from Genealogical Gleanings in England by Henry F. Waters, A.M., Boston, 1901, published in two volumes by The New England Historic Genealogical Society

Baron of the bishopric of Durham and Lord of Bishopton.

Geoffery "Galfrid" Conyers, Lord of Sockburn and Bishopton, 1213-1238. ,
John Conyers, Sockburn, England.
Sir Humphrey' Conyers, Sockburn, England.
Sir John' Conyers, Sockburn, England.
Roger Conyers, Sockburn, England.
Sir John' Conyers, Sockburn, England; died 1395.
Robert Conyers, Sockburn, England; born 1371; died 1433.
John" Conyers, Hornby, England.
Sir Christopher" Conyers, Hornby, England.
Sir John Conyers, of Hornby Castle; sheriff of the shire;governor of the castle at York; in 1460 joined Richard, Duke of York, against the King.
Sir John" Conyers, of Hornby, England; Knight of the Order of the Garter; died 1490.
Reginald" Conyers, Wakerly, England; died 1514.
Richard" Conyers, Wakerly, England.
Christopher" Conyers, Wakerly, England, baptized 1552.

The History and Antiquities of the County Palatine of Durham, Volume 1
By William Hutchinson

A LIST of the Names of many KNIGHTS of the Bishopric of Durham, between Tyne and Tees, who were at the Battle of Lewes, in the Reign of Henry III.

Sir Ra.Bailiffe (Baliol) de Barnard Caslle
Sir Hugh, his son, de Seliabie
Sir Euil. Bailiffe" (Baliol) de Querrington
Sir Robert Neville de Rabie
Sir Walter Audice (Audrey) de Croxdell
* Sir Robert Hilton de Hilton
Sir Mark Fitch (Marmaduke Fitz-Gef
fray) de Silklworth Sir Robert Bertram de Gretham
Sir William Steeney de Tunstall
Sir William Herrington de Herrington
(Herverton) Sir William Basset de Uffejton
Sir Richard Yreland (Yheland) de Ra
venfholme Sir Hugh Gallon (Gabion) de Tudhouse
(Tudhowe) Sir Ralph Standlaw de Standlaw

Sir Walter Witton de Edgeknowl (Edis knull)
Sir William Heswell de Heswell
Sir John Bradley de Frosterley
•Sir Henry Mosely (Merlay) de Heakeld
(Heafield) Sir William Heyton (Hearon) de Mickel Chilton
Sir John Farnercroft (Farnecroft) de Cockside (de Farnecroft)
Sir Wil. Yreland (Yfreland) de Seaham
Sir John Gilford de Colierley
Sir Roger Eppleden de Eppengdon
Sir Walter Ludworth de Ludworth
Sir John Raington de Sherington (or
Roungton de Monkton
Sir William Fitz-Mondye de Brereton
(or Meundie de Sheorton)
Sir William Karrow de Seaton Karrow,
in parochia de Stranton
* Sir Roger Lumley de Lumley
Sir Jeffrey Park de Blakeston
Sir Adam Fulthorpe de Fulthorpe
Sir Hugh Choppell de Vineyeard
Sir John Egglei'cliffe de Egglescliffe
Sir Ralph Coatham de Coatham
Sir Thomas Aylaliby de Allaby
Sir Henry Rowlee de Elton
Sir Simon Morton de Morton (EalJ Morton)
Sir Randolf Fisliburn de Fithburn
Sir Wil. Monsfort de Blakemarg1.
(per-haps Masters de Brackcnbury)
* Sir Ralph Surtees de Bytonlal (Bitersal alias Dinsdale)
Sir Ralph Middleton de Hatton (de Little
Haughton) * Sir Jeffrey Conyers de Socburne

Sources:

1. 'Parishes: Sockburn', A History of the County of York North Riding:
Volume 1 (1914), pp. 449-454
2. Harleian Society, Vol 80, Knights of Edward I , Vol I (London:
1929) p 234
3. Calendar of Fine Rolls, Vol 1, p 403
4. Calendar of Fine Rolls, Vol 1, p 424
5. Chancery: Certificates of Statute Merchant and Statute Staple, C
241/68/74
6. Calendar of Fine Rolls, Vol 1, p 432
7. 'Parishes: Long Newton', A History of the County of Durham: Volume
3 (1928), pp. 299-304
8. Archaeologica Aeliana, Third Series, Vol 6 (Newcastle:1910) p 45
9. John Hodgson, A History of Northumberland, Vol V (Vol 3, Part 1)
(London: 1820) p 53 & 104
10. Archaeologica Aeliana, Third Series, Vol 6(Newcastle: 1910) p 48
11. 45th Annual Report of the Deputy Keeper of the Public Records
(London: 1885) p 175
12. 'Parishes: Ormesby', A History of the County of York North Riding:
Volume 2 (1923), pp. 276-283
13. 45th Annual Report of the Deputy Keeper of the Public Records

(London: 1885) p 183
14. Archaeologica Aeliana, Third Series, Vol 7(Newcastle: 1910) p 59
15. Surtees Society, Vol 30, Testamenta Eboracensia, Part II (Durham:
1855) p 64n
16. Calendar of Patent Rolls, Henry 6, Vol 1, p 28
17. Complete Peerage, Vol 5, p 277
18. Lincolnshire Archives, Yarborough [YARB 16/1/1]

Title: VCH-Yorkshire North Riding, available inwww.british-history.ac.uk
Repository:
Media: Book
Page: see notes under Robert Conyers, d. 1431

DE YEALAND:Adam (b. 1160)
DE YEALAND:Alicia (b. 1190) England:Lancashire:Lancaster:Yealand Conyers **Alicia de Yealand**, daughter of Adam de Yealand, was born in 1190 in Yealand Conyers, Lancaster, Lancashire, England. Sources:

1. 'Parishes: Sockburn', A History of the County of York North Riding:
Volume 1 (1914), pp. 449-454
2. Harleian Society, Vol 80, Knights of Edward I , Vol I (London:
1929) p 234
3. Calendar of Fine Rolls, Vol 1, p 403
4. Calendar of Fine Rolls, Vol 1, p 424
5. Chancery: Certificates of Statute Merchant and Statute Staple, C
241/68/74
6. Calendar of Fine Rolls, Vol 1, p 432
7. 'Parishes: Long Newton', A History of the County of Durham: Volume
3 (1928), pp. 299-304
8. Archaeologica Aeliana, Third Series, Vol 6 (Newcastle:1910) p 45
9. John Hodgson, A History of Northumberland, Vol V (Vol 3, Part 1)
(London: 1820) p 53 & 104
10. Archaeologica Aeliana, Third Series, Vol 6(Newcastle: 1910) p 48
11. 45th Annual Report of the Deputy Keeper of the Public Records
(London: 1885) p 175
12. 'Parishes: Ormesby', A History of the County of York North Riding:
Volume 2 (1923), pp. 276-283
13. 45th Annual Report of the Deputy Keeper of the Public Records
(London: 1885) p 183
14. Archaeologica Aeliana, Third Series, Vol 7(Newcastle: 1910) p 59
15. Surtees Society, Vol 30, Testamenta Eboracensia, Part II (Durham:
1855) p 64n
16. Calendar of Patent Rolls, Henry 6, Vol 1, p 28
17. Complete Peerage, Vol 5, p 277
18. Lincolnshire Archives, Yarborough [YARB 16/1/1]

Title: VCH-Yorkshire North Riding, available inwww.british-history.ac.uk
Repository:
Media: Book
Page: see notes under Robert Conyers, d. 1431

Sir Geoffery Conyers I and Alicia de Yealand had the following child:

CONYERS I:Sir Humphrey (b. 1215)   +5   i.   **Sir Humphrey Conyers I**, born 1215,
 Sockburn,Durhamshire,EnglandEngland:Durhamshire:Sockburn ; died 1283,
 Sockburn,Durhamshire,EnglandEngland:Durhamshire:Sockburn .

Fifth Generation

5. CONYERS I:Sir Humphrey (b. 1215) England:Durhamshire:Sockburn **Sir Humphrey Conyers I** (Sir Geoffery-4, Roger-3, Roger-2, Roger-1) was born in 1215 in Sockburn,Durhamshire,England.England:Durhamshire:Sockburn He died in 1283 at the age of 68 in Sockburn,Durhamshire,England. Sir Humphrey Conyers

M, #15087, d. after 1283
Father   Sir Sir Geoffery Conyers, Knight of Sockburne
   Sir Humphrey Conyers Gave lands to Rievaulx Abbey. He died after 1283.
Family
Child
Sir John Conyers+ d. 1299

Sources:

[S3957] Unknown author, Burke's Peerage, 1938, p. 2639; Burke's Dormant and Extinct Baronetcies, p. 127.

The following is reprinted from Genealogical Gleanings in England by Henry F. Waters, A.M., Boston, 1901, published in two volumes by The New England Historic Genealogical Society

Baron of the bishopric of Durham and Lord of Bishopton.

Geoffery "Galfrid" Conyers, Lord of Sockburn and Bishopton,1213-1238. ,
John Conyers, Sockburn, England.
Sir Humphrey' Conyers, Sockburn, England.
Sir John' Conyers, Sockburn, England.
Roger Conyers, Sockburn, England.
Sir John' Conyers, Sockburn, England; died 1395.
Robert Conyers, Sockburn, England; born 1371; died 1433.
John" Conyers, Hornby, England.
Sir Christopher" Conyers, Hornby, England.
Sir John Conyers, of Hornby Castle; sheriff of the shire;governor of the castle at York; in 1460 joined Richard, Duke of York, against the King.
Sir John" Conyers, of Hornby, England; Knight of the Order of the Garter; died 1490.
Reginald" Conyers, Wakerly, England; died 1514.
Richard" Conyers, Wakerly, England.
Christopher" Conyers, Wakerly, England, baptized 1552.

Sir Humphrey Conyers
Birth: 1215 Sockburn, Durhamshire, England

Death: 1283 Sockburn, Durhamshire,England

Succeeded his brother John as lord of Sockburn, and Girsby

Spouse: Pernel

Children: John Conyers (- <1304)
    Sir Roger Conyers (- 1298)

Sources:

1. 'Parishes: Sockburn', A History of the County of York North Riding:
Volume 1 (1914), pp. 449-454
2. Harleian Society, Vol 80, Knights of Edward I , Vol I (London:
1929) p 234
3. Calendar of Fine Rolls, Vol 1, p 403
4. Calendar of Fine Rolls, Vol 1, p 424
5. Chancery: Certificates of Statute Merchant and Statute Staple, C
241/68/74
6. Calendar of Fine Rolls, Vol 1, p 432
7. 'Parishes: Long Newton', A History of the County of Durham: Volume
3 (1928), pp. 299-304
8. Archaeologica Aeliana, Third Series, Vol 6 (Newcastle:1910) p 45
9. John Hodgson, A History of Northumberland, Vol V (Vol 3, Part 1)
(London: 1820) p 53 & 104
10. Archaeologica Aeliana, Third Series, Vol 6(Newcastle: 1910) p 48
11. 45th Annual Report of the Deputy Keeper of the Public Records
(London: 1885) p 175
12. 'Parishes: Ormesby', A History of the County of York North Riding:
Volume 2 (1923), pp. 276-283
13. 45th Annual Report of the Deputy Keeper of the Public Records
(London: 1885) p 183
14. Archaeologica Aeliana, Third Series, Vol 7(Newcastle: 1910) p 59
15. Surtees Society, Vol 30, Testamenta Eboracensia, Part II (Durham:
1855) p 64n
16. Calendar of Patent Rolls, Henry 6, Vol 1, p 28
17. Complete Peerage, Vol 5, p 277
18. Lincolnshire Archives, Yarborough [YARB 16/1/1]

<NO SURNAME>:Pernel (b. 1220)
England **Pernel** was born in 1220 in England.England She died in 1283 at the age of 63 in England. Pernel

BIRTH 1220 •England
DEATH 1283 .England

Sources:

1. 'Parishes: Sockburn', A History of the County of York North Riding:
Volume 1 (1914), pp. 449-454
2. Harleian Society, Vol 80, Knights of Edward I , Vol I (London:
1929) p 234
3. Calendar of Fine Rolls, Vol 1, p 403
4. Calendar of Fine Rolls, Vol 1, p 424
5. Chancery: Certificates of Statute Merchant and Statute Staple, C

241/68/74

6. Calendar of Fine Rolls, Vol 1, p 432

7. 'Parishes: Long Newton', A History of the County of Durham: Volume 3 (1928), pp. 299-304

8. Archaeologica Aeliana, Third Series, Vol 6 (Newcastle:1910) p 45

9. John Hodgson, A History of Northumberland, Vol V (Vol 3, Part 1) (London: 1820) p 53 & 104

10. Archaeologica Aeliana, Third Series, Vol 6(Newcastle: 1910) p 48

11. 45th Annual Report of the Deputy Keeper of the Public Records (London: 1885) p 175

12. 'Parishes: Ormesby', A History of the County of York North Riding: Volume 2 (1923), pp. 276-283

13. 45th Annual Report of the Deputy Keeper of the Public Records (London: 1885) p 183

14. Archaeologica Aeliana, Third Series, Vol 7(Newcastle: 1910) p 59

15. Surtees Society, Vol 30, Testamenta Eboracensia, Part II (Durham: 1855) p 64n

16. Calendar of Patent Rolls, Henry 6, Vol 1, p 28

17. Complete Peerage, Vol 5, p 277

18. Lincolnshire Archives, Yarborough [YARB 16/1/1]

Sir Humphrey Conyers I and Pernel had the following child:

CONYERS I:Sir John (b. 1250)   +6   i.   **Sir John Conyers I**, born 1250, Sockburn Hall,Sockburn,Durhamshire,EnglandEngland:Durhamshire:Sockburn:Sockburn Hall ; died 1299, Conyers Manor,Hutton Conyers,Yorkshire,EnglandEngland:Yorkshire:Hutton Conyers:Conyers Manor .

Sixth Generation

6. CONYERS I:Sir John (b. 1250) England:Durhamshire:Sockburn:Sockburn Hall **Sir John Conyers I** (Sir Humphrey-5, Sir Geoffery-4, Roger-3, Roger-2, Roger-1) was born in 1250 in Sockburn Hall,Sockburn,Durhamshire,England.England:Yorkshire:Hutton Conyers:Conyers Manor He died in 1299 at the age of 49 in Conyers Manor,Hutton Conyers,Yorkshire,England. Sir John Conyers

M, #15086, d. 1299
Father   Sir Humphrey Conyers d. a 1221
    Sir John Conyers married Scolastica de Cotham, daughter of Ralph de Cotam. Sir John Conyers died in 1299.
Family
Scolastica de Cotham
Children
Roger de Conyers, Knight of Sockburne+ d. 1323
Jane Conyers+ b. c 1265

Sources:

[S3957] Unknown author, Burke's Peerage, 1938, p. 2639;Burke's Dormant and Extinct Baronetcies, p. 127.

The following is reprinted from Genealogical Gleanings in England by Henry F. Waters, A.M., Boston, 1901, published in two volumes by The New England Historic Genealogical Society

Baron of the bishopric of Durham and Lord of Bishopton.

Geoffery "Galfrid" Conyers, Lord of Sockburn and Bishopton, 1213-1238. ,
John Conyers, Sockburn, England.
Sir Humphrey' Conyers, Sockburn, England.
Sir John' Conyers, Sockburn, England.
Roger Conyers, Sockburn, England.
Sir John' Conyers, Sockburn, England; died 1395.
Robert Conyers, Sockburn, England; born 1371; died 1433.
John" Conyers, Hornby, England.
Sir Christopher" Conyers, Hornby, England.
Sir John Conyers, of Hornby Castle; sheriff of the shire; governor of the castle at York; in 1460 joined Richard, Duke of York, against the King.
Sir John" Conyers, of Hornby, England; Knight of the Order of the Garter; died 1490.
Reginald" Conyers, Wakerly, England; died 1514.
Richard" Conyers, Wakerly, England.
Christopher" Conyers, Wakerly, England, baptized 1552.

Sir John Conyers

Birth: 1250
Death: 1299
Father: Humphrey Conyers
Mother: Pernel

Sir Roger de Conyers, knight [2]
protection for 4 years going to Holy Land, 10 Feb 1271[2]
Holding 1 knight's fee in Northumberland [2]
Distrained to receive knighthood 1278 [2]
Quittance of eyre, Northumberland 27 Dec 1278 [2]
Safe conduct for him, sent by King to Rothelan, 28 Apr 1279 [2]
Protection till Michaelmas 31 Mar 1282 [2]

He and his wife dead at the date of his father-in-law, Ralph de
Cotum's ipm, when Ralph's heirs were his daughter Alice and John
Conyers, son of his daughter Scolastica [4]

Spouse: Scolastica de Cotum
Death: bef. 14 Sep 1298 (date of writ for father's ipm) [3]
Father: Sir Ralph de Cotum
Mother: Christian

Sources:

1. 'Parishes: Sockburn', A History of the County of York North Riding:
Volume 1 (1914), pp. 449-454
2. Harleian Society, Vol 80, Knights of Edward I , Vol I (London:

1929) p 234

3. Calendar of Fine Rolls, Vol 1, p 403

4. Calendar of Fine Rolls, Vol 1, p 424

5. Chancery: Certificates of Statute Merchant and Statute Staple, C 241/68/74

6. Calendar of Fine Rolls, Vol 1, p 432

7. 'Parishes: Long Newton', A History of the County of Durham: Volume 3 (1928), pp. 299-304

8. Archaeologica Aeliana, Third Series, Vol 6 (Newcastle:1910) p 45

9. John Hodgson, A History of Northumberland, Vol V (Vol 3, Part 1) (London: 1820) p 53 & 104

10. Archaeologica Aeliana, Third Series, Vol 6 (Newcastle: 1910) p 48

11. 45th Annual Report of the Deputy Keeper of the Public Records (London: 1885) p 175

12. 'Parishes: Ormesby', A History of the County of York North Riding: Volume 2 (1923), pp. 276-283

13. 45th Annual Report of the Deputy Keeper of the Public Records (London: 1885) p 183

14. Archaeologica Aeliana, Third Series, Vol 7 (Newcastle:1910) p 59

15. Surtees Society, Vol 30, Testamenta Eboracensia, Part II (Durham: 1855) p 64n

16. Calendar of Patent Rolls, Henry 6, Vol 1, p 28

17. Complete Peerage, Vol 5, p 277

18. Lincolnshire Archives, Yarborough [YARB 16/1/1]

Sir John Conyers I, Lord of Sockburn
BIRTH   1250 • Sockburn Hall,Sockburn,Durhamshire,England
DEATH   1299 • Conyers Manor,Hutton Conyers,Yorkshire,England

Sockburn is a village and civil parish to the south of Darlington in County Durham, England. It is situated at the apex of a meander of the River Tees, known locally as the Sockburn Peninsula. Today, all that remains of the village is an early nineteenth-century mansion, a ruined church and a farmhouse built in the late eighteenth century.
Sockburn was once a larger parish. The ancient parish included the townships of Sockburn in County Durham, and Girsby and Over Dinsdale, both on the opposite bank of the River Tees in the North Riding of Yorkshire.[1] In 1866 Girsby and Over Dinsdale became separate civil parishes.[2] By 1961 the parish had a population of only 32.[3] At the 2011 Census the population of the civil Parish remained less than 100. Details could be found in the parish of Neasham.
In antiquity, Higbald, Bishop of Lindisfarne was crownedat Sockburn in 780 or 781 and Eanbald, Archbishop of York, in 796.
For many centuries the estate was in the hands of the Conyers family. In medieval times a Sir John Conyers is said to have slain a dragon or "worm" that was terrorising the district. The stone under which the Sockburn Worm was reputedly buried is (or at least until recently was) still visible, and the falchion with which it was said to have been slain is in Durham Cathedral Treasury. As Sockburn was the most southerly point in the Durham diocese, the sword was ceremonially presented by the Lord of the Manorto each new Bishop of Durham when he entered his diocese for the first time at the local ford or the nearby Croft-on-Tees bridge. This custom died out in the early nineteenth century, but was revived by Bishop Jenkins in 1984, the Mayor of Darlington doing the honours.
The Conyers family died out in the seventeenth century,and their manor house fell into ruin. The estate came into the hands of the Blackett family, industrialists from Newcastle. A new farmhouse was built in the late eighteenth century. In 1799, this was occupied by Tom Hutchinson, who is said to have once bred a seventeen and a half stone sheep, and his sisters Mary and Sara. They were distant relatives of the family of William Wordsworth.He lodged with them for six months in 1799, and eventually married Mary. His friend Samuel Taylor Coleridge also stayed there, and fell in love with Sara,but he was already married; his feeling for Sara found expression in his poem"Love", which contains references to the church and the dragon

legend.

Sources:

William Page (editor) (1914). "Parishes: Sockburn". A History of the County of York North Riding: Volume 1.Institute of Historical Research. Retrieved 5 September 2011.
Illustrated article about the Conyers Falchion and the Sockburn Worm legend, with bibliography. Retrieved 2007-05-29.
Information and photos of the project to restore Sockburn Hall. Retrieved 2007-07-19
DE COTAM:Ralph
DE COTUM:Scolastica **Scolastica de Cotum**, daughter of Ralph de Cotam, died before 14 Sep 1298. Scolastica de Cotham

F, #15880
Father   Ralph de Cotam
    Scolastica de Cotham married Sir John Conyers, son of Sir Humphrey Conyers.
Family
Sir John Conyers d. 1299
Children
Roger de Conyers, Knight of Sockburne+ d. 1323
Jane Conyers+ b. c 1265

Sources:

[S4414] Unknown author, Burke's Dormant and Extinct Baronetcies, p. 127.

Scolastica de Cotum
Death: bef. 14 Sep 1298 (date of writ for father's ipm) [3]
Father: Sir Ralph de Cotum
Mother: Christian

Sources:

1. 'Parishes: Sockburn', A History of the County of York North Riding:
Volume 1 (1914), pp. 449-454
2. Harleian Society, Vol 80, Knights of Edward I , Vol I (London:
1929) p 234
3. Calendar of Fine Rolls, Vol 1, p 403
4. Calendar of Fine Rolls, Vol 1, p 424
5. Chancery: Certificates of Statute Merchant and Statute Staple, C
241/68/74
6. Calendar of Fine Rolls, Vol 1, p 432
7. 'Parishes: Long Newton', A History of the County of Durham: Volume
3 (1928), pp. 299-304
8. Archaeologica Aeliana, Third Series, Vol 6 (Newcastle:1910) p 45
9. John Hodgson, A History of Northumberland, Vol V (Vol 3, Part 1)
(London: 1820) p 53 & 104

Sir John Conyers I and Scolastica de Cotum had the following child:

CONYERS IV:Sir Roger (b. 1280) +7   i.   **Sir Roger Conyers IV**, born 1280, Sokeburne, Durham,
                EnglandEngland:Durham:Sokeburne ; died 1323, Sokeburne, Durham,
                EnglandEngland:Durham:Sokeburne .

Seventh Generation

7. CONYERS IV:Sir Roger (b. 1280) England:Durham:Sokeburne **Sir Roger Conyers IV** (Sir John-6, Sir Humphrey-5, Sir Geoffery-4, Roger-3, Roger-2, Roger-1) was born in 1280 in Sokeburne, Durham, England.England:Durham:Sokeburne He died in 1323 at the age of 43 in Sokeburne, Durham, England. Roger de Conyers, Knight of Sockburne

M, #15084, d. 1323
Father Sir John Conyers d. 1299
Mother Scolastica de Cotham
    Roger de Conyers, Knight of Sockburne was born at of Sockburne, Durham, England. He died in 1323.
Family
Child
Sir John de Conyers, Knight of Sockburn+4,2,3 b. b 1323,d. c 6 Mar 1396

Sources:

[S3955] Unknown author, Burke's Peerage, 1938, p. 2639.
[S16] Douglas Richardson, Magna Carta Ancestry, 2nd Edition, Vol. IV, p. 146.
[S4] Douglas Richardson, Royal Ancestry, Vol. V, p. 94.
[S5] Douglas Richardson, Plantagenet Ancestry, p. 697.

The following is reprinted from Genealogical Gleanings in England by Henry F. Waters, A.M., Boston, 1901, published in two volumes by The New England Historic Genealogical Society

Baron of the bishopric of Durham and Lord of Bishopton.

Geoffery "Galfrid" Conyers, Lord of Sockburn and Bishopton, 1213-1238. ,
John Conyers, Sockburn, England.
Sir Humphrey' Conyers, Sockburn, England.
Sir John' Conyers, Sockburn, England.
Roger Conyers, Sockburn, England.
Sir John' Conyers, Sockburn, England; died 1395.
Robert Conyers, Sockburn, England; born 1371; died 1433.
John" Conyers, Hornby, England.
Sir Christopher" Conyers, Hornby, England.
Sir John Conyers, of Hornby Castle; sheriff of the shire; governor of the castle at York; in 1460 joined Richard, Duke of York, against the King.
Sir John" Conyers, of Hornby, England; Knight of the Order of the Garter; died 1490.
Reginald" Conyers, Wakerly, England; died 1514.
Richard" Conyers, Wakerly, England.
Christopher" Conyers, Wakerly, England, baptized 1552.

Sources:

1. 'Parishes: Sockburn', A History of the County of York North Riding:
Volume 1 (1914), pp. 449-454

2. Harleian Society, Vol 80, Knights of Edward I , Vol I(London: 1929) p 234

3. Calendar of Fine Rolls, Vol 1, p 403

4. Calendar of Fine Rolls, Vol 1, p 424

5. Chancery: Certificates of Statute Merchant and Statute Staple, C 241/68/74

6. Calendar of Fine Rolls, Vol 1, p 432

7. 'Parishes: Long Newton', A History of the County of Durham: Volume 3 (1928), pp. 299-304

8. Archaeologica Aeliana, Third Series, Vol 6 (Newcastle:1910) p 45

9. John Hodgson, A History of Northumberland, Vol V (Vol3, Part 1) (London: 1820) p 53 & 104

10. Archaeologica Aeliana, Third Series, Vol 6(Newcastle: 1910) p 48

11. 45th Annual Report of the Deputy Keeper of the Public Records (London: 1885) p 175

12. 'Parishes: Ormesby', A History of the County of York North Riding: Volume 2 (1923), pp. 276-283

13. 45th Annual Report of the Deputy Keeper of the Public Records (London: 1885) p 183

14. Archaeologica Aeliana, Third Series, Vol 7 (Newcastle: 1910) p 59

15. Surtees Society, Vol 30, Testamenta Eboracensia, Part II (Durham: 1855) p 64n

16. Calendar of Patent Rolls, Henry 6, Vol 1, p 28

17. Complete Peerage, Vol 5, p 277

18. Lincolnshire Archives,Yarborough [YARB 16/1/1]

DE FAYE:Joan (b. 1280)

England:Durham:Durham **Joan De Faye** was born in 1280 in Durham, Durham, England.England:Durham:Durham She died in 1355 at the age of 75 in Durham, Durham, England. Sources:

1. 'Parishes: Sockburn', A History of the County of York North Riding: Volume 1 (1914), pp. 449-454

2. Harleian Society, Vol 80, Knights of Edward I , Vol I (London: 1929) p 234

3. Calendar of Fine Rolls, Vol 1, p 403

4. Calendar of Fine Rolls, Vol 1, p 424

5. Chancery: Certificates of Statute Merchant and Statute Staple, C 241/68/74

6. Calendar of Fine Rolls, Vol 1, p 432

7. 'Parishes: Long Newton', A History of the County of Durham: Volume 3 (1928), pp. 299-304

8. Archaeologica Aeliana, Third Series, Vol 6 (Newcastle:1910) p 45

9. John Hodgson, A History of Northumberland, Vol V (Vol 3, Part 1) (London: 1820) p 53 & 104

10. Archaeologica Aeliana, Third Series, Vol 6(Newcastle: 1910) p 48

11. 45th Annual Report of the Deputy Keeper of the Public Records (London: 1885) p 175

12. 'Parishes: Ormesby', A History of the County of York North Riding: Volume 2 (1923), pp. 276-283

13. 45th Annual Report of the Deputy Keeper of the Public Records (London: 1885) p 183

14. Archaeologica Aeliana, Third Series, Vol 7(Newcastle: 1910) p 59

15. Surtees Society, Vol 30, Testamenta Eboracensia, Part II (Durham: 1855) p 64n

16. Calendar of Patent Rolls, Henry 6, Vol 1, p 28

17. Complete Peerage, Vol 5, p 277
18. Lincolnshire Archives,Yarborough [YARB 16/1/1]

Sir Roger Conyers IV and Joan De Faye had the following child:

CONYERS II:Sir John (b. 1322)   +8   i.   **Sir John Conyers II**, born bef 1322, Sockburn, Darlington, Durham, EnglandEngland:Durham:Darlington:Sockburn ; died Feb 1394/95.

Eighth Generation

8. CONYERS II:Sir John (b. 1322) England:Durham:Darlington:Sockburn **Sir John Conyers II** (Sir Roger-7, Sir John-6, Sir Humphrey-5, Sir Geoffery-4, Roger-3, Roger-2, Roger-1) was born before 1322 in Sockburn, Darlington, Durham, England. He died Feb 1394/95. Sir John de Conyers, Knight of Sockburn

M, #15082, b. before 1323, d. circa 6 March 1396
Father   Roger de Conyers, Knight of Sockburne 2,3,6 d. 1323
    Sir John de Conyers, Knight of Sockburn was born before 1323 at of Sockburn, Durham,England. He married Elizabeth de Aton, daughter of Sir William de Aton, Lord Vesci, 2nd Baron Aton, Sheriff of Yorkshire and Isabel de Percy, after 1363; They had 1 son (Robert, Esq.) 7,2,8,3,4,5,6 Sir John de Conyers, Knight of Sockburn died circa 6 March 1396. 2,3,6
Family
Elizabeth de Aton
Children
Elizabeth Conyers+9,10
Robert Conyers, Esq., Sheriff of Durham, Lord Sockburne +2,3,6 b. c 1371, d. 25 Apr 1431

Sources:

[S3953] Unknown author, Burke's Peerage, 1938, p. 2639.
[S5] Douglas Richardson, Plantagenet Ancestry, p. 697.
[S16] Douglas Richardson, Magna Carta Ancestry, 2nd Edition, Vol. IV, p. 146.
[S6] Douglas Richardson, Plantagenet Ancestry: 2nd Edition, Vol. I, p. 406.
[S4] Douglas Richardson, Royal Ancestry, Vol. I, p. 570.
[S4] Douglas Richardson, Royal Ancestry, Vol. V, p. 94.
[S5] Douglas Richardson, Plantagenet Ancestry, p.157-158.
[S16] Douglas Richardson, Magna Carta Ancestry, 2nd Edition, Vol. IV, p. 96.
[S61] Unknown author, Family Group Sheets, Family History Archives, SLC.
[S9737] Unknown author, Foster's Yorkshire Pedigrees.

The following is reprinted from Genealogical Gleanings in England by Henry F. Waters, A.M., Boston, 1901, published in two volumes by The New England Historic Genealogical Society

Baron of the bishopric of Durham and Lord of Bishopton.

Geoffery "Galfrid" Conyers, Lord of Sockburn and Bishopton, 1213-1238. ,
John Conyers, Sockburn, England.

Sir Humphrey' Conyers, Sockburn, England.
Sir John' Conyers, Sockburn, England.
Roger Conyers, Sockburn, England.
Sir John' Conyers, Sockburn, England; died 1395.
Robert Conyers, Sockburn, England; born 1371; died 1433.
John" Conyers, Hornby, England.
Sir Christopher" Conyers, Hornby, England.
Sir John Conyers, of Hornby Castle; sheriff of the shire;governor of the castle at York; in 1460 joined Richard, Duke of
York, against the King.
Sir John" Conyers, of Hornby, England; Knight of the Order of the Garter; died 1490.
Reginald" Conyers, Wakerly, England; died 1514.
Richard" Conyers, Wakerly, England.
Christopher" Conyers, Wakerly, England, baptized 1552.

Sir John de Conyers

Death: Feb 1395/95 England

Knight of Sockburn, Durham

Second son of Roger de Conyers
Second husband of Elizabeth de Aton, youngest daughter of Sir William de Aton and Isabel de Percy.
Family links:
 Spouse:
  Elizabeth de Aton Conyers (____ - 1402)

Burial:
Greyfriars Abbey Church (Defunct)
York
York Unitary Authority
North Yorkshire, England

Sources:

Title: VCH-Yorkshire North Riding, available in www.british-history.ac.uk
Repository:
Media: Book
Page: see notes under Robert Conyers, d. 1431
1. 'Parishes: Sockburn', A History of the County of York North Riding:
Volume 1 (1914), pp. 449-454
2. Harleian Society, Vol 80, Knights of Edward I , Vol I(London:
1929) p 234
3. Calendar of Fine Rolls, Vol 1, p 403
4. Calendar of Fine Rolls, Vol 1, p 424
5. Chancery: Certificates of Statute Merchant and Statute Staple, C
241/68/74
6. Calendar of Fine Rolls, Vol 1, p 432
7. 'Parishes: Long Newton', A History of the County of Durham: Volume
3 (1928), pp. 299-304
8. Archaeologica Aeliana, Third Series, Vol 6 (Newcastle:1910) p 45
9. John Hodgson, A History of Northumberland, Vol V (Vol 3, Part 1)
(London: 1820) p 53 & 104

10. Archaeologica Aeliana, Third Series, Vol 6 (Newcastle: 1910) p 48
11. 45th Annual Report of the Deputy Keeper of the Public Records
(London: 1885) p 175
12. 'Parishes: Ormesby', A History of the County of York North Riding:
Volume 2 (1923), pp. 276-283
13. 45th Annual Report of the Deputy Keeper of the Public Records
(London: 1885) p 183
14. Archaeologica Aeliana, Third Series, Vol 7(Newcastle: 1910) p 59
15. Surtees Society, Vol 30, Testamenta Eboracensia, Part II (Durham:
1855) p 64n
16. Calendar of Patent Rolls, Henry 6, Vol 1, p 28
17. Complete Peerage, Vol 5, p 277
18. Lincolnshire Archives,Yarborough [YARB 16/1/1]
ALTON:Elizabeth
Elizabeth Alton died on 25 Apr 1402–1 May 1402. Elizabeth de Aton

F, #15083
Father   Sir William de Aton, Lord Vesci, 2nd Baron Aton, Sheriff of Yorkshire 2,8,9,4,10,11,7 b. c 1299, d. 10 Feb 1388
Mother Isabel de Percy 2,8,9,4,10,11,7 d. b 25 May 1368
    Elizabeth de Aton married Sir William Playce, son of Sir Thomas Playz and Joan de Syggeston, circa 1360; They had 1
son (William).8,4,5,7 Elizabeth de Aton married Sir John de Conyers, Knight of Sockburn, son of Roger de Conyers, Knight
of Sockburne, after 1363; They had 1 son (Robert, Esq.)2,8,3,4,5,6,7 Elizabeth de Aton left a will on 25 April 1402;
Requested burial in the Church of Friars Minor, York,Yorkshire. 8,4,7 Her estate was probated on 1 May 1402.8,4,7
Family 1
Sir William Playce d. c 1363
Child
William Place 8 d. a 30 Mar 1396
Family 2
Sir John de Conyers, Knight of Sockburn b. b 1323, d. c 6 Mar 1396
Children
Elizabeth Conyers+12
Robert Conyers, Esq., Sheriff of Durham, Lord Sockburne +8,4,7 b. c 1371, d. 25 Apr 1431

Sources:

[S3954] Unknown author, The Complete Peerage, by Cokayne, Vol. I, p. 326; Burke's Peerage, 1938, p. 2639.
[S5] Douglas Richardson, Plantagenet Ancestry, p. 157-158.
[S16] Douglas Richardson, Magna Carta Ancestry, 2nd Edition, Vol. IV, p. 96.
[S16] Douglas Richardson, Magna Carta Ancestry, 2nd Edition, Vol. IV, p. 146.
[S6] Douglas Richardson, Plantagenet Ancestry: 2nd Edition, Vol. I, p. 406.
[S4] Douglas Richardson, Royal Ancestry, Vol. I, p. 570.
[S4] Douglas Richardson, Royal Ancestry, Vol. V, p. 94.
[S5] Douglas Richardson, Plantagenet Ancestry, p. 697.
[S16] Douglas Richardson, Magna Carta Ancestry, 2nd Edition, Vol. IV, p. 95.
[S6] Douglas Richardson, Plantagenet Ancestry: 2nd Edition, Vol. I, p. 405-406.
[S4] Douglas Richardson, Royal Ancestry, Vol. I, p.569-570.
[S61] Unknown author, Family Group Sheets, Family History Archives, SLC.

Elizabeth de Aton Conyers

Death: Apr., 1402,England

Youngest daughter and heiress of Sir William de Aton and Isabel de Percy. Granddaughter of Sir Henry Percy and Idoine de Clifford.

Wife of Sir William Playce of Gristhorpe, son and heir to Thomas Playce and Joan de Syggeston. They married before 1365 and had one son,William.

Sir William died shortly before 04 Feb 1371.

Secondly, she was the wife of Sir John de Conyers, son of Roger de Conyers. They had one son, Robert.

Elizabeth left a will dated 25 April 1402, proved 01 May 1402.

 Family links:
 Parents:
  William de Aton (1299 - 1387)
  Isabel de Percyde Aton
  Spouse:
  John de Conyers (_____ - 1396)*
  Children:
  Robert Conyers (_____ - 1431)*

Burial:
Greyfriars Abbey Church (Defunct)
York
York Unitary Authority
North Yorkshire, England

sources:

1. 'Parishes: Sockburn', A History of the County of York North Riding:
Volume 1 (1914), pp. 449-454
2. Harleian Society, Vol 80, Knights of Edward I , Vol I(London:
1929) p 234
3. Calendar of Fine Rolls, Vol 1, p 403
4. Calendar of Fine Rolls, Vol 1, p 424
5. Chancery: Certificates of Statute Merchant and Statute Staple, C
241/68/74
6. Calendar of Fine Rolls, Vol 1, p 432
7. 'Parishes: Long Newton', A History of the County of Durham: Volume
3 (1928), pp. 299-304
8. Archaeologica Aeliana, Third Series, Vol 6 (Newcastle:1910) p 45
9. John Hodgson, A History of Northumberland, Vol V (Vol 3, Part 1)
(London: 1820) p 53 & 104
10. Archaeologica Aeliana, Third Series, Vol 6(Newcastle: 1910) p 48
11. 45th Annual Report of the Deputy Keeper of the Public Records
(London: 1885) p 175
12. 'Parishes: Ormesby', A History of the County of York North Riding:
Volume 2 (1923), pp. 276-283
13. 45th Annual Report of the Deputy Keeper of the Public Records
(London: 1885) p 183
14. Archaeologica Aeliana, Third Series, Vol 7(Newcastle: 1910) p 59
15. Surtees Society, Vol 30, Testamenta Eboracensia, PartII (Durham:
1855) p 64n
16. Calendar of Patent Rolls, Henry 6, Vol 1, p 28
17. Complete Peerage, Vol 5, p 277
18. Lincolnshire Archives,Yarborough [YARB 16/1/1]

Sir John Conyers II and Elizabeth Alton had the following child:

CONYERS I:Robert (b. 1371)   +9   i.   **Robert Conyers I**, born 1371, Sockburn, Darlington, Durham, EnglandEngland:Durham:Darlington:Sockburn ; died 25 Apr 1431.

Ninth Generation

9. CONYERS I:Robert (b. 1371) England:Durham:Darlington:Sockburn **Robert Conyers I** (Sir John-8, Sir Roger-7, Sir John-6, Sir Humphrey-5, Sir Geoffery-4, Roger-3, Roger-2, Roger-1) was born in 1371 in Sockburn, Darlington, Durham, England. He died on 25 Apr 1431 at the age of 60. The following is reprinted from Genealogical Gleanings in England by Henry F. Waters, A.M., Boston, 1901, published in two volumes by The New England Historic Genealogical Society

Baron of the bishopric of Durham and Lord of Bishopton.

Geoffery "Galfrid" Conyers, Lord of Sockburn and Bishopton, 1213-1238. ,
John Conyers, Sockburn, England.
Sir Humphrey' Conyers, Sockburn, England.
Sir John' Conyers, Sockburn, England.
Roger Conyers, Sockburn, England.
Sir John' Conyers, Sockburn, England; died 1395.
Robert Conyers, Sockburn, England; born 1371; died 1433.
John" Conyers, Hornby, England.
Sir Christopher" Conyers, Hornby, England.
Sir John Conyers, of Hornby Castle; sheriff of the shire;governor of the castle at York; in 1460 joined Richard, Duke of York, against the King.
Sir John" Conyers, of Hornby, England; Knight of the Order of the Garter; died 1490.
Reginald" Conyers, Wakerly, England; died 1514.
Richard" Conyers, Wakerly, England.
Christopher" Conyers, Wakerly, England, baptized 1552.

Robert Conyers

Death: Apr. 25,1431, England
Son of Sir John de Conyers and Elizabeth de Aton. Grandson of Roger de Conyers, William de Aton and Isabel de Percy. Husband of Isabel Pert, daughter and co-heiress to William Pert of Tiverington, Yorkshire and Joan le Scrope, daughter of Sir Stephen. They had one son and seven daughters.
Robert left a will dated 18 April 1431, proved 18 May 1431.
 Family links:
 Parents:
  John de Conyers (____ - 1396)
  Elizabeth de Aton Conyers (____ - 1402)

Burial:
Neasham Priory
Sockburn
Darlington Unitary Authority
County Durham, England

Sources:
[S10802] Unknown author, *The Lineage and Ancestry of HRH Prince Charles, by Gerald Paget, Vol. II, p. 405.*
[S16] Douglas Richardson, *Magna Carta Ancestry, 2nd Edition*, Vol. I, p. 291.
[S4] Douglas Richardson, *Royal Ancestry*, Vol. I, p. 492.

[S5] Douglas Richardson, *Plantagenet Ancestry*, p. 144.
Title: VCH-Yorkshire North Riding, available in www.british-history.ac.uk
Repository:
Media: Book
Title: Magna Carta Ancestry, by Douglas Richardson, 2005, Genealogical Publishing Co.
Page: 798
Title: VCH-Yorkshire North Riding, available in www.british-history.ac.uk
Repository:
Media: Book
Text: 1431
1. 'Parishes: Sockburn', A History of the County of York North Riding:
Volume 1 (1914), pp. 449-454
2. Harleian Society, Vol 80, Knights of Edward I , Vol I(London:
1929) p 234
3. Calendar of Fine Rolls, Vol 1, p 403
4. Calendar of Fine Rolls, Vol 1, p 424
5. Chancery: Certificates of Statute Merchant and Statute Staple, C
241/68/74
6. Calendar of Fine Rolls, Vol 1, p 432
7. 'Parishes: Long Newton', A History of the County of Durham: Volume
3 (1928), pp. 299-304
8. Archaeologica Aeliana, Third Series, Vol 6 (Newcastle:1910) p 45
9. John Hodgson, A History of Northumberland, Vol V (Vol3, Part 1)
(London: 1820) p 53 & 104
10. Archaeologica Aeliana, Third Series, Vol 6 (Newcastle: 1910) p 48
11. 45th Annual Report of the Deputy Keeper of the Public Records
(London: 1885) p 175
12. 'Parishes: Ormesby', A History of the County of York North Riding:
Volume 2 (1923), pp. 276-283
13. 45th Annual Report of the Deputy Keeper of the Public Records
(London: 1885) p 183
14. Archaeologica Aeliana, Third Series, Vol 7(Newcastle: 1910) p 59
15. Surtees Society, Vol 30, Testamenta Eboracensia, Part II (Durham:
1855) p 64n
16. Calendar of Patent Rolls, Henry 6, Vol 1, p 28
17. Complete Peerage, Vol 5, p 277
18. Lincolnshire Archives,Yarborough [YARB 16/1/1]

Robert Conyers, Esq., Sheriff of Durham, Lord Sockburne

M, #15078, b. circa 1371, d. 25 April 1431
Father   Sir John de Conyers, Knight of Sockburn 2,3,6 b. b 1323, d. c 6 Mar 1396
Mother Elizabeth deAton 2,3,6
    RobertConyers, Esq., Sheriff of Durham, Lord Sockburne was born circa 1371 at of Sockburn, Durham, England; Age 25
in 1396. 2,3,5 He married Isabel Pert,daughter of William Pert and Joan le Scrope, circa 1404; They had 1 son (Sir
Christopher) and 7 daughters (Joan, wife of Sir Philip Dymoke; Elizabeth;Isabel, wife of Thomas Clervaux; Margaret;
Katherine; Cecily; & Beatrice).2,3,4,5 Robert Conyers, Esq., Sheriff of Durham, Lord Sockburne left a will on 18 April
1431. 2,3,5 He died on 25 April 1431; Buried at Sockburn,Durham.2,3,5 His estate was probated on 18 May 1431. 2,3,5
Family
Isabel Pert b. c 1387, d. bt 1427 - 25 Apr 1431
Children
Isabel Conyers+7,3,8,5
Joan Conyers+9,2,10,3,11,5 b. c 1405, d. a 1431

Sir Christopher Conyers+12,3,5 b. c 1422, d. 13 Mar 1487

Sources:

[S3951] Unknown author, Lineage and Ancestry of HRH Prince Charles by Paget, Vol. II, p. 405; Plantagenet Ancestry of 17th Century Colonists, by David Faris, p. 94.
[S5] Douglas Richardson, Plantagenet Ancestry, p. 697.
[S16] Douglas Richardson, Magna Carta Ancestry, 2nd Edition, Vol. IV, p. 146.
[S4] Douglas Richardson, Royal Ancestry, Vol. III, p.312.
[S4] Douglas Richardson, Royal Ancestry, Vol. V, p.94-95.
[S4] Douglas Richardson, Royal Ancestry, Vol. V, p. 94.
[S16] Douglas Richardson, Magna Carta Ancestry, 2nd Edition, Vol. I, p. 533.
[S4] Douglas Richardson, Royal Ancestry, Vol. II, p. 295.
[S5] Douglas Richardson, Plantagenet Ancestry, p. 605.
[S16] Douglas Richardson, Magna Carta Ancestry, 2nd Edition, Vol. III, p. 428.
[S4] Douglas Richardson, Royal Ancestry, Vol. IV, p. 461.
[S5] Douglas Richardson, Plantagenet Ancestry, p. 698.

PERT:William
LE SCROPE:Joan PERT:Isabel (b. 1387) **Isabel Pert**, daughter of William Pert and Joan le Scrope, was born in 1387. She died in 1427–25 Apr 1431 at the age of 40. Isabel Pert

F, #15079, b. circa 1387, d. between 1427 and 25 April 1431
Father   William Pert 2,3,6,5 b. c 1350, d. b 1390
Mother Joan le Scrope 2,3,6,5 d. 20 Sep 1427
    Isabel Pert was born circa 1387; Age 40 in 1427.2,3,5 She married Robert Conyers, Esq.,Sheriff of Durham, Lord Sockburne, son of Sir John de Conyers, Knight of Sockburn and Elizabeth de Aton, circa 1404; They had 1 son (Sir Christopher)and 7 daughters (Joan, wife of Sir Philip Dymoke; Elizabeth; Isabel, wife of Thomas Clervaux; Margaret; Katherine; Cecily; & Beatrice). 2,3,4,5 Isabel Pert died between 1427 and 25 April 1431. 2,3,5
Family
Robert Conyers, Esq., Sheriff of Durham, Lord Sockburneb. c 1371, d. 25 Apr 1431
Children
Isabel Conyers+7,3,8,5
Joan Conyers+9,2,10,3,11,5 b. c 1405, d. a 1431
Sir Christopher Conyers+12,3,5 b. c 1422, d. 13 Mar 1487

Sources:

[S3754] Unknown author, Burke's Dormant and Extinct Baronetcies, p. 128.
[S5] Douglas Richardson, Plantagenet Ancestry, p. 697.
[S16] Douglas Richardson, Magna Carta Ancestry, 2nd Edition, Vol. IV, p. 146.
[S4] Douglas Richardson, Royal Ancestry, Vol. III, p.312.
[S4] Douglas Richardson, Royal Ancestry, Vol. V, p.94-95.
[S4] Douglas Richardson, Royal Ancestry, Vol. III, p.311-312.
[S16] Douglas Richardson, Magna Carta Ancestry, 2nd Edition, Vol. I, p. 533.
[S4] Douglas Richardson, Royal Ancestry, Vol. II, p. 295.
[S5] Douglas Richardson, Plantagenet Ancestry, p. 605.
[S16] Douglas Richardson, Magna Carta Ancestry, 2nd Edition, Vol. III, p. 428.
[S4] Douglas Richardson, Royal Ancestry, Vol. IV, p. 461.
[S5] Douglas Richardson, Plantagenet Ancestry, p. 698.
[S10802] Unknown author, *The Lineage and Ancestry of HRH Prince Charles, by Gerald Paget, Vol. II, p. 405.*

[S16] Douglas Richardson, *Magna Carta Ancestry, 2nd Edition*, Vol. I, p. 291.

[S4] Douglas Richardson, *Royal Ancestry*, Vol. I, p. 492.

[S5] Douglas Richardson, *Plantagenet Ancestry*, p. 144.

Title: VCH-Yorkshire North Riding, available in www.british-history.ac.uk

Repository:

Media: Book

Title: Magna Carta Ancestry, by Douglas Richardson, 2005, Genealogical Publishing Co.

Page: 798

Title: VCH-Yorkshire North Riding, available in www.british-history.ac.uk

Repository:

Media: Book

Text: 1431

1. 'Parishes: Sockburn', A History of the County of York North Riding:
Volume 1 (1914), pp. 449-454

2. Harleian Society, Vol 80, Knights of Edward I, Vol I (London:
1929) p 234

3. Calendar of Fine Rolls, Vol 1, p 403

4. Calendar of Fine Rolls, Vol 1, p 424

5. Chancery: Certificates of Statute Merchant and Statute Staple, C
241/68/74

6. Calendar of Fine Rolls, Vol 1, p 432

7. 'Parishes: Long Newton', A History of the County of Durham: Volume
3 (1928), pp. 299-304

8. Archaeologica Aeliana, Third Series, Vol 6 (Newcastle:1910) p 45

9. John Hodgson, A History of Northumberland, Vol V (Vol 3, Part 1)
(London: 1820) p 53 & 104

10. Archaeologica Aeliana, Third Series, Vol 6(Newcastle: 1910) p 48

11. 45th Annual Report of the Deputy Keeper of the Public Records
(London: 1885) p 175

12. 'Parishes: Ormesby', A History of the County of York North Riding:
Volume 2 (1923), pp. 276-283

13. 45th Annual Report of the Deputy Keeper of the Public Records
(London: 1885) p 183

14. Archaeologica Aeliana, Third Series, Vol 7 (Newcastle: 1910) p 59

15. Surtees Society, Vol 30, Testamenta Eboracensia, Part II (Durham:
1855) p 64n

16. Calendar of Patent Rolls, Henry 6, Vol 1, p 28

17. Complete Peerage, Vol 5, p 277

18. Lincolnshire Archives,Yarborough [YARB 16/1/1]

Robert Conyers I and Isabel Pert had the following child:

CONYERS III:Sir John   +10   i.   **Sir John Conyers III**, died Jun 1438–Jul 1438.

Tenth Generation

10. CONYERS III:Sir John **Sir John Conyers III** (Robert-9, Sir John-8, Sir Roger-7, Sir John-6, Sir Humphrey-5, Sir Geoffery-4, Roger-3, Roger-2, Roger-1) died in Jun 1438–Jul 1438. In 1391 an indenture was sealed between Richard Scrope and John Conyers "whereby Richard has sold to John the wardship of the person and lands of Margaret, cousin and heir to Thomas St Quentin, knight, of Hornby, in Richmondshire, which pertains to him because of the minority of Margaret. John has paid 200 marks to Richard for the wardship". Michael Prestwich, ed. Liberties and Identities in the Medieval British Isles, Melanie Devine, The Lordship of Richmond in the Later Middle Ages,

Sources:

(Boydell Press: 2008) pp. 105-6: Citing; NYCRO, MS ZBO, Bolton Cartulary, fo. 56r.

John Conyers married his ward, Margaret St. Quintin, who in 1391 was a minor (less than 14 years old).

The following is reprinted from Genealogical Gleanings in England by Henry F. Waters, A.M., Boston, 1901, published in two volumes by The New England Historic Genealogical Society

Baron of the bishopric of Durham and Lord of Bishopton.

Geoffery "Galfrid" Conyers, Lord of Sockburn and Bishopton, 1213-1238. ,
John Conyers, Sockburn, England.
Sir Humphrey' Conyers, Sockburn, England.
Sir John' Conyers, Sockburn, England.
Roger Conyers, Sockburn, England.
Sir John' Conyers, Sockburn, England; died 1395.
Robert Conyers, Sockburn, England; born 1371; died 1433.
John" Conyers, Hornby, England.
Sir Christopher" Conyers, Hornby, England.
Sir John Conyers, of Hornby Castle; sheriff of the shire;governor of the castle at York; in 1460 joined Richard, Duke of York, against the King.
Sir John" Conyers, of Hornby, England; Knight of the Order of the Garter; died 1490.
Reginald" Conyers, Wakerly, England; died 1514.
Richard" Conyers, Wakerly, England.
Christopher" Conyers, Wakerly, England, baptized 1552.

Sir John Conyers

M, #15076, d. between June 1438 and July 1438
Father   Sir Robert Conyers
Mother Juliana Percy
    Sir John Conyers was born at of Hornby, Yorkshire, England. He married Margaret St.Quinton, daughter of Anthony St. Quinton and Elizabeth Gascoigne. Sir John Conyers died between June 1438 and July 1438.
Family
Margaret St. Quinton d. c 1426
Children
Elizabeth Conyers+
Sir Christopher Conyers, Sheriff of Yorkshire+ b. c 1393

Sources:

[S16] Douglas Richardson, Magna Carta Ancestry, 2nd Edition, Vol. I, p. 291.
[S4] Douglas Richardson, Royal Ancestry, Vol. I, p. 492.
[S5] Douglas Richardson, Plantagenet Ancestry, p. 144.

John Conyers of Hornby

17 Aug 1403, Robert and John Conyers, brothers, were appointed custodians of the castle of Skelton, the manors of Skelton and Marske, and all the other lands of Thomas Faucomberge knight incos. York and Northumberland

Sources:

1. 'Parishes: Sockburn', A History of the County of York North Riding: Volume 1 (1914), pp. 449-454
2. Harleian Society, Vol 80, Knights of Edward I , Vol I (London: 1929) p 234
3. Calendar of Fine Rolls, Vol 1, p 403
4. Calendar of Fine Rolls, Vol 1, p 424
5. Chancery: Certificates of Statute Merchant and Statute Staple, C 241/68/74
6. Calendar of Fine Rolls, Vol 1, p 432
7. 'Parishes: Long Newton', A History of the County of Durham: Volume 3 (1928), pp. 299-304
8. Archaeologica Aeliana, Third Series, Vol 6 (Newcastle:1910) p 45
9. John Hodgson, A History of Northumberland, Vol V (Vol 3, Part 1) (London: 1820) p 53 & 104
10. Archaeologica Aeliana, Third Series, Vol 6 (Newcastle: 1910) p 48
11. 45th Annual Report of the Deputy Keeper of the Public Records (London: 1885) p 175
12. 'Parishes: Ormesby', A History of the County of York North Riding: Volume 2 (1923), pp. 276-283
13. 45th Annual Report of the Deputy Keeper of the Public Records (London: 1885) p 183
14. Archaeologica Aeliana, Third Series, Vol 7(Newcastle: 1910) p 59
15. Surtees Society, Vol 30, Testamenta Eboracensia, Part II (Durham: 1855) p 64n
16. Calendar of Patent Rolls, Henry 6, Vol 1, p 28
17. Complete Peerage, Vol 5, p 277
18. Lincolnshire Archives,Yarborough [YARB 16/1/1]

ST. QUINTON:Anthony
ST. QUINTON:Margaret **Margaret St. Quinton**, daughter of Anthony St. Quinton, died in 1426. Margaret St. Quinton

F, #15077, d. circa 1426
Father   Anthony St. Quinton d. 1443
Mother Elizabeth Gascoigne
    Margaret St. Quinton married Sir John Conyers, son of Sir Robert Conyers and Juliana Percy.Margaret St. Quinton was born at of Hornby, Yorkshire, England. She died circa 1426.
Family
Sir John Conyers d. bt Jun 1438 - Jul 1438
Children
Elizabeth Conyers+
Sir Christopher Conyers, Sheriff of Yorkshire+ b. c 1393

Sources:

[S16] Douglas Richardson, Magna Carta Ancestry, 2nd Edition, Vol. I, p. 291.

[S4] Douglas Richardson, Royal Ancestry, Vol. I, p. 492.

[S5] Douglas Richardson, Plantagenet Ancestry, p. 144.

Sources:

1. 'Parishes: Sockburn', A History of the County of York North Riding: Volume 1 (1914), pp. 449-454

2. Harleian Society, Vol 80, Knights of Edward I , Vol I (London: 1929) p 234

3. Calendar of Fine Rolls, Vol 1, p 403

4. Calendar of Fine Rolls, Vol 1, p 424

5. Chancery: Certificates of Statute Merchant and Statute Staple, C 241/68/74

6. Calendar of Fine Rolls, Vol 1, p 432

7. 'Parishes: Long Newton', A History of the County of Durham: Volume 3 (1928), pp. 299-304

8. Archaeologica Aeliana, Third Series, Vol 6 (Newcastle:1910) p 45

9. John Hodgson, A History of Northumberland, Vol V (Vol 3, Part 1) (London: 1820) p 53 & 104

10. Archaeologica Aeliana, Third Series, Vol 6(Newcastle: 1910) p 48

11. 45th Annual Report of the Deputy Keeper of the Public Records (London: 1885) p 175

12. 'Parishes: Ormesby', A History of the County of York North Riding: Volume 2 (1923), pp. 276-283

13. 45th Annual Report of the Deputy Keeper of the Public Records (London: 1885) p 183

14. Archaeologica Aeliana, Third Series, Vol 7(Newcastle: 1910) p 59

15. Surtees Society, Vol 30, Testamenta Eboracensia, Part II (Durham: 1855) p 64n

16. Calendar of Patent Rolls, Henry 6, Vol 1, p 28

17. Complete Peerage, Vol 5, p 277

18. Lincolnshire Archives,Yarborough [YARB 16/1/1]

Sir John Conyers III and Margaret St. Quinton had the following child:

CONYERS I:Sir Christopher (b. 1393)   +11   i.   **Sir Christopher Conyers I**, born 1393, EnglandEngland ; died 1460, EnglandEngland .

Eleventh Generation

11. CONYERS I:Sir Christopher (b. 1393) England **Sir Christopher Conyers I** (Sir John-10, Robert-9, Sir John-8, Sir Roger-7, Sir John-6, Sir Humphrey-5, Sir Geoffery-4, Roger-3, Roger-2, Roger-1) was born in 1393 in England.England He died in 1460 at the age of 67 in England. April 21, 1423 -- Christopher Conyers was named as a co-executor of his father's, John Conyer, will in an Order dated at Westminster:
 John Beker of Richmond, co. York, 'wryght', for not appearing before the same, to answer Margaret late the wife of John Conyers of Horneby, Christopher son of John Conyers of Horneby, Robert Conyers, knight, brother of John Conyers of Horneby, Richard de Norton, Thomas de Langton, Christopher de Boynton and William de Haukeswell, clerk, executors of the will of John Conyers of Horneby, touching a plea of detinue of 40s. Yorks.' [CPR 1 Henry VI, p. 28, mem. 8]

He was named as the possible member of a commission concerning the IPM of Sir Henry FitzHugh in 1425.
January 24, 1425/26 after the Feast of St. Hilary -- date of Christopher Conyers's will in which he named 4 children as well as his wife:
 - to Elene my wife, if she overlyve me, the third part of my godes. - To John, my sonne, xl marc. - Johan and ____ my daughters. - To my son Thomas and his heirs my purchased lands, etc., in Hornby, Brokeholme,... - John, now mine eldest son, under 21. - My mother dame Margaret Conyers, John Pigot, and Richard Welden, exrs. ' [Testa. Ebor. III:288]

sources:

John Ravilious on Gen-Medieval," Posting. October 29, 2008 -http://archiver.rootsweb.ancestry.com/th/read/gen-medieval/2008-10/1225323689
http://our-royal-titled-noble-and-commoner-ancestors.com/ *Our Royal, Titled, Noble and Commoner Ancestors & Cousins*] database online, compiled by Mr. Marlyn Lewis, follows Douglas Richardson's *Magna Carta Ancestry*. It includes Magna Carta Surety Barons and many of their descendants. Sir Christopher Conyers, Sheriff of Yorkshire
Douglas Richardson. Magna Carta Ancestry: A Study in Colonial and Medieval Families. Royal Ancestry Series. 2nd Edition. 4 Volumes. 2011. Pages 146 - 147.http://amzn.com/1461045207. Editor Kimball G. Everingham, (Salt Lake City, Utah
Ancestry.com family trees
Frederick Lewis Weis. The Magna Charta Sureties, 1215: The Barons Named in the Magna Charta. Contributions by Walter Lee Sheppard and William Ryland Beall.
The Baronetage of England, or, the History of the English Baronets, and such Baronets of Scotland as are of English Familites. Rev. William Betham. 1815.
Sir John Conyers. Wikipedia. https://en.wikipedia.org/wiki/Sir_John_Conyers.
The Visitation of Yorkshire in the years 1563 and 1564.

The following is reprinted from Genealogical Gleanings in England by Henry F. Waters, A.M., Boston, 1901, published in two volumes by The New England Historic Genealogical Society

Baron of the bishopric of Durham and Lord of Bishopton.

Geoffery "Galfrid" Conyers, Lord of Sockburn and Bishopton, 1213-1238. ,
John Conyers, Sockburn, England.
Sir Humphrey' Conyers, Sockburn, England.
Sir John' Conyers, Sockburn, England.
Roger Conyers, Sockburn, England.
Sir John' Conyers, Sockburn, England; died 1395.
Robert Conyers, Sockburn, England; born 1371; died 1433.
John" Conyers, Hornby, England.
Sir Christopher" Conyers, Hornby, England.
Sir John Conyers, of Hornby Castle; sheriff of the shire;governor of the castle at York; in 1460 joined Richard, Duke of York, against the King.
Sir John" Conyers, of Hornby, England; Knight of the Order of the Garter; died 1490.
Reginald" Conyers, Wakerly, England; died 1514.
Richard" Conyers, Wakerly, England.
Christopher" Conyers, Wakerly, England, baptized 1552.

Sir Christopher Conyers, Sheriff of Yorkshire

M, #15074, b. circa 1393

Father   Sir John Conyers d. bt Jun 1438 - Jul 1438

Mother Margaret St.Quinton d. c 1426

Sir Christopher Conyers, Sheriff of Yorkshire was born circa 1393 at of Hornby Castle,Yorkshire, England. He married Eleanor Rolleston, daughter of Thomas Rolleston, Esq. and Beatrice Haulay, before September 1415. 2,6 Sir Christopher Conyers,Sheriff of Yorkshire married Margaret Waddeley, daughter of Robert Waddeley, circa 1447.3,7

Family 1

Eleanor Rolleston b. c 1390, d. 6 Aug 1444

Children

Sir John Conyers, Sheriff of Yorkshire, Constable of Middleham, Bailiff & Steward of Richmond Liberty, Steward of the lord ship of Middleham+9,2,6 d. 14 Mar 1490

Sir Richard Conyers+

Elizabeth Conyers+10 b. c 1413

Roger Conyers, Esq.+ b. c 1419

Joan Conyers+ b. c 1423

Isabel Conyers+11,4,8 b. c 1433

Margaret Conyers+ b. c 1435

Family 2

Margaret Waddeley

Child

Margaret Conyers+12,13,3,5,7 b. c 1451, d. 1500

Sources:

[S3949] Unknown author, Lineage and Ancestry of HRH Prince Charles by Paget, Vol. II, p. 407; Plantagenet Ancestry of 17th Century Colonists, by David Faris, p. 70.

[S16] Douglas Richardson, Magna Carta Ancestry, 2nd Edition, Vol. I, p. 530-531.

[S16] Douglas Richardson, Magna Carta Ancestry, 2nd Edition, Vol. III, p. 400.

[S16] Douglas Richardson, Magna Carta Ancestry, 2nd Edition, Vol. IV, p. 128.

[S4] Douglas Richardson, Royal Ancestry, Vol. II, p. 248.

[S4] Douglas Richardson, Royal Ancestry, Vol. II, p. 288.

[S4] Douglas Richardson, Royal Ancestry, Vol. IV, p.431-432.

[S4] Douglas Richardson, Royal Ancestry, Vol. V, p. 69.

[S5] Douglas Richardson, Plantagenet Ancestry, p. 227.

[S40] Roots Web's World Connect Project.

[S5] Douglas Richardson, Plantagenet Ancestry, p. 695.

[S5] Douglas Richardson, Plantagenet Ancestry, p. 218.

[S5] Douglas Richardson, Plantagenet Ancestry, p.597-598.

Christopher Conyers (bailiff of Richmond)

Christopher Conyers of Hornby, Lancashire (d. 1461 x1465), was a member of the fifteenth century English gentry, prominent in the local politics of northern England (specifically Yorkshire) and the early years of the Wars of the Roses.

The son and heir of John Conyers of Hornby (d. c. 1438),he married Ellen, the daughter (and coheiress of Thomas Rolleston in November 1415. After Ellen's death in 1433, he married one Margaret Waddesley. Between his two wives he produced twenty-five children, twelve being sons; 'unusually,'notes Rosemary Horrox, he was able to provide for many of his younger sons,rather than just the eldest, as was usual. Horrox puts this down to the fact that his heir had married the daughter and coheir of Philip, Lord Darcy, which provided Conyers with a source of income, as well as the fact that he arranged good marriages for many of them. His ability to do so, she continues,demonstrates his 'good standing' in the region. This standing is also reflected in his acting as a feoffee for local man John Waddesford of Kirklington, NorthYorkshire, and bearing witness to the exchange of deeds in a property exchange between Richard Clairvaux and John, Lord Scrope of Bolton.

Although never knighted or made Sheriff of his county, he was appointed bailiff of the Honour of Richmond in 1436, during the earl of Salisbury's tenure of the Honour. The same year, Conyers acted as feoffee to use of Salisbury's will, (due to Salisbury's appointment to royal service in France, in the latter days of the Hundred Years' War) which meant that if his mother died whilst the earl was abroad, her estates would be controlled by Conyers and others on Salisbury's behalf, rather than temporarily returning to the king.

In 1464 he was commissioned (alongside Salisbury's son,the earl of Warwick, and Lords Greystoke and Fitzhugh) to recapture castles in Northumberland (Bamburgh, Alnwick and Dunstanburgh) that were held by the remnants of the Lancastrian army.

Sources:

Horrox, Rebecca. "Conyers, Christopher". Oxford Dictionary of National Biography (online ed.). Oxford University Press.doi:10.1093/ref:odnb/61160. (Subscription or UK public library membership required.)
Pollard, J., The North-East of England During Wars of the Roses : Lay Society, War and Politics, 1450-1500 (Oxford, 1990), 111
Pollard, J., The North-East of England During Wars of the Roses : Lay Society, War and Politics, 1450-1500 (Oxford, 1990), 113
Jacobs E.F., The Fifteenth Century, 1399-1485 (Oxford,1969), 323
Hicks, M.A., Warwick the Kingmaker (Oxford, 1998), 246n.98

ROLLESTON:Eleanor (b. 1390)
England **Eleanor Rolleston** was born in 1390 in England.England She died on 6 Aug 1444 at the age of 54 in England.
Eleanor Rolleston

F, #15075, b. circa 1390, d. 6 August 1444
Father   Thomas Rolleston, Esq.2,3,4 b. c 1368
Mother Beatrice Haulay d. 1400
     Eleanor Rolleston was born circa 1390 at of Mablethorpe, Lincolnshire, England. She married Sir Christopher Conyers, Sheriff of Yorkshire, son of Sir John Conyers and Margaret St. Quinton, before September 1415.3,4 Eleanor Rolleston died on 6 August 1444.
Family
Sir Christopher Conyers, Sheriff of Yorkshire b. c 1393
Children
Sir John Conyers, Sheriff of Yorkshire, Constable of Middleham, Bailiff & Steward of Richmond Liberty, Steward of the lord ship of Middleham+2,3,4 d. 14 Mar 1490
Sir Richard Conyers+
Elizabeth Conyers+5 b. c 1413
Roger Conyers, Esq.+ b. c 1419
Joan Conyers+ b. c 1423
Isabel Conyers+6 b. c 1433
Margaret Conyers+ b. c 1435

Sources:

[S3950] Unknown author, Plantagenet Ancestry of 17th Century Colonists, by David Faris, p. 70; Burke's Peerage, 1938, p. 2639.
[S5] Douglas Richardson, Plantagenet Ancestry, p. 227.
[S16] Douglas Richardson, Magna Carta Ancestry, 2nd Edition, Vol. I, p. 530-531.

[S4] Douglas Richardson, Royal Ancestry, Vol. II, p. 288.

[S40] RootsWeb's World Connect Project.

[S5] Douglas Richardson, Plantagenet Ancestry, p. 695.

Sir Christopher Conyers I and Eleanor Rolleston had the following child:

CONYERS IV (KNIGHT OF THE GARTER) # 227:Sir John   +12   i.   **Sir John Conyers IV (KNIGHT OF THE GARTER) # 227**, died 14 Mar 1490, EnglandEngland .

Twelfth Generation

12. CONYERS IV (KNIGHT OF THE GARTER) # 227:Sir John England **Sir John Conyers IV (KNIGHT OF THE GARTER) # 227** (Sir Christopher-11, Sir John-10, Robert-9, Sir John-8, Sir Roger-7, Sir John-6, Sir Humphrey-5, Sir Geoffery-4, Roger-3, Roger-2, Roger-1) died on 14 Mar 1490 in England. Sir John Conyers (died 1490), one of twenty-five children of Christopher Conyers (died 1460), was a pre-eminent member of the gentry of Yorkshire, northern England, during the fifteenth century Wars of the Roses.
Life and career.
Based in Hornby Castle, he was originally retained by hispatron, the regional magnate Richard Neville, Earl of Salisbury at a fee of £86s. 8d. By 1465, he was Steward of the Honour of Richmondshire and was being retained, along with his brothers William and Richard, by Salisbury's son and successor as regional magnate, the earl of Warwick, for which he received £136s. 8d. He accompanied Salisbury on his journey from Middleham to Ludlow in September 1459, and took part in the Battle of Blore Heath on the 23rd of that month. He later took part in Warwick's rebellion against Edward IV in 1469 and the Battle of Edgecote, raising his 'Wensleydale connection, and possibly even being the ringleader, 'Robin of Redesdale.' He submitted to the King in March 1469. After Edward's successful return to power in 1471 he was a Justice of the Peace for Yorkshire's North Riding. A loyal retainer and probable ducal councillor of Edward's brother, Richard, Duke of Gloucester, later King Richard III, (who retained him for £20 annually) he was made a knight of the body, at200 marks per annum annuity, and substantial estates in Yorkshire, "where he was very active on local commissions." He was also elected to the Order of the Garter. In August 1485 he appears to have fought in and survived the Battle of Bosworth in the army of Richard III, and was later granted offices in Richmondshire by the new king, Henry VII in February 1486, as a result of 'good and faithful service.' He supported Henry during the first rebellion of his reign, in spring 1486, a position that has been called 'particularly significant' and, according to Michael Hicks, it 'was a momentous decision'.

Sources:

Ross, C.D., Richard III, London 1981, p.50

Ross, C.D., Richard III, London 1981, p.50

Ross, C.D., Richard III, London 1981, p.50

Pollard, A.J., North-Eastern England During the Wars of the Roses, Oxford 1990, p.128

Griffiths, R.A., The Reign of King Henry VI: The Exercise of Royal Authority, Berkeley 1981, p.847 n.276

Ross, C.D., Edward IV, Trowbridge 1974, p.141

Ross, C.D., Edward IV, Trowbridge 1974, p.128

Hicks, M.A., 'Dynastic Change and Northern Society: The Fourth Earl of Northumberland, 1470-89,' Northern History XIV (1978), p. 89,n.52

Ross, C.D., Richard III, London 1981, p.50

Ross, C.D., Richard III, London 1981, p.57

Skidmore, C., Bosworth: The Birth of the Tudors, Croydon2013, p.363

Hicks, M.A., The Wars of the Roses, London 2012, p.342

The following is reprinted from Genealogical Gleanings in England by Henry F. Waters, A.M., Boston, 1901, published in two volumes by The New England Historic Genealogical Society

Baron of the bishopric of Durham and Lord of Bishopton.

Geoffery "Galfrid" Conyers, Lord of Sockburn and Bishopton, 1213-1238. ,
John Conyers, Sockburn, England.
Sir Humphrey' Conyers, Sockburn, England.
Sir John' Conyers, Sockburn, England.
Roger Conyers, Sockburn, England.
Sir John' Conyers, Sockburn, England; died 1395.
Robert Conyers, Sockburn, England; born 1371; died 1433.
John" Conyers, Hornby, England.
Sir Christopher" Conyers, Hornby, England.
Sir John Conyers, of Hornby Castle; sheriff of the shire;governor of the castle at York; in 1460 joined Richard, Duke of York, against the King.
Sir John" Conyers, of Hornby, England; Knight of the Order of the Garter; died 1490.
Reginald" Conyers, Wakerly, England; died 1514.
Richard" Conyers, Wakerly, England.
Christopher" Conyers, Wakerly, England, baptized 1552.

Sir John Conyers, Sheriff of Yorkshire, Constable of Middleham, Bailiff & Steward of Richmond Liberty, Steward of the lord ship of Middleham

M, #12932, d. 14 March 1490
Father   Sir Christopher Conyers, Sheriff of Yorkshire 2,4,10 b. c 1393
Mother Eleanor Rolleston 2,4,10 b. c 1390, d. 6 Aug 1444
    Sir John Conyers, Sheriff of Yorkshire, Constable of Middleham, Bailiff & Steward of Richmond Liberty, Steward of the lordship of Middleham Eminent in the War of the Roses. He was born at of Hornby, North Riding, Yorkshire, England. He married Margery Darcy, daughter of Sir Philip Darcy, 6th Baron Darcy, Lord Meinell and Eleanor Fitz Hugh, before 20 November 1431; They had 7 sons (Sir John; Richard; Christopher; Henry; Philip; Robert; & William, Esq.) and 5 daughters (Eleanor, wife of Sir Thomas Markenfield; Elizabeth, wife of Sir William FitzWilliam; Margaret, wife of Richard Ascue; Margery, wife of Rowland Place, Esq. & of Robert Wycliffe; & Joan).2,15,3,5,7,8,9,10,11,13,14 Sir John Conyers, Sheriff of Yorkshire, Constable of Middleham, Bailiff &Steward of Richmond Liberty, Steward of the lordship of Middleham died on 14 March 1490; Buried at Hornby, Yorkshire.2,4,10
Family
Margery Darcy b. 1 Sep 1418, d. bt 20 Mar 1469 - 20 Apr 1469
Children
Thomas Conyers+
Richard Conyers, Lord of Horden Manor in Durham+
Elizabeth Conyers+2,6,12
Sir John Conyers+2,4,10 b. c 1432, d. 26 Jul 1469
Eleanor Conyers+2,16,4,7,10,13 b. c 1445, d. 5 Jun 1493
Margery Conyers+3,4,9,10 b. c 1447, d. a 4 May 1493

SOURCES:

[S3652] Unknown author, Plantagenet Ancestry of 17th Century Colonists, by David Faris, p. 70;Burke's Peerage, 1938, p. 738, 2639.
[S5] Douglas Richardson, Plantagenet Ancestry, p. 227.

[S16] Douglas Richardson, Magna Carta Ancestry, 2nd Edition, Vol. I, p. 215.
[S16] Douglas Richardson, Magna Carta Ancestry, 2nd Edition, Vol. I, p. 530-531.
[S16] Douglas Richardson, Magna Carta Ancestry, 2nd Edition, Vol. II, p. 28.
[S16] Douglas Richardson, Magna Carta Ancestry, 2nd Edition, Vol. II, p. 446.
[S16] Douglas Richardson, Magna Carta Ancestry, 2nd Edition, Vol. III, p. 132.
[S16] Douglas Richardson, Magna Carta Ancestry, 2nd Edition, Vol. IV, p. 237.
[S4] Douglas Richardson, Royal Ancestry, Vol. I, p. 380.
[S4] Douglas Richardson, Royal Ancestry, Vol. II, p. 288.
[S4] Douglas Richardson, Royal Ancestry, Vol. II, p. 391.
[S4] Douglas Richardson, Royal Ancestry, Vol. III, p.385.
[S4] Douglas Richardson, Royal Ancestry, Vol. IV, p. 62.
[S4] Douglas Richardson, Royal Ancestry, Vol. V, p. 217.
[S15] Douglas Richardson, Magna Carta Ancestry, p. 259.
[S5] Douglas Richardson, Plantagenet Ancestry, p. 498.

Knights of the Garter, 1348-present

The dates are those of appointment or nomination (app),or investiture or installation (inv).

1 (inv 1348) Edward, Prince of Wales (Founder). Known since 1569 as the "Black Prince." The hero of the battles of Crécyand Poitiers. He died in his father's lifetime.

2 (inv 1348) Henry (Plantagenet), styled "of Lancaster" (Founder). Earl of Derby. Afterwards Duke of Lancaster. Served in the wars against the Scots, the Dutch, and French. Admiral of the Fleet and Steward of England.

3 (inv 1348) Thomas (Beauchamp), 3rd Earl of Warwick(Founder). Marshal of England. Fought at the battles of Crécy and Poitiers.

4 (inv 1348) Sir John de Grailly, Vicomte de Benanges et Castillon. Captal (i.e. Governor) de Buch. One of the Founders of the Order.Fought under the Black Prince at Poitiers.

5 (inv 1348) Ralph, 1st Earl of Stafford (Founder).Served in the Scotch and French wars and in important diplomatic missions in European countries.

6 (inv 1348) William (de Montacute), 2nd Earl of Salisbury. One of the Founders of the Order. In the wars of his time he was chiefly distinguished in naval actions. He was the last survivor of the Founders.

7 (inv 1348) Roger (Mortimer), 2nd Earl of March(Founder). Attended the King into France while yet under age and served later in expeditions under John of Gaunt.

8 (inv 1348) Sir John de Lisle, afterwards 1st Lord Lislede Rougemont. One of the Founders of the Order. Granted a manor at the age of 17 to enable him to serve in the wars, in which he won great fame.

9 (inv 1348) Sir Bartholomew Burghersh (Founder). Served with distinction in the French wars.

10 (inv 1348) Sir John Beauchamp (Founder). Afterwards Lord Beauchamp de Warwick. He carried the Standard Royal at the battle of Crécy Present at the surrender of Calais and the battle of Sluys.

11 (inv 1348) John, 2nd Lord Mohun. One of the Founders of the Order. Served in the wars under the Black Prince.

12 (inv 1348) Sir Hugh Courtenay. One of the Founders of the Order. Served with the King in France.

13 (inv 1348) Sir Thomas Holland (Founder). Afterwards 1st Earl of Kent. Married the "Fair Maid of Kent", widow of the Black Prince. In chief command of the van at the battle of Crécy.

14 (inv 1348) Sir John Grey (Founder). Distinguished in the French wars.

15 (inv 1348) Sir Richard Fitz-Simon (Founder). One of the three who stood over the Black Prince when struck down at the battle of Crécy

16 (inv 1348) Sir Miles Stapleton. One of the Founders of the Order. Fought at the siege of Calais and at the Battle of Crécy.

17 (inv 1348) Sir Thomas Wale (Founder). Attended Edward III into Flanders in 1339 and served in the expedition to Brittany in 1342.

18 (inv 1348) Sir Hugh Wrottesley (Founder). On service in Flanders in 1338.

19 (inv 1348) Sir Male Loryng. One of the Founders of the Order. Distinguished at the battle of Blurs. Attended the Black Prince into Gascony. Fought at the battle of Poitiers.

20 (inv 1348) Sir John Chandos. One of the Founders of the Order. Fought at Crécy and Poitiers.

21 (inv 1348) Sir James Audley (Founder). Fought at the battle of Sluys, and with great distinction at Poitiers, where he was severely wounded.

22 (inv 1348) Sir Otho Holland (Founder). Brother of Thomas Holland, Earl of Kent, also a Founder; whom he accompanied into Brittany, where he was taken prisoner. Later he was Governor of the Channel Islands.

23 (inv 1348) Sir Henry Earn (Founder). Entrusted by the Black Prince with a mission to Brabant.

24 (inv 1348) Sir Sanchet D'Abrichecourt. One of the Founders of the Order.

25 (inv 1348) Sir Walter Paveley. One of the Founders of the Order.

26 (app c.1359) Sir William Fitz Waryne.

27 (inv c.1348) Robert (Ufford), 1st Earl of Suffolk.Employed in various missions in France, Flanders, Scotland, and Italy. Fought at the battle of Poitiers.

28 (inv 1349) William (de Bohun), 1st Earl of Northampton. Present at the naval victory of Sluys and also at the battle of Crécy

29 (app c.1352) Reginald, 1st Lord Cobham of Sterborough.One of the three knights in charge of Edward, Prince of Wales, at Crécy Foughtalso at Poitiers, and conducted the French king as prisoner to the English camp.

30 (app c.1356) Sir Richard de la Vache. One of the Knights specially summoned by Edward III in 1347 to support him in arms.

31 (inv 1358) Thomas, Lord Ughtred. Admiral of the Fleet northwards. Served in the wars in Scotland and France.

32 (inv 1359) Sir Walter Manny. In the suite of Philippa of Hainault, coming to England as bride of Edward III. Served as Admiral of the King's fleet at the battle of Sluys.

33 (app c.1359) Sir Frank van Hale. With Sir W. Manny in the suite of the Earl of Derby. Present at the attack on Bergerac.

34 (inv 1360) Sir Thomas Ufford. Served with the Black Prince in Navarre and Spain, and commanded a ship at the battle of Sluys.

35 (inv 1360) Lionel (Plantagenet), styled "of Antwerp," Duke of Clarence, 3rd son of Edward III.

36 (inv 1360) John (Plantagenet), styled "of Gaunt." Afterwards Duke of Lancaster, and King of Castile and Leon. 4th son of Edward III.

37 (app c.1360) Edmund (Plantagenet). Styled "of Langley," Earl of Cambridge. Afterwards Duke of York. Youngest son of Edward III, and great-grandfather of Edward IV. Saw active service in France and Spain.

38 (inv 1361) Edward, 5th Lord le Despencer. Present atthe battle of Poitiers.

39 (app c.1361) Sir John Sully. Fought at Crécy

40 (app c.1361) William 4th Lord Latimer. Distinguished in the wars in France.

41 (app c.1365) Humphrey (de Bohun), 7th Earl of Hereford.

42 (inv 1365) Sir Ingelram de Couci (Enguerrand deCoucy). Afterwards created Earl of Bedford. Married Isabella, daughter of Edward III.

43 (inv 1366) Henry (Percy), 1st Earl of Northumberland. Possibly degraded 1407.

44 (app c.1368) Ralph, 4th Lord Bassett of Drayton. Served in the French wars under the Black Prince and Richard II.

45 (inv 1368) Sir Richard Pembrugge. Present at the battle of Crécy and the siege of Calais.

46 (inv 1369) John, 3rd Lord Nevill of Raby. Admiral of the King's fleet. Served in the wars against the Scots and French.

47 (inv 1369) Sir Robert de Namur. Commanded a ship atthe battle of Sluys. Married Elizabeth of Hainault, sister of Queen Philippa.

48 (inv 1369) John (Hastings), 2nd Earl of Pembroke.Captain of the English forces in Gascony. Prisoner at Santander after the battle of Rochelle.

49 (inv c.1369) Sir Thomas Grandison. Served in the French wars.

50 (app c.1370) Guy, Lord Bryan. Bore the King's bannerat the defence of Calais.

51 (inv 1372) Sir Guichard d'Angle, afterwards Earl of Huntingdon. Fighting on the French side at Poitiers, he was captured wounded.Brought to England, he supported the English cause.

52 (inv 1372) Sir Alan Buxhull. Served in Brittany.Constable of the Tower of London.

53 (app c.1373) Thomas (Beauchamp), 4th Earl of Warwick.Fought in the French campaign under John of Gaunt. Possibly degraded 1397,restored 1400.

54 (inv 1375) John (de Montfort), Duke of Brittany.Married Mary, 4th daughter of Edward III.

55 (app c.1376) Sir Thomas Banastre. Attended the Black Prince into Spain and fought at the battle of Najara. Perished in a wreck in the Irish Sea on an expedition to Brittany.

56 (inv 1375) William (Ufford), 2nd Earl of Pembroke. Admiral of the North. Served in the French wars.

57 (inv 1375) Hugh, 2nd Earl of Stafford. Served in the wars in France and elsewhere.

58 (inv 1376) Thomas (Holland), 2nd Earl of Kent. Marshal of England. Served in the French wars under his stepfather, the Black Prince.

59 (inv 1376) Sir Thomas Percy. Afterwards created Earl of Worcester. Served with Sir John Chandos in France. Joined his nephew Percy(Hotspur) and was taken prisoner at the battle of Shrewsbury and beheaded.

60 (inv 1376) Sir William Beauchamp; afterwards 1st Lord Bergavenny. Served with distinction in the French wars. Afterwards Captain of Calais.

61 (inv 1376) Richard (Plantagenet), styled "of Bordeaux." Prince of Wales. Subsequently Richard II, King of England.

62 (inv 1377) Henry (Plantagenet), styled "of Bolingbroke, " Earl of Derby. Afterwards Duke of Lancaster. Subsequently Henry IV, King of England.

63 (inv 1377) Sir John Barley. Served in Brittany under Thomas of Woodstock.

64 (inv 1377) Sir Lewis Clifford. Served in France.Incurred disfavour as a Lollard.

65 (app c.1380) Sir Bermond Arnaud de Preissac. Soudan dela Trau.

66 (inv 1380) Thomas (Plantagenet), styled "of Woodstock." Duke of Gloucester. 6th son of Edward III. Murdered at Calais 1397.

67 (app c.1381) Sir Thomas Felton. Fought at the battles of Crécy and Poitiers.

68 (inv 1381) John (Holland), Earl of Huntingdon; afterwards 1st Duke of Exeter. Half-brother of Richard II.

69 (inv 1381) Sir Simon de Burley. Served in the wars in France. Entrusted by the Black Prince with the tutorship of Richard II. Stow ascribes to him the origin of Wat Tyler's rebellion. Beheaded in 1388.

70 (inv 1381) Sir Bryan Stapleton. Served in the French wars.

71 (inv 1382) Sir Richard Burley. Fought in Gascony under John of Gaunt.

72 (inv 1383) Thomas (de Mowbray), Earl of Nottingham.Afterwards 1st Duke of Norfolk and created Earl Marshal. Present at the naval victory over the Spanish and French in 1387.

73 (inv 1384) Robert (Vere), 9th Earl of Oxford and Duke of Ireland. Once the favourite of Richard II, he died in exile and poverty at Louvain. He was attainted in 1387, possibly degraded 1388.

74 (inv 1386) Richard (Fitzalan), 4th Earl of Arundel. Admiral of the West and South. Served in the French wars. Sided with the Duke of Gloucester against the King. Beheaded 1397.

75 (inv 1386) Sir Nicholas Samesfield. in the retinue of the Black Prince and witness to his will. The King's Standard-bearer.

76 (inv 1387) Edward (Plantagenet), 2nd Duke of York;eldest son of Edmund of Langley.

77 (inv 1388) Sir Henry Percy, called Hotspur; eldest son of Henry, 1st Earl of Northumberland. Present at the capture of Berwick-on-Tweed in 1378. Served later in further wars against the Scots and taken prisoner at the battle of Otterburn. Employed for a time in the war in France. Engaged in the suppression of the Welsh under Owen Glendower. Killed at the battle of Shrewsbury.

78 (app c.1388) John, 1st Lord Devereux. Governor of Calais, and served in the French wars in Aquitaine.

79 (app c.1388) Sir Peter Courtenay. Knighted by the Prince of Wales at Vittoria before the battle of Najara. Standard-bearer to Edward III, Captain of Calais. Governor of Windsor Castle.

80 (inv c.1388) Thomas le Despencer, 6th Lord le Despencer; afterwards Earl of Gloucester. Engaged in a plot to surprise Windsor Castle with 500 horse, seize Henry IV, and proclaim King Richard. Captured at Bristol and beheaded.

81 (inv 1390) William, Duke of Gueldres and Juliers.

82 (inv 1390) William VI, Count of Holland, Duke of Bavaria.

83 (app c.1392) John, 2nd Lord Bourchier. Fought at Poitiers and served with the Black Prince in Gascony; also with Thomas of Woodstock in France. Governor of Flanders.

84 (app c.1393) John, 4th Lord Beaumont. Warden of the West Marshes, and Admiral of the North. Served in the French wars.

85 (inv 1394) William (le Scrope), 1st Earl of Wiltshire.Lord Treasurer of England. Beheaded after the surrender of Bristol to Henry IV in 1399.

86 (inv c.1395) Sir William Arundel. Served with Richard II in Ireland. Constable of Rochester Castle.

87 (app c.1396) Sir John Beaufort. Afterwards 1st Earl of Somerset and Marquess of Dorset. Eldest son of John of Gaunt and Katharine Swynford. Admiral of the North.

88 (inv 1397) Thomas (Holland), 3rd Earl of Kent.Afterwards Duke of Surrey. Marshal of England. Conspired against Henry IV and was beheaded.

89 (app c.1397) John (de Montacute), 3rd Earl of Salisbury. Joined in a conspiracy for the restoration of Richard II in 1399, but was captured and beheaded.

90 (inv 1397) Albert (or Robert) Count Palatine, Duke of Bavaria, nephew of Edward III.

91 (app c.1397) Sir Simon Felbrigg. In the retinue of John of Gaunt at the relief of Brest. Fought at the battle of Agincourt.

92 (inv c.1399) Sir Philip de la Vache. Served in the French wars.

93 (inv 1399) Henry (Plantagenet), Prince of Wales.Afterwards Henry V, King of England.

94 (inv 1399) Thomas (Plantagenet), styled "of Lancaster." Duke of Clarence. 2nd son of Henry IV.

95 (app c.1400) John (Plantagenet). Styled "of Lancaster." Third son of Henry IV. Afterwards Duke of Bedford. Protector of England in the absence of Henry V in France. Regent of France during them in ority of Henry VI.

96 (inv 1399) Humphrey (Plantagenet), styled "of Lancaster." Duke of Gloucester. 4th son of Henry IV. Protector of England during the minority of Henry VI.

97 (inv 1400) Thomas (Fitz alan), 5th Earl of Arundel.

98 (app c.1400) Sir Thomas Beaufort. Youngest son of John of Gaunt and Katharine Swynford. Afterwards Earl of Dorset and Duke of Exeter.Captain of Calais. Lord Chancellor.

99 (app 1403) Richard (Beauchamp), 5th Earl of Warwick.Captured the banner of Owen Glendower, and fought at the battle of Shrewsbury.Tutor and Governor of the young King Henry VI.

100 (app c.1400) William, 5th Lord Willoughby de Eresby.

101 (inv 1400) Sir Thomas Rempston. Fought at the battle of Agincourt.

102 (inv 1400) John I, King of Portugal. Married Philippa, sister of Henry IV, King of England.

103 (app c.1401) Sir Thomas Erpyngham. Fought at Agincourt.

104 (inv 1402) Edmund, 5th Earl of Stafford. Lord High Constable. Killed at the battle of Shrewsbury.

105 (inv 1402) Ralph (Nevill), 1st Earl of Westmorland.

106 (inv 1403) Edmund (Holland), 4th Earl of Kent. Admiral of the West and North.

107 (app c.1403) Richard, 4th Lord Grey of Codnor.

108 (inv 1403) William, 7th Lord Ros of Hamlake.

109 (inv 1404) Sir John Stanley.

110 (inv 1404) Eric VII, King of Denmark, Norway and Sweden. Married Philippa, daughter of Henry IV.

111 (inv 1405) John, 5th Lord Lovell of Tichmarsh.

112 (app c.1406) Hugh, 2nd Lord Burnell.

113 (inv 1408) Edward, 3rd Lord Cherleton of Powys.

114 (app c.1408) Gilbert, 5th Lord Talbot. Afterwards Lord Strange of Blackmere. Defeated the insurgent Welsh in 1407. Served in the French wars. Captain General of the Marches in Normandy.

115 (app c.1408) Henry 3rd Lord Fitz Hugh. Served in the French wars with Henry V.

116 (inv 1408) Sir Robert Umfraville. Mainly occupied in Scottish affairs. Present at the burning of Peebles.

117 (app c.1410) Sir John Cornwall. Afterwards Lord Fanhope. Fought at the battle of Agincourt. Married Elizabeth, daughter of John of Gaunt, widow of John, Earl of Exeter, and sister of Henry IV.

118 (inv 1409) Henry, 3rd Lord Scrope of Masham. Conspired with the French in a plot against the King. Beheaded 1415.

119 (inv 1411) Thomas, 4th Lord Morley. Captain-General of all the forces in France.

120 (inv 1413) Sir John D'Abrichecourt.

121 (app c.1414) Thomas (de Montacute), 4th Earl of Salisbury. Mortally wounded at the siege of Orleans.

122 (inv 1414) Thomas, 1st Lord Camoys. Commanded the left wing at the battle of Agincourt.

123 (inv 1415) Sir William Harington.

124 (inv 1415) William, 4th Lord Zouche of Hatingworth.

125 (inv 1415) John (Holland), Earl of Huntingdon; afterwards 3rd Duke of Exeter. He married Elizabeth daughter of John of Gaunt and sister of Henry IV.

126 (inv 1415) Richard (de Vere), 11th Earl of Oxford.Held a command at the battle of Agincourt.

127 (inv 1415) Sigismund, Emperor.

128 (inv 1416) Robert, 6th Lord Willoughby de Eresby.Fought at Agincourt.

129 (inv 1417) Sir John Blount.

130 (inv 1417) Sir John Robessart.

131 (app c.1418) Hugh (Stafford), 4th Lord Bourchier. Served with Henry V in Normandy.

132 (app c.1415) Sir William Phelipp. Afterwards 6th Lord Bardolf Fought at Agincourt.

133 (inv 1419) John (Grey) Earl of Tankerville. Distinguished in the French wars.

134 (inv 1420) Sir Walter Hungerford. Afterwards 1st Lord Hungerford. Served in the wars in France.

135 (app 1421) Sir Lewis Robessart. Afterwards Lord Robessart or Lord Bourchier. Standard-bearer to Henry V.

136 (app 1421) Sir Hertong von Clux.

137 (inv 1421) John, 7th Lord Clifford; killed at the siege of Meaux.

138 (app 1421) John (de Mowbray), Earl Marshal;afterwards 3rd Duke of Norfolk. He served in the French wars, but was absent from Agincourt through sickness.

139 (app 1421) William (de la Pole), 3rd Earl of Suffolk,afterwards 1st Duke of Suffolk. Served for 24 years in the wars. In command at the victory of Verneuil, and at the siege of Orleans. Taken prisoner by Joan of Arc. Assassinated 1450.

140 (inv 1422) Philip II, Duke of Burgundy. Elected but then declined the honour.

141 (app 1424) John, 7th Lord Talbot. Afterwards 1st Earl of Shrewsbury. Marshal of France, Fought in the French wars under Henry V.Taken prisoner by Joan of Arc. Killed in battle at Chastillon, near Bordeaux in 1453.

142 (inv 1425) Thomas, 7th Lord Scales. Distinguished in the French wars, and in the suppression of Jack Cade's rebellion.

143 (inv 1426) Sir John Fastolf. Served in the wars in France. Possibly degraded 1429, restored 1429.

144 (inv 1427) Peter, Duke of Coimbra, 3rd son of John I,King of Portugal, by Philippa his wife. sister of Henry IV, King of England.

145 (app 1429) Humphrey, 6th Earl of Stafford. Afterwards 1st Duke of Buckingham. Served in the wars in France. Captain of Calais. Killed at the battle of Northampton, fighting as a Lancastrian.

146 (inv 1429) Sir John Radcliffe. Constable of Bordeaux,1419-23.

147 (inv 1432) John (Fitzalan), 7th Earl of Arundel. Governor of Rouen and served in the French wars. Created Duke of Touraine in France by the Duke of Bedford, the Regent.

148 (inv 1433) Richard (Plantagenet), 3rd Duke of York.Grandson of Edmund of Langley. Protector of England. Killed at the battle of Wakefield.

149 (app 1435) Edward, King of Portugal, Son of Philippa, sister of Henry IV, King of England.

150 (inv 1436) Edmund. (Beaufort), Count Morteign; afterwards 2nd Duke of Somerset. Constable of England. Regent of France. Killed at the first battle of St. Albans.

151 (app c.1436) Sir John Grey, afterwards 4th Lord Greyde Ruthyn. Served in.the French wars.

152 (app c.1438) Richard (Nevill), 5th Earl of Salisbury.Lord Chancellor. Taken prisoner at the battle of Wakefield and beheaded, 1460.

153 (inv 1438) Albert, Duke of Austria. Afterwards Emperor (not installed).

154 (app c.1438) Sir Gaston de Foix, Comte de Longuevilleet Benanges, Captal de Buch. Distinguished in the French wars.

155 (app c.1439) William (Nevill), Lord Fauconberge. Afterwards Earl of Kent. Served with distinction in the French wars.

156 (app c.1439) John (Beaufort), 3rd Earl of Somerset.Afterwards 1st Duke of Somerset. Father of Margaret, Countess of Richmond,mother of Henry VII.

157 (inv 1439) Sir Ralph Boteler. Afterwards 6th Lord Sudeley. Distinguished in the wars in France.

158 (inv 1440) John, 1st Viscount Beaumont. Distinguished both in war and at Court. He was the first to be advanced to the dignity of a Viscount in England.

159 (inv 1445) Sir John Beauchamp. Afterwards 1st Lord Beauchamp of Powyk. Lord Treasurer.

160 (inv 1442) Henry, Duke of Viseu, 4th son of John I, King of Portugal, and nephew of Henry IV. "Henry the Navigator."

161 (inv 1445) Sir Thomas Hoo. Afterwards Lord Hoo and Hastings. Fought with distinction in France. Keeper of the Seals in France and Chancellor of France.

162 (inv 1445) Alvaro Vasquez d' Almada, Countd' Avranches.

163 (inv 1446) Sir John de Foix, Captal de Buch.

164 (inv 1447) Alphonso V, King of Portugal.

165 (inv 1447) Sir Francis Surrienne, Sire de Lunée.

166 (inv 1450) Alphonso V, King of Aragon, Naples, and Sicily.

167 (inv 1450) William, Duke of Brunswick. (Notinstalled.)

168 (inv 1450) Casimir IV, King of Poland. (Notinstalled, but placed here in 1467. See Beltz, page 400.)

169 (app 1450) Richard (Wydville), 1st Lord Rivers. Afterwards 1st Earl Rivers. In command of the forces during the French wars.Lord High Constable. Treasurer of the Exchequer. Beheaded 1469. Father of Elizabeth, Queen of Edward IV.

170 (inv 1451) John (de Mowbray), 4th Duke of Norfolk.

171 (app c.1450) Henry, Viscount Bourchier, Count of Eu. Afterwards 1st Earl of Essex.

172 (inv 1453) Sir Edward Hull, slain in 1453 before being installed.

173 (inv 1457) John, 2nd Earl of Shrewsbury. Served in France with his father.

174 (inv 1457) Thomas, 1st Lord Stanley. Chief Governor of Ireland.

175 (inv 1457) Lionel, 6th Lord Welles. Captain of the forces at Calais. Chief Governor of Ireland. Killed at the battle of Towton, fighting as a Lancastrian.

176 (inv 1457) Frederick III, Emperor. (Not installed.)

177 (inv 1459) James (Butler), 2nd Earl of Wiltshire and 5th Earl of Ormonde.

178 (inv 1459) John (Sutton), 5th Lord Dudley.

179 (inv c.1450) John (Bourchier), 1st Lord Berners. Grandson of Thomas of Woodstock, 6th son of Edward III. Fought for Henry VI at the first battle of St. Albans. Afterwards changed sides.

180 (inv 1459) Jasper (Tudor), Earl of Pembroke and Duke of Bedford. Uncle of Henry VII. Degraded in 1461, reinstalled c. 1485.

181 (inv c.1461) Richard (Nevill), 1st Earl of Warwick.Famous in the Wars of the Roses as the "Kingmaker." Killed at the battle of Barnet. Probably degraded 1468.

182 (inv c.1461) William, 1st Lord Bonville. Knighted while with the army in France. Executed after the second battle of St.

Albans.

183 (inv 1461) Sir Thomas Kiriell.

184 (inv 1461) Sir John Wenlock. Afterwards 1st Lord Wenlock. Killed at the battle of Tewkesbury. fighting as a Lancastrian.

185 (app c.1461) George (Plantagenet), Duke of Clarence.Lord-Lieutenant of Ireland. Rebelled against his brother Edward IV, with his father-in-law, Richard, Earl of Warwick, the "King-maker." Returned to his allegiance. Convicted of treason on the accusation of his brother Richard,Duke of Gloucester,afterwards Richard III, he is said to have been drowned in a butt of Malmsey.

186 (app c.1461) Sir William Chamberlaine. Distinguished in the French wars under the Duke of Bedford.

187 (inv c.1461) John (Tiptoft), Earl of Worcester.Constable of England. Supporter of Edward IV. On the restoration to power of Henry VI he was beheaded for high treason.

188 (inv 1462) William, 1st Lord Hastings. In command at the battle of Barnet. Beheaded in 1483.

189 (inv c.1461) John (Nevill), Lord Montagu. Afterwards Marquess of Montagu.

190 (inv c.1461) William, Lord Herbert; afterwards 1stEarl of Pembroke. A staunch Yorkist. Captured Harlech Castle. Taken prisoner at Edgcote and beheaded.

191 (inv 1461) Sir John Astley.

192 (inv c.1463) Ferdinand I, King of Sicily and Naples.

193 (inv c.1463) Gaillard (de Durfort), seigneur de Durasand Blanquefort, died 1481. Married Anne de La Pole. Possibly degraded 1476, orresigned.

194 (app 1462) John, 5th Lord Scrope of Bolton. Fought asa Yorkist. Also in expeditions to France and Scotland.

195 (inv c.1463) Francesco Sforza, Duke of Milan.

196 (app c.1462) James, 9th Earl of Douglas. Acted with the Duke of York in rebellion against Henry VI. Joined the Duke of Albany in an invasion of Scotland and was taken prisoner.

197 (app c.1462) Sir Robert Harcourt. Killed fighting for the Lancastrian cause in 1470.

198 (app c.1465) Richard (Plantagenet) Duke of Gloucester. Afterwards RICHARD III, King of England. Killed at the battle of Bosworth.

199 (app c.1466) Anthony (Wydville), 2nd Lord Scales.Afterwards 2nd Earl Rivers, Beheaded at Pomfret Castle by Richard III. Brother of Elizabeth, Queen of Edward IV.

200 (inv c.1467) Inigo (d'Avalos), Conte di Monteoderisio.(Not installed.)

201 (inv c.1468) Charles, Duke of Burgundy. Surnamed"The Bold." Killed in action against the Duke of Lorraine at Nancy.He married the Princess Margaret, daughter of Richard, Duke of York, sister of Edward IV, King of England.

202 (inv c.1471) William (Fitz alan), 9th Earl of Arundel. Fought as a Yorkist at the second battle of St. Albans.

203 (app 1472) John (de Mowbray), 5th Duke of Norfolk and Earl Marshal. One of the leaders in the invasion of France in 1475.

204 (inv 1472) John (Stafford), created Earl of Wiltshire. Son of Humphrey, 1st Duke of Buckingham.

205 (app 1472) Walter (Devereux), 7th Lord Ferrets of Chartley. Killed at the battle of Bosworth, fighting for Richard III.

206 (app 1472) Walter (Blount), 1st Lord Mountjoy. Lord High Treasurer. Fought for Edward IV at the battle of Towton.

207 (inv 1472) John (Howard), 1st Duke of Norfolk. Warned in the following distich: "Jockey of Norfolk be not too bold,/ For Dickonthy master is bought and sold" he was killed at Bosworth at Richard's side.

208 (app c.1472) John (de la Pole), 2nd Duke of Suffolk.Married Elizabeth, sister of Edward IV. A staunch Yorkist.

209 (inv 1474) Thomas (Arundel), Lord Maltravers.Afterwards 10th Earl of Arundel.

210 (inv 1474) Sir William Parr. Fought as a Yorkist on the side of the Nevills at Banbury.

211 (app c.1474) Henry (Stafford), 2nd Duke of Buckingham. Beheaded in 1483 for plotting for Richmond against Richard III,whom he formerly supported.

212 (app 1474) Federigo (da Montefeltro), 1st Duke of Urbino. Took active part in the war for the Angev in succession to Naples.

213 (app 1474) Henry (Percy), 4th Earl of Northumberland. In command at the capture of Berwick-on-Tweed. Taken prisoner at the battle of Bosworth. Assassinated in 1489 by the mob for levying an unpopular tax.

214 (app 1475) Edward (Plantagenet) PRINCE OF WALES. Afterwards EDWARD V, King of England. Murdered with his brother Richard, Duke of York, in the Tower of London.

215 (app 1475) Richard (Plantagenet), 5th Duke of York. 2nd son of Edward IV. Murdered in the Tower of London with his brother Edward V.

216 (inv 1476) Thomas (Grey), 1st Marquess of Dorset.Commanded the forces assisting the Emperor Maximilian against the French.Degraded 1483, restored 1485.

217 (inv 1476) Sir Thomas Montgomery.

218 (inv 1480) Ferdinand V, King of Castile. (Stall voided through non-installation.)

219 (inv 1480) Hercules (d'Este), Duke of Modena and Ferrara.

220 (inv 1482) John II, King of Portugal, not installed,and election void. Re-elected 1488.

221 (app 1483) Francis, 9th Lord Lovell of Tichmarsh. Afterwards Viscount Lovell. Fought at the battle of Bosworth for Richard III.Degraded 1485."Lovell, the dogge," See note s.v. Sir Richard Radcliffe.

222 (inv 1483) Thomas (Howard), 3rd Earl of Surrey.Degraded 1485; restored in 1491.

223 (inv 1483) Sir Richard Radcliffe. Confidential adviser of Richard III. Associated with Catesby and Lovell, he was satirised in the famous couplet: "The catte. the ratte and Lovell our dogge Rulyth all Englande under a hogge." The "hogge" refers to Richard III, whose badge was a white boar. Radcliffe was killed at Bosworth.

224 (inv 1483) Thomas, 2nd Lord Stanley. Afterwards 1st Earl of Derby. At the battle of Bosworth he deserted the cause of Richard III, and is said to have placed the crown on Richmond's head on the field of battle.

225 (app c.1483) Sir Thomas Borough (or Burgh).Afterwards 1st Lord Borough of Gainsborough.

226 (app c.1484) Sir Richard Tunstall.

227 (inv c.1483) Sir John Conyers (d. 1490)

228 (inv 1486) John (de Vere), 13th Earl of Oxford. In command at the battle of Bosworth in support of Henry VII, and later against Simnel's rebellion.

229 (app c.1486) John, Lord Cheyney. Struck down at the battle of Bosworth by Richard III, but not killed.

230 (app c.1487) John, 1st Lord Dynham.

231 (app c.1487) Giles, 1st Lord Daubeny. Governor of Calais.

232 (inv 1487) Sir William Stanley, 2nd son of Thomas, 1st Lord Stanley. Beheaded for alleged share in the Perkin Warbeck conspiracy.

233 (app c.1487) George (Stanley) 9th Lord Strange of Knockyrt. Eldest son of Thomas, 1st Earl of Derby, and died in his father's lifetime.

234 (inv 1488) George (Talbot), 4th Earl of Shrewsbury.Fought with distinction against Lambert Simnel at the battle of Stoke.

235 (inv 1488) Sir Edward Wydville, afterwards Lord Wydville.

236 (inv 1488) John, 1st Viscount Welles, Captain in the forces of his nephew, the Earl of Richmond, afterwards Henry VII.

237 (inv 1489) Sir John Savage. Acted with Sir Rhys ap Thomas in support of Henry Tudor, afterwards Henry VII.

238 (app c.1488) Sir Robert Willoughby. Afterwards 1st Lord Willoughby de Broke. Fought at the battle of Bosworth for Henry VII.

239 (app c.1490) Maximilian, King of the Romans.Afterwards the Emperor Maximilian I. In alliance with Henry VIII, he defeated the French at the battle of the Spurs, 1513.

240 (inv c.1491) Arthur (Tudor) Prince of Wales. Son of Henry VII. Died before his father.

241 (app c.1494) Edward (Courtenay), 1st Earl of Devon.Fought at Bosworth, and defended Exeter against Perkin Warbeck in 1497.

242 (inv 1493) Alphonso, Duke of Calabria. Afterwards Alphonso II, King of Sicily and Naples.

243 (inv 1493) John, King of Denmark, Norway and Sweden.(Not installed.)

244 (inv 1493) Sir Edward Poynings. Supporter of the Earl of Richmond. Commanded a force sent to aid Maximilian against rebels in the Netherlands. Famous Lord Deputy of Ireland, responsible for the measures knownas Poynings' Law.

245 (app c.1495) Sir Gilbert Talbot, 3rd son of John 2nd Earl of Shrewsbury. Captain of Calais. Sent by Henry VII on a mission to Rome.

246 (inv c.1495) Henry (Tudor), Duke of York. Created PRINCE OF WALES in 1502 on the death of his brother Arthur. Afterwards HENRY VIII, King of England.

247 (app c.1495) Henry Algernon (Percy), 5th Earl of Northumberland. Fought at the battle of the Spurs.

248 (inv 1495) Edward (Stafford), 3rd Duke of Buckingham.Degraded 1521.

249 (inv c.1496) Charles (Somerset), 1st Earl of Worcester.

250 (inv 1496) Edmund (de la Pole), 8th Earl of Suffolk. On accepting the accession of Henry VII he surrendered his claim to the Dukedom of Suffolk. Degraded 1500. Beheaded 1513.

251 (c.1496d) Henry (Bourchier), 2nd Earl of Essex. Bore the Sword of State at the Field of the Cloth of Gold.

252 (inv 1498) Sir Thomas Lovell. Supporter of Henry VII,and fought at the battle of Bosworth. Speaker of the House of Commons. He built the gate-house at Lincoln's Inn.

253 (app 1499) Sir Richard Pole.

254 (app c.1500) Sir Richard Guildford. A trusty councillor of Henry VII. Died on a pilgrimage to the Holy Land.

255 (inv 1500) Sir Reginald Bray. A close friend of Henry VII.

256 (inv 1501) Thomas (Grey), 2nd Marquess of Dorset. one of the eight "Challengers" at the Field of the Cloth of Gold.

257 (inv 1503) Philip, Archduke of Austria. Afterwards Philip I, King of Castile.

258 (inv 1505) Gerald (FitzGerald), 8th Earl of Kildare. Surnamed "Gerald the Great." Supporter of Lambert Simnel. Defeated Perkin Warbeck near Galway,

259 (app c.1504) Guidobaldo (da Montefeltro), 2nd Duke of Urbino.

260 (app 1505) Richard (Grey), 3rd Earl of Kent. Present at the Field of the Cloth of Gold.

261 (inv c.1505) Lord Henry Stafford. Afterwards 3rd Earl of Wiltshire. 2nd son of Henry, 2nd Duke of Buckingham.

262 (app c.1505) Sir Rhys ap Thomas Fitz-Urian. An ardent supporter of Henry VII.

263 (inv 1507) Sir Thomas Brandon.

264 (app 1508) Charles, Archduke of Austria. Afterwards the Emperor Charles V.

265 (inv 1509) Thomas, 1st Lord Darcy. Warden of the Scots Marshes. Joined in the Pilgrimage of Grace. Convicted of high treason and beheaded. Degraded 1537.

266 (inv 1509) Edward (Sutton), 6th Lord Dudley.

267 (app 1510) Emanuel, King of Portugal. (Not installed.)

268 (inv 1510) Sir Thomas Howard. Afterwards 3rd Duke of Norfolk. Fought at Flodden. Degraded 1547, restored 1553.

269 (inv 1510) Sir Henry Marny. Afterwards Lord Marny. Lord Privy Seal. Fought at the battles of Stoke and Blackheath.

270 (inv 1510) Thomas (West), 8th Lord de la Warr. Favoured Henry VIII's divorce and had large grants of monastic lands.

271 (inv 1513) George (Nevill), 5th Lord Bergavenny.Served in the wars in France.

272 (app 1513) Sir Edward Howard. (Died before installation.)

273 (inv 1513) Sir Charles Brandon. Afterwards Duke of Suffolk. He married Mary, the younger daughter of Henry VII and widow of Louis XII, King of France.

274 (app 1514) Giuliano de Medici, Duc de Nemours, brother of Pope Leo X. (Not installed.)

275 (inv 1514) Sir Edward Stanley. Afterwards 1st Lord Monteagle. Commanded the English army at Flodden. Younger son of Thomas, 1st Earl of Derby.

276 (inv 1518) Thomas, 3rd Lord Dacre of Gillesland.Fought at the Battle of Flodden.

277 (inv 1518) Sir William Sandys. Afterwards Lord Sandys of the Vyne.

278 (inv 1521) Henry (Courtenay), created Marquess of Exeter. Assisted in the suppression of the Pilgrimage of Grace. Later he was accused of conspiracy, found guilty and beheaded. Degraded 1539.

279 (inv 1524) Ferdinand, Archduke of Austria. Afterwards the Emperor Ferdinand I. Brother of the Emperor Charles V.

280 (inv 1522) Sir Richard Wingfield. Soldier and diplomatist; in high favour with Henry VIII.

281 (inv 1523) Sir Thomas Boleyn. Afterwards Earl of Wiltshire and Ormonde. Father of Anne Boleyn and grandfather of Queen Elizabeth.

282 (inv 1523) Walter (Devereux), 9th Lord Ferrers. Present at the capture of Boulogne. Afterwards 1st Viscount Hereford.

283 (inv 1525) Arthur (Plantagenet), Viscount Lisle.Natural son of Edward IV.

284 (inv 1524) Robert (Radclyffe), 10th Lord Fitz Walter.Afterwards 1st Earl of Sussex. Present at the sieges of Tournay and The rouenne.

285 (inv 1525) William (Fitzalan), 11th Earl of Arundel.

286 (inv 1525) Thomas (Manners), 1st Earl of Rutland.Present with Henry VIII at the Field of the Cloth of Gold. Son and heir of George, 12th Lord Ros.

287 (inv 1525) Sir Henry Fitzroy. Afterwards Duke of Richmond and Somerset. Son of Henry VIII and Elizabeth Blount.

288 (inv 1525) Ralph (Nevill), 4th Earl of Westmorland.Present at the Field of the Cloth of Gold.

289 (inst 1526) William (Blunt), Lord Mountjoy.

290 (inv 1526) Sir William Fitz william. Afterwards 1st Earl of Southampton. Served with distinction against the Scots and French, and on important diplomatic missions.

291 (inv 1526) Sir Henry Guildford. A favourite courtier of Henry VIII.

292 (inv 1527) Francis I, King of France.

293 (inv 1527) John (de Vere), 15th Earl of Oxford. Knighted at the battle of the Spurs.

294 (inst 1531) Henry (Percy), earl of Northumberland.

295 (inv 1533) Anne (de Montmorency), Comte de Beaumont,later duc de Montmorency. Afterwards Duc de Montmorency. Constable of France.Mortally wounded at the battle of St. Denis in 1567.

296 (inv 1532) Philippe (de Chabot), Comte de Charny and Buzançais , d. 1543 (Neublanche in English rolls).

297 (inv 1535) James V, King of Scotland. Father of Mary,Queen of Scots and nephew of Henry VIII.

298 (inv 1536) Sir Nicholas Carew. A favourite courtier of Henry VIII. Entrusted with various diplomatic missions. Attainted and beheaded. Degraded 1539.

299 (inv 1537) Henry (Clifford), 1st Earl of Cumberland.

300 (inv 1537) Thomas, Lord Cromwell. Afterwards Earl of Essex. Began life as a cloth-dresser. Rose under Wolsey's

influence. Not orious in connection with the suppression of the monasteries. Lost favour with Henry VIII after introducing Anne of Cleves. Condemned as a traitor and beheaded.Degraded 1540.

301 (inv 1539) Sir John Russell. Afterwards 1st Earl of Bedford. Lord High Admiral, Lord Privy Seal. Appointed to conduct Philip II of Spain to England.

302 (inv 1539) Sir Thomas Cheyney.

303 (inv 1539) Sir William Kingston. Fought at the battle of Flodden. Took part in the tilting at the Field of the Cloth of Gold.

304 (inv 1540) Thomas, Lord Audley of Walden. Lord Chancellor.

305 (inv 1540) Sir Anthony Browne. An executor of the will of Henry VIII.

306 (inv 1541) Edward (Seymour), Earl of Hertford. Afterwards Duke of Somerset. Brother of Queen Jane Seymour and Uncle of Edward VI, and Protector of England during his minority. Took part in many military operations in Scotland and France. Found guilty of conspiracy and beheaded.

307 (inv 1541) Henry (Howard), Earl of Surrey. Son and heir of Thomas, 3rd Duke of Norfolk. Field-Marshal of the army in France, but more famous as a poet. Executed for high treason, aged 30. Degraded 1547.

308 (inv 1541) Sir John Gage. Statesman and military commander.

309 (inv 1541) Sir Anthony Wingfield. Served in the French wars. Present at the Field of the Cloth of Gold.

310 (inv 1543) John (Dudley), 7th Viscount Lisle.Afterwards Earl of Warwick and Duke of Northumberland. Beheaded 1553.

311 (inv 1543) William (Paulet), Lord St. John of Basing.Afterwards 1st Marquess of Winchester. High Treasurer of England. Joined in the overthrow of the Protector Somerset.

312 (inv 1543) William (Parr) Marquess of Northampton.Brother of Katharine Parr, Queen of Henry VIII. Originally appointed in 1543, he was degraded from the Order in 1552 as a supporter of Lady Jane Grey's cause, but re-elected in 1559.

313 (inv 1544) Sir John Wallop. Soldier and diplomatist.

314 (inv 1544) Henry (Fitz alan), 12th Earl of Arundel.Present at the capture of Boulogne. Married, firstly, Catherine daughter of Thomas, 1st Marquess of Dorset, K.G., aunt of Lady Jane Grey.

315 (inv 1544) Sir Anthony St. Leger. Lord Deputy of Ireland.

316 (inv 1545) Francis (Talbot), 5th Earl of Shrewsbury.Took part in the Scottish invasion. Lord President of the Council of the North.

317 (inv 1545) Thomas, Lord Wriothesley. Afterwards 1st Earl of Southampton. Lord Chancellor.

318 (inv 1547) Henry (Grey), 3rd Marquess of Dorset. Afterwards Duke of Suffolk. Father of Lady Jane Grey; and having proclaimed her Queen after the death of Edward VI, was attainted. Degraded 1554.

319 (inv 1547) Edward (Stanley), 3rd Earl of Derby."With his death the glory of hospitality seemed to fall asleep."-Camden.

320 (inv 1547) Thomas, Lord Seymour of Sudeley. Brother of Somerset, the Protector against whom he conspired. Executed at the Tower.Degraded 1549.

321 (inv 1547) Sir William Paget. Afterwards 1st Lord Paget de Beaudesert. Degraded 1552, restored 1553.

322 (inv 1549) Francis (Hastings), 2nd Earl of Huntingdon.

323 (inv 1549) George (Brooke), 9th Lord Cobham. Knighted in the French wars.

324 (inv 1549) Thomas (West), 9th Lord De la Warr. Served in the wars in France.

325 (inv 1549) Sir William Herbert. Afterwards 1st Earl of Pembroke. Took part against the Protector Somerset. Supporter of Queen Mary I.

326 (inv 1551) Henry II, King of France.

327 (inv 1551) Edward, 9th Lord Clinton. Afterwards 1st Earl of Lincoln. Lord High Admiral of England.

328 (inv 1551) Thomas, 1st Lord Darcy of Chiche. Supporter of Lady Jane Grey.

329 (inv 1553) Henry (Nevill), 5th Earl of Westmorland.

330 (inv 1552) Sir Andrew Dudley. Degraded 1553.

331 (inv 1554) Philip, Prince of Spain. Afterwards Philip II, King of Spain. Married Mary I, Queen of England. Duly elected a Knight of the Garter, but installed as joint Sovereign and had no stall-plate.

332 (inv 1554) Henry (Radclyffe), 2nd Earl of Sussex. In command against the Scots, 1547.

333 (inv 1555) Emanuel Philibert, 10th Duke of Saxony.

334 (inv 1554) William, 1st Lord Howard of Effingham. Lord High Admiral.

335 (inv 1555) Sir Edward Hastings. Afterwards Lord Hastings of Lough borough. Brother of Francis, 2nd Earl of Huntingdon. Founded a hospital at Stoke Poges where he died without issue in 1572.

336 (inv 1555) Anthony (Browne), 1st Viscount Montagu. Served with the army in Picardy. Ambassador to the Holy See.

337 (inv 1558) Thomas (Radclyffe), 3rd Earl of Sussex.Chief Governor of Ireland.

338 (inv 1557) William 13th Lord Grey of Wilton. Distinguished in the wars in France, and wounded at the battle of Pinkie.

339 (inv 1557) Sir Robert Rochester. Loyal adherent of Mary I. (Died before installation.)

340 (inv 1559) Thomas (Howard), 4th Duke of Norfolk.Degraded 1572.
Aspired unsuccessfully to marriage with Mary, Queen of Scots. Condemned for high treason and beheaded.

341 (inv 1559) Henry (Manners), 2nd Earl of Rutland.

342 (inv 1559) Sir Robert Dudley, Afterwards Earl of Leicester. A favourite courtier of Queen Elizabeth, and husband of Amy Robsart.

343 (inv 1560) Adolphus, Duke of Holstein.

344 (inv 1561) George (Talbot), 6th Earl of Shrewsbury. Supporter of the claim of Lady Jane Grey. Had the custody of Mary Queen of Scots for 17 years.

345 (inv 1561) Henry (Carey), 1st Lord Hunsdon. Son of William Carey and Mary Boleyn.

346 (inv 1563) Thomas (Percy), 1st Earl of Northumberland. Degraded 1569.
Shared in the rebellion of the four northern Earls in 1568. Driven into Scotland he was betrayed by the Regent, the Earl of Mar, and beheaded.

347 (inv 1563) Ambrose (Dudley), 2nd Earl of Warwick.Brother of the Earl of Leicester and Lord Guilford Dudley.
Convicted of high treason as a supporter of Lady Jane Grey, but pardoned.

348 (inv 1566) Charles IX, King of France.

349 (inv 1564) Francis (Russell), 2nd Earl of Bedford.

350 (inv 1564) Sir Henry Sidney. Father of Sir Philip Sidney. Fought at the battle of Flodden. Present at the Field of the Cloth of Gold.

351 (inv 1568) Maximilian II, Emperor.

352 (inv 1570) Henry (Hastings), 3rd Earl of Huntingdon. Joint custodian of Mary Queen of Scots.

353 (inv 1570) William (Somerset), 3rd Earl of Worcester.Supporter of Lady Jane Grey.

354 (inv 1572) Francis, Duke of Montmorency.

355 (inv 1549) Walter (Devereux), 1st Earl of Essex and Eu. Said to have been poisoned by Lord Leicester, who married his widow.Robert, 2nd Earl of Essex, a favourite courtier of Queen Elizabeth, was his son.

356 (inv 1572) William (Cecil), 1st Lord Burghley (d.1598). For 40 years leading Minister of Queen Elizabeth.

357 (inv 1572) Arthur, 14th Lord Grey of Wilton. Chief Governor of Ireland.

358 (inv 1572) Edmund (Brydges), 2nd Lord Chandos of Sudeley. Served in the wars in Scotland and France.

359 (inv 1574) Henry (Stanley), 4th Earl of Derby.

360 (inv 1574) Henry (Herbert), 2nd Earl of Pembroke.Married Mary, sister of Sir Philip Sidney: "Sidney's sister, Pembroke'smother."

361 (inv 1575) Henry III, King of France.

362 (inv 1575) Charles, 2nd Lord Howard of Effingham. Afterwards Earl of Nottingham. Lord High Admiral. In command of the fleet at the capture of Cadiz and the defeat of the Spanish Armada.

363 (inv 1578) Rudolph II, Emperor.

364 (inv 1582) Frederick II, King of Denmark and Norway.

365 (inv 1582) John Casimir, Count Palatine of the Rhine, Duke of Bavaria.

366 (inv 1585) Edward (Manners), 3rd Earl of Rutland.

367 (inv 1584) William (Brooke), 7th Lord Cobham.

368 (inv 1585) Henry, 9th Lord Scrope of Bolton. Marshal of the army at the siege of Leith.

369 (inv 1588) Robert (Devereux), 2nd Earl of Essex. Degraded 1601.
A favourite courtier of Queen Elizabeth. Fought at the battle of Zutphen when Sir Philip Sidney was killed. Lord Lieutenant of Ireland, and Earl Marshal of England. Condemned and beheaded for high treason.The story of the Queen's ring is apocryphal.

370 (inv 1588) Thomas (Butler), 10th Earl of Ormonde and Ossory. Suppressed various rebellions in Ireland.

371 (inv 1588) Sir Christopher Hatton. Lord Chancellor of England. A favourite courtier of Queen Elizabeth.

372 (inv 1589) Henry (Radclyffe), 4th Earl of Sussex.

373 (inv 1589) Thomas (Sackville), 1st Lord Buckhurst. Afterwards 1st Earl of Dorset.

374 (inv 1590) Henry IV, King of France.

375 (inv 1590) James VI, King of Scotland. Afterwards James I, King of England.

376 (inv 1592) Gilbert (Talbot), 7th Earl of Shrewsbury.

377 (inv 1592) George (Clifford), 3rd Earl of Cumberland. Navigator and mathematician,

378 (inv 1593) Henry (Percy), 3rd Earl of Northumberland. Served at the siege of Ostend under Sir Francis Vere. Heavily fined and imprisoned in the Tower of London for suspected complicity in the "Gunpowder" Plot.

379 (inv 1593) Edward (Somerset), 4th Earl of Worcester.

380 (inv 1593) Thomas, 5th Lord Borough (or Burgh) of Gainsborough. Lord Deputy of Ireland.

381 (inv 1593) Edmund. 3rd Lord Sheffield. Afterwards 1st Earl of Mulgrave. Served in the fleet against the Spanish Armada.

382 (inv 1593) Sir Francis Knollys. First cousin of Queen Elizabeth and prominent in her reign. A consistent champion of the Puritans.

383 (inv 1597) Frederick, Duke of Württemberg.

384 (inv 1597) Thomas, 1st Lord Howard de Walden.Afterwards 1st Earl of Suffolk. Served in the Fleet against the Spanish Armada.

385 (inv 1597) George Carey, 2nd Lord Hunsdon (1546/7-1603). First cousin to Queen Elizabeth.

386 (inv 1597) Charles (Blount), 8th Lord Mountjoy, afterwards Earl of Devonshire (1563-1606). Quelled the Irish Rebellion under the Earl of Tyrone.

387 (inv 1597) Sir Henry Lee (1533-1611). "Personal Champion" to Queen Elizabeth.

388 (inv 1599) Robert (Radclyffe), 5th Earl of Sussex.

389 (inv 1599) Henry (Brooke), 8th Lord Cobham. Degraded 1604.
Joined in the plot in support of Lady Arabella Stuart's claim to the throne, known as "the Treason of Maine." Condemned to death, his achievements as K.G. were taken down and kicked out of the west doors of St. George's Chapel, 16 Feb. 1604.

390 (inv 1599) Thomas, 10th Lord Scrope of Bolton.

391 (inv 1601) William (Stanley), 6th Earl of Derby.

392 (inv 1601) Thomas (Cecil), 2nd Lord Burghley (d.1622). Afterwards 1st Earl of Exeter. Lord President of the Council of the North. Present at the storming of Edinburgh in 1573. Suppressed the rebellion of the Earl of Essex.

393 (inv 1603) Henry Frederick (Stuart), Duke of Rothesay. Afterwards PRINCE OF WALES. Eldest son of James I. Died in his father's lifetime.

394 (inv 1605) Christian IV, King of Denmark and Norway.Brother of Anne, Queen of James I of England.

395 (inv 1603) Ludovick (Stuart), 2nd Duke of Lennox.Afterwards also 1st Duke of Richmond.

396 (inv 1603) Henry (Wriothesley), 3rd Earl of Southampton. Served under Essex in the attack upon Cadiz.

397 (inv 1603) John (Erskine), 2nd Earl of Mar.Companion, from boyhood, of James I. Accompanied him to England in 1603. High Treasurer of England.

398 (inv 1603) William (Herbert), 3rd Earl of Pembroke.He and his brother Philip are "the incomparable pair" to whom the First Folio of Shakespeare's Works is dedicated.

399 (inv 1605) Ulric, Duke of Schleswig-Holstein, son of the king of Denmark and Norway.

400 (inv 1605) Henry (Howard), Earl of Northampton. Lord Privy Seal.

401 (inv 1608) Robert (Cecil), 1st Earl of Salisbury (d.1612). 2nd son of Lord Burghley. Chief Minister of James I. He built Hatfield House.

402 (inv 1606) Thomas, 3rd Viscount Howard of Bindon.

403 (inv 1608) George (Home), 1st Earl of Dunbar. Attended James VI to England. Chancellor of the Exchequer.

404 (inv 1605) Philip (Herbert), 1st Earl of Montgomery.Afterwards 4th Earl of Pembroke.

405 (inv 1611) Charles (Stuart), Duke of York. Afterwards Prince of Wales and subsequently CHARLES I, King of England.

406 (inv 1611) Thomas, 14th Earl of Arundel and Surrey. Afterwards 1st Earl of Norfolk. Famous as an art collector.

407 (inv 1611) Robert (Kerr), Viscount Rochester.Afterwards 1st Earl of Somerset. Accused of complicity in the Overbury Plot.

408 (inv 1612) Frederick Casimir, Duke of Bavaria, Count Palatine of the Rhine. Afterwards King of Bohemia. Married Elizabeth, daughter of James I.

409 (inv 1613) Maurice of Nassau, Prince of Orange.

410 (inv 1615) Thomas (Erskine), Viscount Fentun. Afterwards 1st Earl of Kellie. Rescued James VI of Scotland (James I of England) from Lord Gowrie's Plot.

411 (inv 1615) William Lord Knollys of Grays. Afterwards 1st Earl of Banbury.

412 (inv 160) Francis, (Manners), 6th Earl of Rutland.Concerned in the rebellion of the Earl of Essex, but escaped with a heavy fine.As Admiral of the Fleet, he conducted Charles, Prince of Wales, from Spain in 1623.

413 (inv 1616) Sir George Villiers. Afterwards 1st Duke of Buckingham. The favourite courtier of James I and Charles I. Assassinated at Portsmouth 1628.

414 (inv 1616) Robert (Sidney), Viscount Lisle.Afterwards 1st Earl of Leicester. Served in the wars in the Netherlands.

415 (inv 1623) James 2nd Marquess of Hamilton.

416 (inv 1624) Esmé (Stuart), 3rd Duke of Lennox.

417 (inv 1625) Christian, Duke of Brunswick-Wolfenbüttel.

418 (inv 1625) William, (Cecil), 2nd Earl of Salisbury(d. 1668).

419 (inv 1625) James (Hay), 1st Earl of Carlisle. A favourite courtier of James I.

420 (inv 1625) Edward (Sackville), 4th Earl of Dorset.

421 (inv 1625) Henry (Rich) Earl of Holland. Supporter of Charles I. Taken prisoner at Nonsuch and beheaded in Palace Yard, Westminster,in 1649.

422 (inv 1625) Thomas (Howard), Viscount Andover. Afterwards 1st Earl of Berkshire.

423 (inv 1625) Claude de Lorraine, Duc de Chevreuse.

424 (inv 1628) Gustavus Adolphus II, King of Sweden. Surnamed "the Great." Killed at the battle of Lützen.

425 (inv 1628) Henry Frederick de Nassau, Prince of Orange. Grandfather of William III, King of England.

426 (inv 1628) Theophilus (Howard), 2nd Earl of Suffolk,

427 (inv 1629) William (Compton), 1st Earl of Northampton.

428 (inv 1630) Richard, 1st Lord Weston of Neyland. Afterwards 1st Earl of Portland. Lord High Treasurer.

429 (inv 1630) Robert (Bertie), 1st Earl of Lindsey. Died of wounds received at the battle of Edgehill.

430 (inv 1630) William (Cecil), 2nd Earl of Exeter (d.1640).

431 (app 1630) James, 3rd Marquess of Hamilton. Afterwards 1st Duke of Hamilton. In command of the Scotch forces he was defeated by Cromwell in 1648 and beheaded in Palace Yard.

432 (inv 1633) Prince Charles Ludovic, Count Palatine of the Rhine, Duke of Bavaria. Son of Frederick, King of Bohemia and the Princess Elizabeth, daughter of James I.

433 (inv 1633) James (Stuart), 4th Duke of Lennox. Afterwards also 1st Duke of Richmond.

434 (inv 1633) Henry (Danvers), Earl of Danby.

435 (inv 1633) William (Douglas), 8th Earl of Morton.Loyal supporter of Charles I in the Civil War.

436 (inv 1635) Algernon (Percy), 10th Earl of Northumberland. Lord High Admiral.

437 (inv 1638) Charles (Stuart), Duke of Cornwall.Shortly afterwards styled PRINCE OF WALES. Subsequently CHARLES II, King of England.

438 (inv 1640) Thomas (Wentworth), 1st Earl of Strafford.Opposed the King's forced loan. Later supported him. Lord Lieutenant of Ireland. Impeached for high treason and beheaded.

439 (inv 1661) James (Stuart), Duke of York. Afterwards JAMES II, King of England.

440 (inv 1645) Prince Rupert, Count Palatine of the Rhine. Duke of Bavaria. Supporter of Charles I in the Civil War. Brother of 432. Elected 1642; installation dispensed with at Oxford 1645.

441 (inv 1645) William of Nassau, Prince of Orange. Married Mary, daughter of Charles I, King of England, by whom she had William III, joint sovereign of England.

442 (inv 1645) Sir Bernard de Foix, Captal de Buch,

443 (app 1649) Maurice, Count Palatine of the Rhine. (Not installed.)

444 (inv 1661) James (Butler), 1st Marquess of Ormonde. Afterwards 1st Duke of Ormonde.

445 (inv 1661) Edward, Count Palatine of the Rhine, Duke of Bavaria. Son of Frederick, King of Bohemia, and the Princess Elizabeth.daughter of James I.

446 (inv 1661) George (Villiers), 2nd Duke of Buckingham.One of the five Ministers who formed the "Cabal."

447 (app 1650) William (Seymour), 1st Marquess of Hertford. Afterwards 2nd Duke of Somerset, the attainder of his ancestor Edward, 1st Duke, being reversed in 1660. Conspicuous for his bravery in the defence of Sherborne Castle and at the battle of Lansdowne. One of the four who offered their lives to the Commons in lieu of King Charles I. (Not installed.)

448 (inv 1661) Thomas (Wriothesley), 4th Earl of Southampton. Lord High Treasurer.

449 (app 1650) William, 2nd Duke of Hamilton. In command of the royal forces in Scotland. Mortally wounded at the battle of Worcester. (Not installed.)

450 (inv 1661) William (Cavendish), created Duke of Newcastle-upon-Tyne. Companion of Charles II during his long exile.

451 (app 1650) James (Graham), 1st Marquess of Montrose (1612-50). Fought in Scotland as a royalist. (Not installed.)

452 (app 1650) James (Stanley). 7th Earl of Derby.Powerful supporter of the royalist cause, and known as "the Loyal Earl." His wife, Charlotte de la Trémouille, is famous for her heroic defence of Lathom House. The Earl was taken prisoner at the battle of Worcester and beheaded. (Not installed.)

453 (inv 1661) George (Digby), 2nd Earl of Bristol.

454 (app 1653) Henry (Stuart), Duke of Gloucester.Brother of Charles II. (Not installed.)

455 (inv 1661) Henry Charles (de la Trémouille) Prince of Tarento.

456 (inv 1661) William Henry of Nassau, Prince of Orange.Afterwards William III, King of England.

457 (inv 1661) Frederick William, Margrave of Brandenburg, Duke of Prussia.

458 (inv 1661) John Gaspar Ferdinand de Marchin, Comte de Graville.

459 (inv 1661) Sir George Monck. Afterwards 1st Duke of Albemarle. The chief instrument in the Restoration of King Charles II.

460 (inv 1661) Edward (Montagu), 1st Earl of Sandwich.The patron and friend of Samuel Pepys. As joint General of the Fleet he was with Monck in escorting Charles II back to England from France in 1660.

461 (inv 1661) Aubrey (de Vere), 20th (and last) Earl of Oxford. Imprisoned in the Tower of London as party to a plot against the Protector Cromwell.

462 (inv 1661) Charles (Stuart), 4th Duke of Richmond and Lennox, and last of this creation.

463 (inv 1661) Montagu (Bertie), 2nd Earl of Lindsey.Fought as a Royalist; taken prisoner at Edgehill, and wounded at Naseby.

464 (inv 1661) Edward (Montagu), 2nd Earl of Manchester.Fought as a zealous Parliamentarian in the Civil War. Speaker of the House of Commons and House of Lords.

465 (inv 1661) William (Wentworth), 2nd Earl of Strafford.

466 (inv 1663) Christian V, King of Denmark and Norway.

467 (inv 1663) James (Scott), Duke of Monmouth and Duke of Buccleuch. Son of Charles II and Lucy Walters. Served in the French Army.Rebelled against James II, and assumed the title of King. Defeated at Sedgemoor and beheaded. Degraded 1685.

468 (app 1666) James (Stuart), Duke of Cambridge, 2nd son of James II. Died aged 3. (Not installed.)

469 (inv 1671) Charles XI, King of Sweden.

470 (inv 1671) John George II, Duke of Saxony.

471 (inv 1671) Christopher (Monck) 2nd Duke of Albemarle.

472 (inv 1672) John (Maitland) Duke of Lauderdale. One of the five Ministers who formed the "Cabal."

473 (inv 1672) Henry (Somerset), 3rd Marquess of Worcester. Afterwards 1st Duke of Beaufort. Lord-President of Wales. Instrumental in the return of Charles II to England in 1660.

474 (inv 1672) Henry (Jermyn), Earl of St. Albans.

475 (inv 1672) William (Russell), 5th Earl of Bedford.Afterwards 1st Duke of Bedford. Fought as a Royalist at the first battle ofNewbury.

476 (inv 1672) Henry (Bennet), Earl of Arlington. One of the five Ministers who formed the "Cabal."

477 (inv 1672) Thomas (Butler) Earl of Ossory. Son of James 1st Duke of Ormonde, but died in his father's lifetime. Served in various actions against the Dutch Fleet.

478 (inv 1673) Charles (Palmer, afterwards Fitzroy) Earl of Southampton. Afterwards Duke of Southampton. Son of Charles II and Barbara,Duchess of Cleveland.

479 (inv 1674) John (Sheffield), 3rd Earl of Mulgrave.Afterwards Duke of Buckingham and of Normanby. Served with the Fleet at the battle of Solebay, and with the Forces at Tangier, Lord Privy Seal.

480 (inv 1677) Henry (Cavendish), 2nd Duke of Newcastle-on-Tyne.

481 (inv 1677) Thomas (Osborne), 2nd Earl of Danby. Afterwards 1st Duke of Leeds. Lord President of the Council. Took an active part in the Revolution that brought William III to the throne.

482 (inv 1680) Henry (Fitzroy), 1st Duke of Grafton. Son of Charles II and Barbara, Duchess of Cleveland.

483 (inv 1680) James (Cecil), 3rd Earl of Salisbury (d.1683).

484 (inv 1680) Charles II, Count Palatine of the Rhine,Duke of Bavaria.

485 (inv 1681) Charles (Lennox), 1st Duke of Richmond.Son of Charles II and Louise, Duchess of Portsmouth.

486 (inv 1682) William, 3rd Duke of Hamilton.

487 (inv 1684) Prince George of Denmark and Norway.Consort of the Princess ANNE, afterwards Queen of England.

488 (inv 1684) Charles (Seymour) 6th Duke of Somerset.Supporter of the Prince of Orange, and contributed largely to the undisputed succession of the House of Hanover.

489 (inv 1684) George (Palmer, afterwards Fitzroy), Duke of Northumberland. 3rd son of Charles II and Barbara, Duchess of Cleveland.

490 (inv 1685) Henry (Howard), 7th Duke of Norfolk(1654-1701). Constable of Windsor Castle.

491 (inv 1685) Henry (Mordaunt), 2nd Earl of Peterborough. Served in the action off Solebay.

492 (inv 1685) Laurence (Hyde), Earl of Rochester, 2nd son of Edward, 1st Earl of Clarendon and uncle of Queen Anne. First Lord of the Treasury.

493 (inv 1685) Louis (de Duras), 2nd Earl of Feversham. Marquis de Blanquefort in France. Nephew of Turenne. Naturalized in England in 1665. Friend of Charles II and James II. Commanded at the battle of Sedgemoor.

494 (inv 1687) Robert (Spencer), 2nd Earl of Sunderland. Diplomatist. Lord President of the Council.

495 (app 1688) James (Fitzjames), Duke of Berwick. Son of James II and Arabella Churchill. Served with distinction in the French army.(Not installed.)

496 (inv 1689) James (Butler), 2nd Duke of Ormonde.Viceroy of Ireland. Degraded 12 July 1716 (last formal degradation).

497 (inv 1689) Frederick Armand, 1st Duke of Schomberg. Killed at the battle of the Boyne.

498 (inv 1689) William (Cavendish), 4th Earl of Devonshire. Afterwards 1st Duke of Devonshire.

499 (inv 1694) Frederick III, Margrave of Brandenburg(1657-1713). Became in 1701 Frederick I, King of Prussia. Married the Princess Sophia, sister of George I.

500 (inv 1694) George William, Duke of Brunswick-Luneburg. Afterwards Duke of Zelle. Father of Sophia, Queen of George 1.

501 (inv 1693) John George IV, Duke of Saxony.

502 (inv 1692) Charles (Sackville), 6th Earl of Dorsetand 1st Earl of Middlesex. Supported the cause of William of Orange.

503 (inv 1694) Charles (Talbot), 12th Earl of Shrewsbury.Afterwards 1st Duke of Shrewsbury. Supporter of William III. Viceroy of Ireland. Lord High Treasurer.

504 (inv 1696) William, Duke of Gloucester. Eldest son of George, Prince of Denmark and the Princess Anne, afterwards Queen Anne of England.

505 (inv 1697) William (Bentinck), 1st Earl of Portland(1649-1709). Favourite courtier of William III.

506 (inv 1698) John (Holles), created Duke of Newcastle-upon-Tyne. Married Margaret, daughter and coheiress of Henry(Cavendish), 2nd Duke of Newcastle-upon-Tyne.

507 (inv 1700) Thomas (Herbert), 8th Earl of Pembroke and 5th Earl of Montgomery. Lord High Admiral of England. Viceroy of Ireland.

508 (inv 1700) Arnold Joost (van Keppel), 1st Earl of Albemarle. Attended the Prince of Orange, afterwards William III, to England in 1688.

509 (inv 1703) George Lewis, Duke of Brunswick-Luneburg, Elector of Hanover (1660-1727). Afterwards GEORGE I, King of Great Britain.

510 (inv 1701) James (Douglas), 2nd Duke of Queensberry. Lord Privy Seal and a Lord of the Treasury. Largely instrumental in carrying the Act of Union with Scotland.

511 (inv 1702) Wriothesley (Russell), 2nd Duke of Bedford.

512 (inv 1703) John (Churchill), 1st Duke of Marlborough (1650-1722). The hero of the battles of Blenheim, Ramillies, Oudenarde and Malplaquet.

513 (inv 1703) Meinhardt (de Schomberg), 3rd Duke of Schomberg and Duke of Leinster. Present at the battle of the Boyne, at which his father was killed.

514 (inv 1704) Sidney, Lord Godolphin of Rialton. Afterwards 1st Earl of Godolphin. Lord High Treasurer.

515 (inv 1710) George Augustus, Electoral Prince of Brunswick-Luneburg. Afterwards PRINCE OF WALES. Subsequently GEORGE II, King of Great Britain.

516 (inv 1710) William (Cavendish), 2nd Duke of Devonshire. Lord President of the Council.

517 (inv 1710) John (Campbell), 2nd Duke of Argyll. Fought under Marlborough at Ramillies and Malplaquet. Played an important part in bringing about the Act of Union.

518 (inv 1713) Henry (Somerset), 2nd Duke of Beaufort.

519 (inv 1712) James 4th Duke of Hamilton and 1st Duke of Brandon. Engaged the notorious duel with Lord Mohun in Hyde Park which ended fatally for both.

520 (inv 1713) Henry (Grey). 1st Duke of Kent.

521 (inv 1713) John, 1st Earl Poulett. First Lord of the Treasury.

522 (inv 1713) Robert (Harley), 1st Earl of Oxford and Earl Mortimer. Lord High Treasurer. He and his son founded the famous Harleian Collection of manuscripts now in the British Museum.

523 (inv 1713) Thomas (Wentworth), 3rd Earl of Strafford.

524 (inv 1713) Charles (Mordaunt), 3rd Earl of Peterborough. In command of the forces in Spain during the War of the Spanish Succession.

525 (inv 1714) Charles (Paulet), 2nd Duke of Bolton. Asupporter of the Prince of Orange (William III), bringing him from Holland in 1688.

526 (inv 1714) John (Manners), 2nd Duke of Rutland.

527 (inv 1714) Lionel Cranfield (Sackville), 7th Earl of Dorset. Afterwards 1st Duke of Dorset. Lord Lieutenant of Ireland.

528 (inv 1714) Charles (Montague), 1st Earl of Halifax.Chancellor of the Exchequer. First Lord of the Treasury.

529 (inv 1718) Frederick Lewis, Prince of Brunswick-Luneburg (1707-51). Eldest son of George II. Afterwards PRINCE OF WALES. Father of George III.

530 (inv 1718) Ernest Augustus, Prince of Brunswick-Luneburg. Afterwards Duke of York and Albany, Bishop of Osnaburg.Youngest brother of George I.

531 (inv 1718) Charles (Beauclerk), 1st Duke of St. Albans. Son of Charles II and Eleanor Gwynne.

532 (inv 1718) John, 2nd Duke of Montagu.

533 (inv 1718) Thomas (Pelham-Holles, formerly Pelham), 1st Duke of Newcastle-under-Lyme. First Lord of the Treasury.

534 (inv 1718) James, 3rd Earl of Berkeley. Vice-Admiral of the Red. Commanded a ship in Rooke's engagement off Malaga.

535 (inv 1719) Evelyn (Pierrepont), 1st Duke of Kingston-upon-Hull.Lord Privy Seal. Lord President of the Council.

536 (inv 1720) Charles (Spencer), 3rd Earl of Sunderland. First Lord of the Treasury. Lord President of the Council.

537 (inv 1721) Charles (Fitzroy), 2nd Duke of Grafton.Viceroy of Ireland.

538 (inv 1721) Henry Fiennes (Clinton), 7th Earl of Lincoln.

539 (inv 1722) Charles (Paulet), 3rd Duke of Bolton.

540 (inv 1722) John (Manners), 3rd Duke of Rutland (1696-1779).

541 (inv 1722) John (Ker), 1st Duke of Roxburghe. Prominent in promoting the Union with Scotland.

542 (inv 1724) Richard (Lumley), 2nd Earl of Scarborough(1708-39).

543 (inv 1724) Charles, 2nd Viscount Townshend. Lord President of the Council.

544 (inv 1726) Charles (Lennox), 2nd Duke of Richmond and Duke of Lennox. Served at the battle of Dettingen.

545 (inv 1726) Sir Robert Walpole. Afterwards 1st Earl of Orford. The famous Minister of George I and George II. He was in fact though not in name the first Prime Minister.

546 (inv 1730) William Augustus, Prince of Brunswick-Luneburg (1721-65), 2nd son of George II. Afterwards Duke of Cumberland. Commander-in-Chief of the Forces.

547 (inv 1730) Philip Dormer (Stanhope), 4th Earl of Chesterfield. Ambassador to the Hague. Lord Lieutenant of Ireland. Author of the "Letters to his Son."

548 (inv 1730) Richard (Boyle), 3rd Earl of Burlington and 2nd Earl of Cork.

549 (inv 1733) William Charles Henry, Prince of Orange(1711-51). afterwards William IV de Nassau. Married the Princess Anne, eldest daughter of George II.

550 (inv 1733) William (Cavendish), 3rd Duke of Devonshire. Lord Privy Seal. Lord Lieutenant of Ireland.

551 (inv 1733) Spencer (Compton), Earl of Wilmington. Speaker of the House of Commons.

552 (inv 1738) William (Capel), 3rd Earl of Essex.

553 (inv 1738) James, 1st Earl Waldegrave.

554 (inv 1750) Frederick, Landgrave of Hesse-Cassel (1720-85). Married the Princess Mary, 4th daughter of George II.

555 (inv 1741) Charles (Beauclerk), 2nd Duke of St.Albans. Constable of Windsor Castle.

556 (inv 1741) Charles (Spencer), 3rd Duke of Marlborough (1706-58). Fought at the battle of Dettingen.

557 (inv 1741) Evelyn (Pierrepont), 2nd Duke of Kingston-upon-Hull.

558 (inv 1741) William (Bentinck), 2nd Duke of Portland (1709-62).

559 (inv 1750) Frederick III, Duke of Saxe-Gotha. Brother of Augusta, Princess of Wales, the mother of George III.

560 (app 1746) John Adolphus, Duke of Saxe-Weissenfels.(Not installed.)

561 (inv 1750) George William Frederick, Prince of Brunswick-Luneburg (1738-1820). Afterwards GEORGE III, King of Great Britain.

562 (inv 1750) Charles William Frederick, 8th Margrave of Brandenburg-Anspach.

563 (inv 1750) Thomas (Osborne), 4th Duke of Leeds.

564 (inv 1750) John (Russell), 4th Duke of Bedford (1710-71). Lord Privy Seal. Lord President of the Council.

565 (inv 1750) Wilham Anne (van Keppel), 2nd Earl of Albemarle. Served at the battles of Dettingen, Fontenoy, and Culloden.

566 (inv 1750) John (Carteret), 2nd Earl Granville. Chief Governor of Ireland.

567 (inv 1752) Edward Augustus, Prince of Brunswick-Luneburg (1739-67). Afterwards Duke of York and Albany. 2nd son of Frederick, Prince of Wales.

568 (inv 1752) William V. de Nassau, Prince of Orange.Son of William IV, Prince of Orange, and the Princess Anne, his wife, eldest daughter of George II.

569 (inv 1752) Henry (Fiennes-Clinton, afterwards Pelham-Clinton), 9th Earl of Lincoln. Afterwards 2nd Duke of Newcastle-under-Lyme.

570 (inv 1752) Daniel (Finch), 8th Earl of Winchilsea and 3d Earl of Nottingham (d. 1769)

571 (inv 1752) George (Brudenell, afterwards Montagu), 4th Earl of Cardigan. Afterwards Duke of Montagu. Constable of Windsor Castle.

572 (inv 1757) William (Cavendish), 4th Duke of Devonshire. First Lord of the Treasury and Prime Minister.

573 (inv 1757) Henry (Howard), 4th Earl of Carlisle.

574 (inv 1757) Hugh (Smithson, afterwards Percy), 2nd Earl of Northumberland. Afterwards 1st Duke of Northumberland. Viceroy of Ireland.

575 (inv 1757) Francis (Seymour-Conway), 1st Earl of Hertford. Afterwards 1st Marquess of Hertford. Viceroy of Ireland.

576 (inv 1757) James 2nd Earl Waldegrave.

577 (inv 1760) Ferdinand, Prince of Brunswick-Beyern.

578 (inv 1760) Charles (Watson-Wentworth), 2nd Marquessof Rockingham. First Lord of the Treasury and Prime Minister.

579 (inv 1760) Richard (Grenville-Temple), 2nd Earl Temple. Lord Privy Seal.

580 (inv 1762) William Henry, Prince of Brunswick-Luneburg. Afterwards Duke of Gloucester (1743-1805). 3rd son of Frederick Prince of Wales, and brother of George III.

581 (inv 1762) John (Stuart), 3rd Earl of Bute. First Lord of the Treasury and Prime Minister.

582 (inv 1771) Adolf Friedrich IV, Duke of Mecklenburg-Strelitz (1738-94). Brother of Charlotte, Queen of George

583 (app 1764) George (Montague-Dunk), Earl of Halifax. Viceroy of Ireland. Lord Privy Seal. (Not installed.)

584 (inv 1771) George Augustus Frederick, PRINCE OF WALES (1762-1830). Afterwards GEORGE IV, King of Great Britain.

585 (inv 1771) Charles William Ferdinand, Hereditary Prince, afterwards Duke of Brunswick-Wolfenbüttel. Married the Princess Augusta, eldest daughter of Frederick, Prince of Wales. Killed at the battle of Jena.

586 (inv 1771) George (Keppel), 3rd Earl of Albemarle.

587 (inv 1771) Henry Frederick, Prince ofBrunswick-Luneburg (1745-90). Afterwards Duke of Cumberland and Strathearn. 4th son of Frederick, Prince of Wales, and brother of George III.

588 (inv 1771) George (Spencer), 4th Duke of Marlborough (1739-1817).

589 (inv 1771) Augustus Henry (Fitzroy), 3rd Duke of Grafton (1735-1811).

590 (inv 1771) Granville (Leveson-Gower) Viscount Trentham. Afterwards 1st Marquess of Stafford. Lord President of the Council.

591 (inv 1771) Frederick, Prince of Brunswick-Luneburg,Bishop of Osnaburg (1763-1827). 2nd son of George III. Afterwards Duke of York and Albany.

592 (app 1772) Sir Frederick North. Afterwards 4th Earl of Guilford. First Lord of the Treasury and Prime Minister. (Not installed.)

593 (app 1778) Henry (Howard), 12th Earl of Suffolk, 5th Earl of Berkshire. Lord Privy Seal. (Not installed.)

594 (app 1778) William Henry (Nassau de Zulenstein), 4th Earl of Rochford. (Not installed.)

595 (app 1778) Thomas (Thynne), 3rd Viscount Weymouth. Afterwards 1st Marquess of Bath. Lord Lieutenant of Ireland. (Not installed.)

596 (inv 1801) William Henry, Prince of Brunswick-Luneburg (1765-1837). 3rd son of George III. Afterwards Duke of Clarence, and subsequently WILLIAM IV, King of Great Britain.

597 (inv 1801) Charles (Lennox), 3rd Duke of Richmond and Lennox.

598 (inv 1801) William (Cavendish), 5th Duke of Devonshire (1748-1811).

599 (inv 1801) William (Petty), 3rd Earl of Shelburne.Afterwards 1st Marquess of Lansdowne. First Lord of the Treasury.

600 (app 1782) Charles (Manners), 4th Duke of Rutland(1754-87). Viceroy of Ireland. (Not installed.)

601 (inv 1801) Edward, Prince of Brunswick-Luneburg,afterwards Duke of Kent (1767-1820). 4th son of George III and father of Queen Victoria.

602 (inv 1801) Ernest Augustus, Prince ofBrunswick-Luneburg, 5th son of George III (1771-1851). Afterwards Duke of Cumberland. Succ. 1837 as King of Hanover.

603 (inv 1801) Augustus Frederick, Prince of Brunswick-Luneburg (1773-1843). Afterwards Duke of Sussex. 6th son of George III.

604 (inv 1801) Adolphus Frederick, Prince of Brunswick-Luneburg (1774-1850). Afterwards Duke of Cambridge. 7th son of George III.

605 (inv 1801) William Landgrave of Hesse-Cassel. Son of the Princess Mary, daughter of George II.

606 (inv 1801) Henry (Somerset), 5th Duke of Beaufort (1744-1803).

607 (inv 1801) George (Nugent-Temple-Grenville), 1st Marquess of Buckingham.

608 (inv 1801) Charles, 2nd Earl, afterwards 1st Marquess Cornwallis. Served in the American War. Governor-General of India. Compelled the surrender of Tippoo Sahib.

609 (app 1788) John Frederick (Sackville), 3rd Duke of Dorset. Ambassador to Paris. (Not installed.)

610 (inv 1801) Hugh (Percy), 2nd Duke of Northumberland.

611 (inv 1801) Ernest Lewis, 5th Duke of Saxe-Gotha and Altenburg. Cousin of George III.

612 (app 1790) Francis Godolphin (Osborne), 5th Duke of Leeds. Ambassador to Paris. (Not installed.)

613 (inv 1801) John (Pitt), 2nd Earl of Chatham. Lord Privy Seal. Lord President of the Council.

614 (inv 1801) James (Cecil), 1st Marquess of Salisbury (d. 1823).

615 (inv 1801) John (Fane), 10th Earl of Westmorland. Viceroy of Ireland.

616 (inv 1801) Frederick (Howard), 5th Earl of Carlisle. Lord Privy Seal. Lord-Lieutenant of Ireland.

617 (inv 1801) Henry (Scott), 3rd Duke of Buccleuch. Afterwards also 5th Duke of Queensberry.

618 (inv 1801) William Frederick, Prince of Brunswick-Luneburg. Afterwards 2nd Duke of Gloucester (1776-1834). Nephew of George III.

619 (inv 1801) William Henry (Bentinck, afterwards Cavendish Bentinck), 3rd Duke of Portland (1738-1809). Lord President of the Council and First Lord of the Treasury.

620 (app 1797) Richard 1st Earl Howe. Admiral. Defeated the French fleet in the English Channel. (Not installed.)

621 (inv 1801) George John, 2nd Earl Spencer. Lord Privy Seal.

622 (inv 1801) John Jeffreys (Pratt), 2nd Earl Camden.Afterwards 1st Marquess Camden. Lord Lieutenant of Ireland.

623 (inv 1801) John (Ker), 3rd Duke of Roxburghe.

624 (inv 1805) John Henry (Manners), 5th Duke of Rutland(1778-1857).

625 (inv 1805) Philip (Yorke), 3rd Earl of Hardwick.Viceroy of Ireland.

626 (inv 1805) Henry Charles (Somerset), 6th Duke of Beaufort (1766-1835).

627 (inv 1805) John James (Hamilton), 1st Marquess of Abercorn.

628 (inv 1805) George Augustus (Herbert), 11th Earl of Pembroke and 8th Earl of Montgomery.

629 (inv 1805) George (Finch), 9th Earl of Winchilsea and 4th Earl of Nottingham (1752-1826, nephew of 570)

630 (inv 1805) Philip (Stanhope), 5th Earl of Chesterfield. Ambassador to Spain.

631 (inv 1805) George (Legge), Earl of Dartmouth.

632 (inv 1812) George Granville (Leveson-Gower), 2nd Marquess of Stafford. Afterwards 1st Duke of Sutherland.

633 (inv 1812) Francis Conway (Ingram-Seymour-Conway),2nd Marquess of Hertford.

634 (inv 1812) William (Lowther), 1st Earl of Lonsdale (d. 1844).

635 (inv 1812) Richard Colley, Marquess Wellesley. Elder brother of Arthur, Duke of Wellington. Governor-General of India, with distinguished war services.

636 (inv 1812) Charles (Lennox), 4th Duke of Richmond and Lennox (1764-1819).

637 (inv 1812) James (Graham), 3d Duke of Montrose (1755-1836).

638 (inv 1812) Francis (Rawdon-Hastings), 2nd Earl of Moira. Afterwards Marquess of Hastings. Served the American War. Commander of the Forces in India.

639 (inv 1812) Henry (Pelham-Chnton), 4th Duke of Newcastle-under-Lyme.

640 (inv 1814) Arthur (Wellesley), 1st Duke of Wellington(1769-1852). The hero of the Peninsular War and the battle of Waterloo. First Lord of the Treasury and Prime Minister.

641 (inv 1814) Alexander I, Emperor of all the Russia (1777-1825).

642 (inv 1814) Louis XVIII, King of France (1757-1824).

643 (inv 1814) Francis I, Emperor of Austria (1768-1835).

644 (inv 1814) Frederick William III, King of Prussia(1770-1840). Father of William I, Emperor of Germany.

645 (inv 1814) Robert Banks (Jenkinson), 2nd Earl of Liverpool. First Lord of the Treasury and Prime Minister.

646 (inv 1814) Robert (Stewart), Viscount Castlereagh. Afterwards 2nd Marquess of Londonderry. Secretary of State for Foreign Affairs.Fought a duel with Canning in 1808.

647 (inv 1815) Ferdinand VII, King of Spain (1784-1833).

648 (inv 1814) William Frederick de Nassau, Prince of Orange (1772-1843). Afterwards William I, King of the Netherlands.

649 (inv 1816) Leopold George Frederick, Duke of Saxe-Coburg-Saalfeld (1790-1865). Afterwards Leopold I, King of the Belgians.He married the Princess Charlotte Augusta of Wales, only child of the Regent,afterwards George IV, in the direct line of the British Throne.

650 (inv 1817) Henry, 3rd Earl Bathurst. Secretary of State for Foreign Affairs. Lord President of the Council.

651 (inv 1818) Henry William (Paget), 1st Marquess of Anglesey. Served in the Peninsular War, and at the battle of Waterloo where helost a leg.

652 (inv 1819) Hugh (Percy), 3rd Duke of Northumberland.Viceroy of Ireland.

653 (inv 1820) Richard(Temple-Nugent-Brydges-Chandos-Grenville), 2nd Marquess of Buckingham.Afterwards 1st Duke of Buckingham and Chandos.

654 (inv 1822) Frederick VI, King of Denmark (1768-1839).

655 (inv 1823) João VI, King of Portugal (1767-1826).

656 (inv 1822) George James, 1st Marquess of Cholmondeley.

657 (inv 1822) Francis Charles (Seymour-Conway), 3rd Marquess of Hertford.

658 (inv 1823) Thomas (Thynne), 2nd Marquess of Bath.

659 (inv 1825) Charles X, King of France (1757-1836).

660 (inv 1826) Charles (Sackville-Germaine), 5th Duke of Dorset.

661 (inv 1826) Nicholas I, Emperor of all the Russia (1796-1855).

662 (inv 1827) George William Frederick (Osborne), 6th Duke of Leeds.

663 (inv 1827) William George Spencer (Cavendish), 6th Duke of Devonshire (1790-1858).

664 (inv 1827) Brownlow (Cecil), 2nd Marquess of Exeter (1795-1867).

665 (inv 1829) Charles (Lennox, afterwards Gordon-Lennox), 5th Duke of Richmond and Lennox (1791-1860). Fought at the battle of Waterloo.

666 (inv 1829) George, 3rd Earl of Ashburnham.

667 (inv 1831) Bernard Eric Freund, Duke of Saxe-Meiningen. Brother of Adelaide, Queen of William IV.

668 (inv 1830) Wilhelm I, King of Württemberg (1781-1864).

669 (inv 1830) John (Russell), 6th Duke of Bedford(1766-1839). Lord Lieutenant of Ireland.

670 (inv 1831) Charles, 2nd Earl Grey. First Lord of the Treasury and Prime Minister of Reform Bill fame.

671 (inv 1831) Augustus William Maximilian Frederick Lewis, reigning Duke of Brunswick-Wolfenbüttel.

672 (inv 1834) Bernard Edward (Howard), 12th Duke of Norfolk (1765-1842). Earl Marshal.

673 (inv 1834) George Henry (Fitzroy), 4th Duke of Grafton (1760-1844).

674 (inv 1835) Walter Francis (Montagu-Douglas-Scott),5th Duke of Buccleuch and 7th Duke of Queensberry (1806-84). Lord Privy Seal.Lord President of the Council.

675 (inv 1835) George Frederick Alexander Charles Ernest Augustus, Prince of Brunswick-Luneburg (1819-78). Succ. 1851 as George V of Hanover. Nephew of King George IV of England.

676 (inv 1835) George Frederick William Charles, Prince of Brunswick-Luneburg. Afterwards 2nd Duke of Cambridge. Commander-in-Chief of the British Army. Served in the Crimean War.

677 (inv 1836) Alexander, 10th Duke of Hamilton and 7th Duke of Brandon (1767-1852). Ambassador to St. Petersburg.

678 (inv 1836) Henry (Petty), 3rd Marquess of Lansdowne. Lord President of the Council.

679 (inv 1837) George (Howard), 6th Earl of Carlisle.Lord Privy Seal.

680 (inv 1837) Edward Adolphus (Seymour), 11th Duke of Somerset (1775-1855).

681 (inv 1837) Charles William Frederick Emicon, Prince of Leiningen. Half-brother of Queen Victoria.

682 (inv 1838) Ernst Anton Karl Ludwig, Reigning Duke of Saxe-Coburg and Gotha (1784-1844). Uncle of Queen Victoria.

683 (inv 1839) Edward (Smith-Stanley), 13th Earl of Derby.

684 (inv 1839) William Harry (Vane), 1st Duke of Cleveland.

685 (inv 1839) Francis Albert Augustus Charles Emanuel,Prince of Saxe-Coburg and Gotha (1819-61). Afterwards Consort of Queen VICTORIA.

686 (inv 1841) George Granville (Leveson-Gower), 2nd Duke of Sutherland.

687 (inv 1841) Robert (Grosvenor), 1st Marquess of Westminster.

688 (inv 1842) Frederick William IV, King of Prussia(1795-1861).

689 (inv 1842) Frederick Augustus II, King of Saxony.

690 (inv 1842) Henry (Somerset), 7th Duke of Beaufort(1792-1853).

691 (inv 1842) Richard Plantagenet(Temple-Nugent-Brydges-Chandos-Grenville), 2nd Duke of Buckingham. Lord Privy Seal.

692 (inv 1842) James Brownlow William (Gascoigne-Cecil,formerly Cecil), 2nd Marquess of Salisbury (1791-1868). Lord Privy Seal. Lord President of the Council.

693 (inv 1842) Henry (Vane), 2nd Duke of Cleveland.

694 (inv 1844) Louis Philippe, King of the French.

695 (inv 1844) Ernst (II) August Karl Johannes Leopold Alexander Eduard, reigning Duke of Saxe-Coburg and Gotha (1818-93). Brother of Prince Albert, the consort of Queen Victoria.

696 (inv 1844) Thomas Philip (Robinson, afterwards Weddell, afterwards de Grey), 2nd Earl de Grey. Lord-Lieutenant of Ireland.

697 (inv 1844) James (Hamilton), 2nd Marquess of Abercorn (1811-85). Cr. 1868 1st Duke of Abercorn. Lord Lieutenant of Ireland.

698 (inv 1844) Charles Chetwynd, 2nd Earl Talbot. Viceroy of Ireland.

699 (inv 1844) Edward (Herbert, formerly Clive), 2nd Earl of Powis.

700 (inv 1846) George Charles (Pratt), 2nd Marquess Camden.

701 (inv 1846) Richard (Seymour-Conway), 4th Marquess of Hertford.

702 (inv 1847) Francis (Russell), 7th Duke of Bedford (1788-1861).

703 (inv 1848) Henry Charles (Howard), 13th Duke of Norfolk (1791-1856). Earl Marshal.

704 (inv 1849) George William Frederick (Villiers) 4th Earl of Clarendon (1800-70). Lord Privy Seal. Lord Lieutenant of Ireland.

705 (inv 1849) Frederick, 4th. Earl Spencer. Commanded a ship at the battle of Navarino.

706 (inv 1851) Constantine Henry (Phipps), 1st Marquess of Normanby. Lord Lieutenant of Ireland. Secretary of State for

the Colonies.

707 (inv 1851) Charles William (Wentworth-Fitz wilham),5th Earl Fitz william.

708 (inv 1853) Algernon (Percy), 4th Duke of Northumberland. Admiral R.N., First Lord of the Admiralty

709 (inv 1853) Charles William (Vane, formerly Stewart),3rd Marquess of Londonderry. Served as a General in the Peninsular War.

710 (inv 1855) George William Frederick (Howard), 7th Earl of Carlisle. Lord Lieutenant of Ireland.

711 (inv 1855) Francis (Leveson-Gower), 1st Earl of Ellesmere.

712 (inv 1855) George (Gordon, afterwards Hamilton-Gordon). 4th Earl of Aberdeen. First Lord of the Treasury and Prime Minister.

713 (inv 1855) Napoleon III, Emperor of the French.

714 (inv 1855) Victor Emmanuel II, King of Sardinia(1820-78). Became in 1860 King of Italy.

715 (inv 1856) Hugh, 2nd Earl Fortescue. Lord Lieutenant of Ireland.

716 (inv 1856) Henry John (Temple), 3rd Viscount Palmerston. First Lord of the Treasury and Prime Minister.

717 (inv 1856) Abdul Medjid, Sultan of Turkey.

718 (inv 1857) Granville George (Leveson-Gower), 2nd Earl Granville. Lord President of the Council.

719 (inv 1857) Richard (Grosvenor), 2nd Marquess of Westminster.

720 (inv 1858) Friedrich Wilhelm Nikolaus Karl, Crown Prince of Prussia (1831-88). Succ. 1888 as Friedrich III, Emperor of Germany. Married Victoria, Princess Royal, eldest daughter of Queen Victoria.

721 (inv 1858) Arthur Richard (Wellesley), 2nd Duke of Wellington (1807-84).

722 (inv 1858) William (Cavendish), 7th Duke of Devonshire (1808-91). Chancellor of the University of Cambridge.

723 (inv 1858) Pedro V, King of Portugal (1837-61).

724 (inv 1858) Albert Edward, PRINCE OF WALES. Afterwards EDWARD VII, King of Great Britain.

725 (inv 1859) Dudley (Ryder), 2nd Earl of Harrowby. Lord Privy Seal.

726 (inv 1859) Edward Geoffrey (Smith-Stanley), 14th Earl of Derby. Chief Secretary for Ireland and afterwards Prime Minister.

727 (inv 1860) Henry Pelham (Pelham-Clinton), 5th Duke of Newcastle.

728 (inv 1861) Wilhelm I, King of Prussia (1797-1888).Became in 1871 Wilhelm I, Emperor of Germany.

729 (inv 1862) Charles, Earl Canning. Governor-General of India in the time of the Mutiny.

730 (inv 1862) Edward Adolphus (Seymour), 12th Duke of Somerset (1804-85).

731 (inv 1862) John, 1st Earl Russell, 3rd son of John, 6th Duke of Bedford (1792-1878), and better known as Lord John Russell. First Lord of the Treasury and Prime Minister (1846-52, 1865-66).

732 (inv 1862) Anthony (Ashley-Cooper), 7th Earl of Shaftesbury. A great philanthropist.

733 (inv 1862) William Thomas Spencer(Wentworth-Fitz william), 6th Earl Fitzwilliam.

734 (inv 1862) Frederick William Lewis Charles, Prince of Hesse. Afterwards Grand Duke Louis IV, of Hesse. Married the Princess Alice, 2nd daughter of Queen Victoria.

735 (inv 1862) Friedrich Wilhelm, reigning Grand-Duke of Mecklenburg-Strelitz (1819-1904).

736 (inv 1863) Prince Alfred Ernest Albert, Duke of Saxony and Prince of Saxe-Coburg-Gotha (1844-1900). Afterwards Duke of Edinburgh, reigning duke of Saxe-Coburg and Gotha 1893. 2nd son of Queen Victoria.

737 (inv 1863) Henry George, 3rd Earl Grey. Secretary of State for the Colonies.

738 (inv 1864) George Granville William (Leveson-Gower), 3rd Duke of Sutherland.

739 (inv 1864) George William Frederick (Brudenell-Bruce) 2nd Marquess of Ailesbury.

740 (inv 1864) Henry (Petty-Fitzmaurice), 4th Marquess of Lansdowne.

741 (inv 1865) John Poyntz, 5th Earl Spencer. Viceroy of Ireland. Lord President of the Council.

742 (inv 1865) Harry George (Vane, afterwards Poulett).4th Duke of Cleveland.

743 (inv 1865) Luís I, King of Portugal (1838-89).

744 (inv 1865) Christian IX, King of Denmark (1818-1906).

745 (inv 1865) Louis III, Grand-Duke of Hesse and the Rhine.

746 (inv 1865) Francis Thomas (de Grey), 7th Earl Cowper.

747 (inv 1866) Henry Richard Charles (Wellesley), 1st Earl Cowley. Diplomatist. Ambassador to France.

748 (inv 1866) Leopold II, King of the Belgians(1835-1909).

749 (inv 1866) Frederick Christian Charles Augustus, Dukeof Schleswig-Holstein (1831-1917). Known in England as Prince Christian. Married the Princess Helena, 3rd daughter of Queen Victoria.

750 (inv 1867) Charles Henry (Gordon-Lennox), 6th Duke of Richmond and 1st Duke of Gordon (1818-1903).

751 (inv 1867) Charles Cecil John (Manners), 6th Duke of Rutland (1815-88).

752 (inv 1867) Henry Charles Fitzroy (Somerset), 8th Duke of Beaufort (1824-99).

753 (inv 1867) Arthur William Patrick Albert, Duke of Saxony, Prince of Coburg-Gotha (1850-1942). Afterwards Duke of Connaught and Strathearn. Governor-General of Canada. 3rd son of Queen Victoria. No other Knight of the Garter throughout the history of the Order has held the honour for so long a period.

754 (inv 1867) Francis Joseph, Emperor of Austria(1830-1916). Removed 13 May 1915.

755 (inv 1867) Alexander II, Emperor of all the Russia (1818-81). Assassinated.

756 (inv 1867) Abdul Aziz, Sultan of Turkey.

757 (inv 1868) John Winston (Spencer-Churchill), 7th Duke of Marlborough (1822-83).

758 (inv 1869) Prince Leopold George Duncan Albert, Duke of Saxony and Prince of Saxe-Coburg-Gotha (1853-84). Afterwards Duke of Albany. 4th son of Queen Victoria.

759 (inv 1869) Stratford (Canning), Viscount Stratford deRedcliffe. Diplomatist.

760 (inv 1869) George Frederick Samuel (Robinson), 2nd Earl of Ripon and 3rd Earl de Grey of Wrest. Afterwards 1st Marquess of Ripon. Lord President of the Council. Viceroy of India.

761 (inv 1870) Hugh Lupus (Grosvenor), 3rd Marquess of Westminster. Afterwards 1st Duke of Westminster.

762 (inv 1871) Pedro II, Emperor of Brazil.

763 (inv 1872) Thomas (Dundas), 2nd Earl of Zetland (d.1873).

764 (inv 1873) Nasred Din, Shah of Persia.

765 (inv 1873) Thomas William (Coke), 2nd Earl of Leicester.

766 (inv 1876) George I, King of the Hellenes (1845-1913).

767 (inv 1877) Prince Friedrich Wilhelm Viktor Albert of Prussia (1859-1941). Succ. 1888 as Wilhelm II, Emperor of Germany. Removed 13 May 1915.

768 (inv 1878) Umberto I, King of Italy (1844-1900).

769 (inv 1878) Prince Ernest Augustus William Adolphus George Frederick of Hanover (1845-1923). 3rd Duke of Cumberland and Teviotdale. Son of George V, King of Hanover. Removed 13 May 1915.

770 (inv 1878) Benjamin (D'Israeli), Earl of Beaconsfield. First Lord of the Treasury and Prime Minister.

771 (inv 1878) Robert Arthur Talbot (Gascoigne-Cecil),3rd Marquess of Salisbury (1830-1903). Lord Privy Seal. First Lord of the Treasury and Prime Minister.

772 (inv 1880) Francis Charles Hastings (Russell), 9thDuke of Bedford (1819-91).

773 (inv 1881) Alexander III, Emperor of all the Russia (1845-1894).

774 (inv 1881) Oscar II, King of Sweden and Norway (1829-1907).

775 (inv 1881) Alfonso XII, King of Spain (1857-85).

776 (inv 1882) Albert, King of Saxony.

777 (inv 1882) William III, King of the Netherlands(1817-90).

778 (inv 1883) Augustus Charles Lennox (Fitzroy), 7th Duke of Grafton (1821-1918). Served in the Crimean War.

779 (inv 1883) Prince Albert Victor Christian Edward, of Wales. Afterwards Duke of Clarence and Avondale. Eldest son of Albert Edward,Prince of Wales.

780 (inv 1884) George Douglas (Campbell), 8th Duke of Argyll. Lord Privy Seal. President of the Council for India.

781 (inv 1884) Edward Henry (Stanley), 15th Earl of Derby. Secretary of State for Foreign Affairs, and for the Colonies.

782 (inv 1884) Prince George Frederick Ernest Albert of Wales. Afterwards PRINCE OF WALES, and subsequently GEORGE V, King of Great Britain.

783 (inv 1885) John (Wodehouse), 1st Earl of Kimberley. Viceroy of Ireland, Lord Privy Seal.

784 (inv 1885) William (Compton), 4th Marquess of Northampton.

785 (inv 1885) William Philip (Molyneux), 4th Earl of Sefton.

786 (inv 1885) Prince Henry Maurice of Battenberg.Married the Princess Beatrice, youngest daughter of Queen Victoria.

787 (inv 1886) Algernon George (Percy), 6th Duke of Northumberland (1810-99).

788 (inv 1886) William (Nevill), 1st Marquess of Abergavenny.

789 (inv 1886) Henry (Fitzalan-Howard), 15th Duke of Norfolk (1847-1917). Earl Marshal.

790 (inv 1887) Rudolph Francis Charles Joseph, Prince Imperial of Austria (1858-89).

791 (inv 1888) Charles Stewart (Vane-Tempest-Stewart),6th Marquess of Londonderry. Viceroy of Ireland.

792 (inv 1889) Prince Albert Wilhelm Heinrich of Prussia(1862-1929). Brother of Wilhelm II, Emperor of Germany (the Kaiser), and grandson of Queen Victoria. Removed 13 May 1915.

793 (inv 1890) Karl, King of Württemberg (1823-91).

794 (inv 1891) Vittorio Emanuele Ferdinando, Prince of Naples (1869-1947). Succ. 1900 as Vittorio Emanuele III, King of Italy. His banner was removed in 1940.

795 (inv 1891) John James Robert (Manners), 7th Duke of Rutland (1818-1906).

796 (inv 1891) George Henry, 5th Earl of Cadogan. Lord Privy Seal.

797 (inv 1892) Ernst Ludwig Karl Albrecht Wilhelm, Grand Duke of Hesse and the Rhine [Hesse-Darmstadt] (1868-1937). Removed 13 May 1915.

798 (inv 1892) Carol I, King of Romania (1839-1914).

799 (inv 1892) Spencer Compton (Cavendish), 8th Duke of Devonshire (1833-1908). Secretary of State for War. Chief Secretary for Ireland. Lord President of the Council.

800 (inv 1892) James (Hamilton), 2nd Duke of Abercorn (1838-1913).

801 (inv 1892) Archibald Philip (Primrose), 5th Earl of Rosebery. Lord President of the Council and Prime Minister.

802 (inv 1893) Nicholas Alexandrovitch, Grand Duke of Russia (1868-1918). Became in 1894 Nicholas II, Emperor of all the Russia.
Assassinated.

803 (inv 1894) Gavin (Campbell), 1st Marquess of Breadalbane. Keeper of the Privy Seal of Scotland.

804 (inv 1894) Alfred Alexander William Ernest Albert,Hereditary Prince of Saxe-Coburg (1874-99). Only son of Alfred, Duke of Edinburgh, 2nd son of Queen Victoria.

805 (inv 1895) Henry Charles Keith (Petty-Fitzmaurice), 5th Marquess of Lansdowne. Secretary of State for Foreign Affairs. Governor-General of Canada.

806 (inv 1895) Carlos I, King of Portugal (1863-1908).Assassinated.

807 (inv 1896) Christian Frederick William Charles, Crown Prince of Denmark (1843-1912). Succ. 1906 as Frederick VIII, King of Denmark.

808 (inv 1897) Frederick Arthur (Stanley), 16th Earl of Derby. Secretary of State for the Colonies. Governor-General of Canada.

809 (inv 1897) William Henry Walter(Montagu-Douglas-Scott), 6th Duke of Buccleuch, and 8th Duke of Queensberry (1831-1914).

810 (inv 1899) Victor Alexander (Bruce), 9th Earl of Elgin and 15th Earl of Kincardine.

811 (inv 1899) Henry George (Percy), 7th Duke of Northumberland (1846-1918).

812 (inv 1900) William John Arthur Charles James(Cavendish-Bentinck), 6th Duke of Portland (1857-1943).

812bis (app 12.2.1901) Alexandra, Queen Consort(1844-1925), daughter of Christian IX, King of Denmark, K.G. Married Edward VII.

813 (inv 1901) Frederick Sleigh, 1st Earl Roberts. Field Marshal; saw active service in India, Afghanistan, and South Africa.

814 (inv 1901) Friedrich Wilhelm Viktor August Ernst,Crown Prince Imperial of Germany (1882-1951). Removed 13 May 1915.

815 (inv 1902) Alfonso XIII, King of Spain (1886-1941).

816 (inv 1902) Herbrand Arthur (Russell), 11th Duke of Bedford (1858-1940).

817 (inv 1902) Charles Richard John (Spencer-Churchill),9th Duke of Marlborough (1871-1934).

818 (inv 1902) Prince Michael Alexandrovitch, hereditary Grand-Duke of Russia (1878-1918). Brother of Nicholas II. Assassinated.

819 (inv 1902) Francis Ferdinand Charles Louis Joseph, Marie, Archduke of Austria (1863-1914). Assassinated.

820 (inv 1902) Prince Emmanuel Philibert Victor Eugene Genes Joseph Marie, Duke of Aosta (1869-1931).

821 (inv 1902) Prince Luís Filipe Maria Carlos, Duke of Braganza, Crown Prince of Portugal (1887-1908). Assassinated.

822 (inv 1902) Prince Leopold Charles Edward GeorgeAlbert, Duke of Albany (1884-1954). Became in 1900 reigning Duke of Saxe-Coburg-Gotha. Removed 13 May 1915.

823 (inv 1902) Prince Arthur Frederick Patrick Albert of Connaught, only son of Arthur, Duke of Connaught, and grandson of Queen Victoria. Governor-General of the Union of South Africa.

824 (inv 1902) Arthur Charles (Wellesley), 4th Duke of Wellington (1849-1934).

825 (inv 1902) Cromartie (Sutherland Leveson-Gower), 4th Duke of Sutherland.

826 (inv 1903) Muzaffer-ed-Din, Shah of Persia.

827 (inv 1904) Wilhelm II, King of Württemberg (1848-1921). Removed 13 May 1915.

828 (app 14.6.1905) Oscar Gustaf Adolf, Prince of Sweden and Norway (1858-1950). Succ. 1907 as Gustaf V, King of Sweden.

829 (app 6.8.1905) Charles Henry (Gordon-Lennox), 7th Duke of Richmond and 2nd Duke of Gordon (1845-1928).

830 (app 4.11.1905, inv 1906) Mutsuhito, Emperor of Japan.

831 (app 7.9.1906) Prince Frederick, Grand-Duke of Baden.

832 (27.9.1906) Charles Robert (Wynn-Carrington), 1stEarl Carrington. Afterwards Marquess of Lincolnshire. Lord Privy Seal.

833 (app 9.11.1906) Haakon VII, King of Norway(1872-1957). Married the Princess Maud, youngest daughter of Edward VII.

834 (app 1.5.1908) Robert Offley Ashburton(Crewe-Milnes), 1st Earl of Crewe. Secretary of State for the Colonies. LordPrivy Seal. Lord President of the Council.

835 (app 27.6.1908) William George Spencer Scott(Compton), 5th Marquess of Northampton.

836 (app 24.2.1909) John George (Lambton), 3rd Earl of Durham.

837 (app 21.7.1909) William Waldegrave, 2nd Earl of Selborne. First Lord of the Admiralty. High Commissioner of South Africa.

838 (app 19.11.1909) Manoel II, King of Portugal(1889-1932).

838bis (app 3.6.1910) Mary, Queen Consort. Daughter of Francis, Duke of Teck. Married George V.

839 (app 15.12.1910, inv 1911) Gilbert John (Elliot), 4th Earl of Minto. Governor-General of Canada. Viceroy of India.

840 (app 10.3.1911) Luitpold, Prince Regent of Bavaria (1821-1912). His banner and crest were never placed in the Chapel.

841 (app 23.6.1910, inv 1911) Edward Albert Christian George Andrew Patrick David, PRINCE OF WALES. Afterwards EDWARD VIII, King of Great Britain. Created Duke of Windsor after his abdication.

842 (app 19.6.1911) Adolf Friedrich V, Grand-Duke of Mecklenburg-Strelitz (1848-1914).

843 (app 19.6.1911, inv 1912) John Douglas Sutherland(Campbell). 9th Duke of Argyll. Governor General of Canada. Married the Princess Louise, 4th daughter of Queen Victoria.

844 (app 19.6.1911) Alexander William George (Duff), 1st Duke of Fife. Governor-General of Canada. Married the Princess Louise, afterwards Princess Royal, eldest daughter of Edward VII.

845 (app 18.9.1912) Yoshihito, Emperor of Japan.

846 (app 12.2.1912, inv 1913) Sir Edward Grey. Afterwards Viscount Grey of Falloden. Secretary of State for Foreign Affairs.

847 (app 19.7.1913) Charles Robert, 6th Earl Spencer.

848 (app 9.5.1914) Christian X, King of Denmark(1870-1947).

849 (app 22.6.1914) William (Lygon), 7th Earl Beauchamp. Lord President of the Council.

850 (app 4.12.1914) Albert I, King of the Belgians(1875-1934).

851 (app 1.1.1915) Edward George Villiers (Stanley), 17th Earl of Derby. Secretary of State for War.

852 (app 1.1.1914, inv 1915) Edwyn Francis(Scudamore-Stanhope), 10th Earl of Chesterfield.

853 (app 3.6.1915) Horatio Herbert, Earl Kitchener of Khartoum. Field Marshal. Served in the Soudan, South Africa, and World War I.Secretary of State for War.

854 (app 1.1.1916) George Nathaniel, Earl Curzon of Kedleston. Afterwards Marquess. Viceroy of India. Chancellor of the University of Oxford.

855 (app 1.1.1916) Victor Christian William (Cavendish),9th Duke of Devonshire (1868-1938). Governor General of Canada.

856 (app 1.1.1916) Charles, Lord Hardinge of Penshurst.Viceroy of India.

857 (app 14.12.1916) Prince Albert Frederick George.Afterwards Duke of York, and subsequently GEORGE VI, King of Great Britain.

858 (app 14.3.1917) James Edward Hubert (Gascoyne-Cecil), 4th Marquess of Salisbury (1861-1947). President of the Board of Trade. Lord Privy Seal.

859 (app 14.3.1917) Thomas Henry (Thynne), 5th Marquess of Bath.

860 (app 3.6.1918) Henry John Brinsley (Manners), 8th Duke of Rutland (1852-1925).

861 (app 9.12.1919) Charles Stewart Henry(Vane-Tempest-Stewart), 7th Marquess of Londonderry.

862 (app 16.2.1921) Alfred, Viscount Milner. Secretary of State for War, and for the Colonies. High Commissioner of South Africa.

863 (app 31.3.1921) Prince Henry William Frederick Albert (1900-74). Cr. 1928 Duke of Gloucester. 3rd son of George V.

864 (app 27.2.1922) Henry George Charles, Viscount Lascelles (1882-1947). Afterwards 6th Earl of Harewood. Married the Princess Victoria. Alexandra Alice Mary, only daughter of King George V, afterwards Princess Royal of England.

865 (app 3.3.1922) Arthur James, Earl Balfour. First Lord of the Treasury and Prime Minister.

866 (app 20.12.1923, inv 1924) Prince George Edward Alexander Edmund. Cr. 1934 Duke of Kent (1902-42). 4th son of George V.

867 (app 4.5.1924) Ferdinand, King of Romania(1865-1927).

868 (app 30.4.1925) Edmund Bernard (Fitzalan-Howard),Viscount Fitz alan of Derwent. Viceroy of Ireland.

869 (app 25.5.1925) Alan Ian (Percy), 8th Duke of Northumberland (1880-1930).

870 (app 9.2.1925) Herbert Henry (Asquith), 1st Earl of Oxford and Asquith. Prime Minister and First Lord of the Treasury.

871 (app 1.12.1925) Sir Joseph Austen Chamberlain. Secretary of State for Foreign Affairs. Lord Privy Seal and Leader of the House of Commons.

872 (app 17.4.1928) Alexander Augustus Frederick William Alfred George Cambridge, Earl of Athlone (1874-1957).

Formerly known as Prince Alexander of Teck. Married the Princess Alice, daughter of Prince Leopold, 4th son of Queen Victoria. Governor-General of the Union of South Africa. Governor of Windsor Castle.

873 (app 17.4.1928) James Albert Edward (Hamilton), 3rd Duke of Abercorn (1869-1953).

874 (app 17.4.1928) William Henry (Grenfell), 1st Lord Desborough (1855-1945).

875 (app 11.10.1928) Hugh Cecil (Lowther), 5th Earl of Lonsdale (1857-1944).

876 (app 3.5. 1929) Hirohito, Emperor of Japan. Removed in 1941, reinstated by warrant 22 May 1971.

877 (app 7.6.1929) Aldred Frederick George Beresford(Lumley), 10th Earl of Scarborough (1857-1960).

878 (app 3.5.1931) Edward Frederick Lindley (Wood), LordIrwin (1881-1959). Afterwards 3rd Viscount and 1st Earl Halifax. Viceroy of India. Secretary of State for Foreign Affairs. Chancellor of the University of Oxford.

879 (app 3.6.1933) Victor Alexander George Robert, 2nd Earl of Lytton (1871-1947).

880 (app 1.1.1934) James Richard, 7th Earl Stanhope and 13th Earl of Chesterfield (1880-1967).

881 (app 1.1.1935) Charles Alfred Worsley (Pelham), 4th Earl of Yarborough (1859-1936).

882 (app 2.12.1935) Leopold III, King of the Belgians (1901-83).

882bis (app 14.12.1936) Elizabeth, Queen Consort(1900-2002). Daughter of Claude (Bowes-Lyon), 14th Earl of Strathmore, K.G.Married King George VI.

883 (app 11.5.1937) George Herbert Hyde (Villiers), 6th Earl of Clarendon (1877-1955).

884 (app 11.5.1937) Bernard Marmaduke (Howard), 16th Duke of Norfolk (1908-75). Earl Marshal.

885 (app 11.5.1937) William Thomas (Cecil), 5th Marquess of Exeter (1876-1956).

886 (app 11.5.1937) Claude George (Bowes-Lyon), 14th Earlof Strathmore and Kinghorne (1855-1944). Father of Elizabeth, Queen Consort of George VI, King of Great Britain.

887 (app 11.5.1937) Henry Hugh Arthur Fitzroy (Somerset), 10th Duke of Beaufort (1900-84).

888 (app 28.5.1937) Stanley, Earl Baldwin of Bewdley (1867-1947). Prime Minister. First Lord of the Treasury. Lord Privy Seal.Chancellor of the University of Cambridge.

889 (app 7.11.1938) George II, King of the Hellenes (1890-1947).

890 (app 15.11.1938) Carol II, King of Romania (1893-1953).

891 (app 19.7.1939) Paul, Prince Regent of Yugoslavia (1883-1976).

892 (app 1.1.1941) Edward William Spencer (Cavendish), 10th Duke of Devonshire (1895-1950).

893 (app 11.6.1942) Lawrence John Lumley (Dundas), 2nd Marquess of Zetland (1876-1961).

894 (app 29.10.1943) Victor Alexander John (Hope), 2nd Marquess of Linlithgow (1887-1952).

894bis (app 24.9.1944) Wilhelmina, Queen of the Netherlands (1880-1962).

895 (app 3.12.1946) Christopher (Addison), 1st Viscount Addison (1869-1951).

896 (app 3.12.1946) Robert Arthur (Gascoyne-Cecil), 5th Marquess of Salisbury (1893-1972).

897 (app 3.12.1946) Louis (Mountbatten), 1st Earl Mountbatten of Burma (1900-79).

898 (app 3.12.1946) Alan Francis (Brooke), 1st Viscount Alan brooke (1883-1963).

899 (app 3.12.1946) Charles Frederick Algernon (Portal),1st Viscount Portal of Hungerford (1893-1971).

900 (app 3.12.1946) Harold Rupert Leofric George(Alexander), 1st Earl Alexander of Tunis (1891-1969).

901 (app 3.12.1946) Bernard Law (Montgomery), 1st Viscount Montgomery of Alamein (1887-1976).

901bis (app 1947) Princess Elizabeth, Duchess of Edinburgh (b. 1926). Subsequently Queen ELIZABETH II.

902 (app 19.11.1947) Prince Philip, Duke of Edinburgh (b.1921).

903 (app 12.3.1948) William Arthur Henry(Cavendish-Bentinck), 7th Duke of Portland (1893-1977).

904 (app 12.3.1948) William George Arthur (Ormsby-Gore), 4th Baron Harlech (1885-1964).

905 (app 12.3.1948) Lawrence Roger (Lumley), 11th Earl of Scarborough (1896-1969).

906 (app 12.3.1948) Betram Francis (Gurdon), 2nd Baron Cranworth (1877-1964).

907 (app 9.4.1951) Gerald (Wellesley), 7th Duke of Wellington (1885-1972).

908 (app 9.4.1951) Hugh William (Fortescue), 5th Earl Fortescue (1888-1958).

909 (app 9.4.1951) Wentworth Henry Canning (Beaumont),2nd Viscount Allendale (1890-1956).

910 (app 8.5.1951) Frederik IX, King of Denmark(1899-1972).

911 (app 5.12.1952) William Spencer (Leverson-Gower), 4th Earl Granville (1880-1953).

912 (app 24.4.1953) Winston Leonard Spencer Churchill (1874-1965).

913 (app 28.6.1954) Gustaf VI Adolf, King of Sweden (1882-1973).

914 (app 14.10.1954) Haile Selassie I, Emperor of Ethiopia (d. 1975).

915 (app 20.10.1954) Robert Anthony (Eden), 1st Earl of Avon (1897-1977).

916 (app 23.4.1955) Rupert Edward Lee (Guinness), 2nd Earl of Iveagh (1874-1967).

917 (app 7.4.1956) Clement Richard (Attlee), 1st Earl Attlee (1883-1967).

918 (app 23.4.1957) Hastings Lionel (Ismay), 1st Baron Ismay (1887-1965).

919 (app 23.4.1957) Michael Guy Percival (Willoughby), 11th Baron Middleton (1887-1970).

919bis (app 25.3.1958) Juliana, Queen of the Netherlands(1909-2004).

920 (app 26.7.1958) Charles Philip Arthur George, Prince of Wales (b. 1948).

921 (app 23.4.1959) William Joseph (Slim), 1st Viscount Slim of Yarralumla (1891-1970).

922 (app 23.4.1959) Hugh Algernon (Percy), 10th Duke of Northumberland (1914-88).

923 (app 29.5.1959) Olav V, King of Norway (1903-91).

924 (app 23.4.1960) William (Pleydell-Bouverie), 7th Earl of Radnor (1895-1968).

925 (app 23.4.1960) Edward Kenelm (Digby), 11th Baron Digby (1894-1964).

926 (app 2.5.1962) John de Vere (Loder), 2nd Baron Wakehurst (1895-1970).

927 (app 14.5.1963) Baudouin I, King of the Belgians (1930-93).

928 (app 9.7.1963) Paul I, King of the Hellenes (1901-64).

929 (app 16.9.1963) Gerald Walter Robert Templer (1898-1979).

930 (app 10.4.1964) Albert Victor (Alexander), 1st Earl Alexander of Hillsborough (1885-1965).

931 (app 10.4.1964) Charles John (Lyttelton), 10th Viscount Cobham (1909-77).

932 (app 23.4.1965) Basil Stanlake (Brooke), 1st Viscount Brookeborough (1888-1973).

933 (app 23.4.1965) Edward Ettindene (Bridges), 1st Baron Bridges (1892-1969).

934 (app 23.4.1968) Derek (Heathcoat Amory), 1st Viscount Amory (1899-1981).

935 (app 23.4.1968) William Philip (Sidney), 1st Viscount De L'Isle (1909-91).

936 (app 10.2.1969) Richard Gardiner (Casey), Baron Casey of Berwick (1890-1976).

937 (app 23.4.1969) Alexander Francis St Vincent (Baring), 6th Baron Ashburton (1898-1991).

938 (app 23.4.1970) Francis Oliver (Lyttelton), 1st Viscount Chandos (1893-1972).

939 (app 23.4.1970) Cameron Fromanteel (Cobbold), 1st Baron Cobbold (1904-87).

940 (app 23.4.1970) Edmund Castell Bacon, 13th Bart (1903-1982).

941 (app 23.4.1970) Sir Cennydd George Traherne (1910-95).

942 (app 23.4.1971) Geoffrey Noel (Waldegrave), 12th Earl Waldegrave (1905-95).

943 (app 23.4.1971) Francis Aunger (Pakenham), 7th Earl of Longford (1905-2001)

944 (app 23.4.1971) Richard Austen (Butler), Baron Butler of Saffron Walden (1902-82).

945 (app 24.4.1972) Hervey (Rhodes), Baron Rhodes (1895-1987).

946 (app 24.4.1972) Evelyn (Baring), 1st Baron Howick of Glendale (1903-73).

947 (app 24.4.1972) Charles Garrett Ponsonby (Moore), 11th Earl of Drogheda (1910-89).

948 (app 13.6.1972) Jean, Grand Duke of Luxembourg (b.1921).

949 (app 23.4.1974) Edward Arthur Alexander (Shackleton), Baron Shackleton (1911-94).

950 (app 23.4.1974) Humphrey (Trevelyan), Baron Trevelyan (1905-85).

951 (app 23.4.1974) John Henry Guy (Nevill), 5th Marquess of Abergavenny (1914-2000)

952 (app 23.4.1976) James Harold (Wilson), Baron Wilson of Rievaux (1916-95). Prime Minister.

953 (app 23.4.1976) Hugh Denis Charles (FitzRoy), 11th Duke of Grafton (b. 1919).

954 (app 23.4.1977) George Rowland Stanley (Baring), 3rd Earl of Cromer (1918-91).

955 (app 23.4.1977) Samuel Charles (Elworthy), Baron Elworthy (1911-93).

956 (app 23.4.1979) Henry Cecil John (Hunt), Baron Hunt (1910-98). Mountaineer.

957 (app 23.4.1979) Paul Meerna Caedwalla Hasluck (1905-93). Governor General of Australia 1969-74.

957bis (app 15.5.1979) Margarethe II, Queen of Denmark(b. 1940).

958 (app 21.4.1980) Sir Keith Jacka Holyoake (1904-83).Prime Minister of New Zealand 1960-72, Governor-General 1977-80.

959 (app 21.4.1980) Sir Richard Amyatt Hull (1907-89).Chief of the Imperial General Staff 1961-65.

960 (app 22.4.1983) Miles Francis Stapleton (Fitz Alan Howard), 17th Duke of Norfolk (1915-2002).

961 (app 22.4.1983) Adm. Terence Thornton (Lewin), Baron Lewin (1920-99).

962 (app 22.4.1983) Gordon William Humphreys (Richardson), Baron Richardson of Duntisbourne (b. 1915). Governor of the Bank of England 1973-83.

963 (app 25.5.1983) Carl XVI Gustaf, King of Sweden (b.1946).

964 (app 23.4.1985) Oswald Constantine John (Phipps), 4th Marquess of Normanby (1912-94).

965 (app 23.4.1985) Peter Alexander Rupert (Carrington), 6th Baron Carrington (b. 1919).

966 (app 9.10.1985) Edward, Duke of Kent (b. 1935).

967 (app 23.4.1987) Leonard James (Callaghan), Baron Callaghan of Cardiff (1912-2005). Prime Minister 1976-79.

968 (app 21.4.1988) Philip William Bryce (Lever), 3rd Viscount Leverhulme (1915-2000).

969 (app 21.4.1988) Quinton McGarel (Hogg), Baron Hailsham of St Marylebone (1907-2001).

970 (app 17.10.1988) Juan Carlos I, King of Spain (b.1938).

970bis (app 28.6.1989) Beatrix, Queen of the Netherlands (b. 1938).

971 (app 23.4.1990) Lavinia Mary, Duchess of Norfolk (1916-95).

972 (app 23.4.1990) Arthur Valerian (Wellesley), 8th Duke of Wellington (b. 1915).

973 (app 23.4.1990) Edwin Noel Westby (Bramall), Baron Bramall (b. 1923). Chief of the General Staff 1979-82.

974 (app 24.4.1992) Edward Richard George Heath (1916-2005). Prime Minister 1970-74.

975 (app 24.4.1992) Matthew White (Ridley), 4th Viscount Ridley (b. 1925). Lord Stewart of the Household.

976 (app 24.4.1992) John Davan (Sainsbury), Baron Sainsbury of Preston Candover (b. 1927).

976bis (app 23.4.1994) Princess Anne, The Princess Royal (b. 1950).

977 (app 23.4.1994) Sir Ninian Martin Stephen (b. 1923). Governor-General of Australia 1982-89.

978 (app 23.4.1994) Robert (Leigh-Pemberton), Baron Kingsdown (b. 1927).

979 (app 23.4.1994) John Francis Harcourt (Baring), 7th Baron Ashburton (b. 1928).

980 (app 22.4.1995) Margaret Hilda (Thatcher), Baroness Thatcher, OM (b. 1925). Prime Minister of the UK 1979-90.

981 (app 22.4.1995) Edmund Percival Hillary, KBE ONZ (b.1919).

982 (app 23.4.1996) Andrew Robert Buxton (Cavendish), 11th Duke of Devonshire (1920-2004).

983 (app 23.4.1996) Timothy James Alan Colman (b. 1929).

984 (app 23.4.1996) Richard Alexander Walter George, Duke of Gloucester (b. 1944).

985 (app 26.5.1998) Akihito, Emperor of Japan (b. 1933).

986 (app 23.4.1999) James (Hamilton), 5th Duke of Abercorn (b. 1934).

987 (app 23.4.1999) Erskine William Gladstone of Fasqueand and Balfour, 7th Bart (b. 1925).

988 (app 23.4.2001) Peter Anthony, Baron Inge (b. 1935).Chief of the General Staff 1992-94.

989 (app 23.4.2001) Sir Anthony Arthur Acland (b. 1930).

990 (app 31.5.2001) King Harald V of Norway (b. 1937).

990bis (app 23.4.2003) Princess Alexandra, the Hon Lady Ogilvy (b. 1936)

991 (app 23.4.2003) Gerald Cavendish, 6th Duke of Westminster, OBE (b. 1951)

992 (app 23.4.2003) Frederick Edward Robin Butler, BaronButler of Brockwell, GCB, CVO (b. 1938)

993 (app 23.4.2003) John Morris, Baron Morris of Aberavon, PC, QC (b. 1931).

994 (app 23.4.2005) Thomas Henry Bingham, The Lord Bingham of Cornhill, PC (b. 1933). Former Lord Chief Justice of England.

995 (app 23.4.2005) John Major, CH, PC (b. 1943). Former Prime Minister.

996 (app 23.4.2005) Lady Mary Soames (b. 1922, daughter of Sir Winston Churchill, n. 912).

997 (app 23.4.2006) HRH The Duke of York , Prince Andrew (b.1960).

998 (app 23.4.2006) HRH The Earl of Wessex , Prince Edward (b. 1964).

DARCY:Sir Philip VI (b. 1398)

FITZHUGH:Eleanor (b. 1391) DARCY:Margery (b. 1418) England **Margery Darcy**, daughter of Sir Philip VI Darcy and Eleanor FitzHugh, was born on 1 Sep 1418 in England.England She died on 20 Mar 1469–20 Apr 1469 at the age of 50 in England. Margery Darcy

F, #12933, b. 1 September 1418, d. between 20 March 1469 and 20 April 1469
Father   Sir Philip Darcy, 6th Baron Darcy, Lord Meinell 2,3,4,14,15,7,8,9,10,11,12,13 b. c 1398, d.2 Aug 1418
Mother Eleanor Fitz Hugh 2,3,14,15,8,10,11,13 b. c 1391, d. 30 Sep 1457

    Margery Darcy was born on 1 September 1418 at Ravensworth, Yorkshire, England; Age 1 in 1419,& 13 in 1431. Born posthumously.2,5,10 She married Sir John Conyers,Sheriff of Yorkshire, Constable of Middleham, Bailiff & Steward of Richmond Liberty, Steward of the lordship of Middleham, son of Sir Christopher Conyers,Sheriff of Yorkshire and Eleanor Rolleston, before 20 November 1431; They had 7 sons (Sir John; Richard; Christopher; Henry; Philip; Robert; & William,Esq.) and 5 daughters (Eleanor, wife of Sir Thomas Markenfield; Elizabeth, wife of Sir William Fitz William; Margaret, wife of Richard Ascue; Margery, wife of Rowland Place, Esq. & of Robert Wycliffe; &Joan).
2,16,4,6,7,8,9,10,11,12,13 Margery Darcy died between 20 March 1469 and 20 April 1469.2,5,10
Family
Sir John Conyers, Sheriff of Yorkshire, Constable of Middleham, Bailiff & Steward of Richmond Liberty, Steward of the lordship of Middleham d. 14 Mar 1490
Children
Thomas Conyers+
Richard Conyers, Lord of Horden Manor in Durham+

Elizabeth Conyers+2
Sir John Conyers+2,5,10 b. c 1432, d. 26 Jul 1469
Eleanor Conyers+2,17,5,7,10,12 b. c 1445, d. 5 Jun 1493
Margery Conyers+4,5,9,10 b. c 1447, d. a 4 May 1493

SOURCES:

[S3653] Unknown author, The Complete Peerage, by Cokayne,Vol. IV, p. 67; Burke's Peerage, 1938, p. 738, 2639;
Plantagenet Ancestry of 17th Century Colonists, by David Faris, p. 70.
[S5] Douglas Richardson, Plantagenet Ancestry, p. 227.
[S5] Douglas Richardson, Plantagenet Ancestry, p. 731.
[S16] Douglas Richardson, Magna Carta Ancestry, 2nd Edition, Vol. I, p. 215.
[S16] Douglas Richardson, Magna Carta Ancestry, 2nd Edition, Vol. I, p. 530-531.
[S16] Douglas Richardson, Magna Carta Ancestry, 2nd Edition, Vol. II, p. 28.
[S16] Douglas Richardson, Magna Carta Ancestry, 2nd Edition, Vol. III, p. 132.
[S16] Douglas Richardson, Magna Carta Ancestry, 2nd Edition, Vol. IV, p. 237.
[S4] Douglas Richardson, Royal Ancestry, Vol. I, p. 380.
[S4] Douglas Richardson, Royal Ancestry, Vol. II, p. 288.
[S4] Douglas Richardson, Royal Ancestry, Vol. II, p. 391.
[S4] Douglas Richardson, Royal Ancestry, Vol. IV, p. 62.
[S4] Douglas Richardson, Royal Ancestry, Vol. V, p. 217.
[S16] Douglas Richardson, Magna Carta Ancestry, 2nd Edition, Vol. I, p. 530.
[S16] Douglas Richardson, Magna Carta Ancestry, 2nd Edition,Vol. II, p. 27-28.
[S15] Douglas Richardson, Magna Carta Ancestry, p. 259.
[S5] Douglas Richardson, Plantagenet Ancestry, p. 498.

Sir John Conyers IV (KNIGHT OF THE GARTER) # 227 and Margery Darcy had the following child:

CONYERS V:Sir John (b. 1432)   +13   i.   **Sir John Conyers V**, born 1432, EnglandEngland ; died 26 Jul 1469,
        EnglandEngland .

Thirteenth Generation

13. CONYERS V:Sir John (b. 1432) England **Sir John Conyers V** (Sir John-12, Sir Christopher-11, Sir John-10, Robert-9,
Sir John-8, Sir Roger-7, Sir John-6, Sir Humphrey-5, Sir Geoffery-4, Roger-3, Roger-2, Roger-1) was born in 1432 in
England.England He died on 26 Jul 1469 at the age of 37 in England. Sir John Conyers

M, #15067, b. circa 1432, d. 26 July 1469
Father   Sir John Conyers, Sheriff of Yorkshire, Constable of Middleham, Bailiff & Steward of Richmond Liberty, Steward
of the lordship of Middleham 2,7,8 d. 14 Mar 1490
Mother Margery Darcy2,7,8 b. 1 Sep 1418, d. bt 20 Mar 1469 - 20 Apr 1469
    Sir John Conyers Thought to be the historic Robin Hood. He was born circa 1432 at of Hornby, Yorkshire, England. 2 He
married Alice Neville, daughter of Sir William Neville, Earl of Kent, 6th Baron Fauconberg, Admiral of England, Ireland, &
Aquitaine and Joan Fauconberg, circa 1460; They had 2 sons (John; & Sir William, 1st Lord Conyers) and 2 daughters
(Margery, wife of Sir William Bulmer; & Anne, wife of Richard, 4th Lord Lumley).2,9,3,4,6 Sir John Conyers died on 26
July 1469 at Battle of Edgcote Field, Banbury,Northamptonshire, England.2,3,5
Family
Alice Neville b. c 1437, d. b 21 Apr 1491
Children
Anne Conyers 10,2
Reginald Converse (Conyers)+ d. 1514
John Conyers 11,12 b. c 1461, d. a 1472

Sir William Conyers, 1st Lord Conyers, Constable of Richmond & Middleton Castles, Bailiff of the Liberty of Richmond+13,3,5 b.21 Dec 1468, d. c 14 Apr 1524
Margery Conyers+2 b. c 1469, d. 10 May 1524

SOURCES:

[S3944] Unknown author, The Complete Peerage, by Cokayne,Vol. V, p. 286; Burke's Peerage, 1938, p. 378, 2639.
[S5] Douglas Richardson, Plantagenet Ancestry, p. 227.
[S16] Douglas Richardson, Magna Carta Ancestry, 2nd Edition, Vol. I, p. 531.
[S16] Douglas Richardson, Magna Carta Ancestry, 2nd Edition, Vol. II, p. 145.
[S4] Douglas Richardson, Royal Ancestry, Vol. II, p.288-289.
[S4] Douglas Richardson, Royal Ancestry, Vol. II, p. 552.
[S16] Douglas Richardson, Magna Carta Ancestry, 2nd Edition, Vol. I, p. 530-531.
[S4] Douglas Richardson, Royal Ancestry, Vol. II, p. 288.
[S5] Douglas Richardson, Plantagenet Ancestry, p. 304.
[S11568] The Complete Peerage of England, Scotland,Ireland, Great Britain, and the United Kingdom, by George Edward Cokayne, Vol.VIII, p. 274-5.
[S16] Douglas Richardson, Magna Carta Ancestry, 2nd Edition, Vol. I, p. 532.
[S4] Douglas Richardson, Royal Ancestry, Vol. II, p. 289.
[S5] Douglas Richardson, Plantagenet Ancestry, p.227-228.

"Robin Hood"

From the turmoil of the Wars of the Roses came Robin of Redesdale or Robin Mend-All, leader of a rebellion in Yorkshire in the spring of 1469. 'Robin of Redesdale' was possibly the pseudonym for Sir John Conyers,who held the key position of steward of the lordship of Middleham, the engine-room of Earl Warwick's power in Yorkshire. At around the same time,there was another rebellion in Yorkshire led by Robin of Holderness, possibly the pseudonym for Robert Hill yard of Wine stead, who appears to have been executed in that same year. Robin of Redesdale's rebellion was supported by Warwick, known as 'Kingmaker', and the former was apparently alongside him at the battle of Edgecote in July of 1469; John Conyers is listed as one of the casualties. Sir John Conyers's apparent assumption of the pseudonym 'Robin of Redesdale' echoed the recent use of the name Robin by leaders of popular protest in Yorkshire – probably an allusion to Robin Hood. In 1485 northern rebel leaders allegedly had the names of Robin of Redesdale, Jack Straw (a leader of the Peasants Revolt in Kent in 1381), and Master Mendall (recalling the Robin Mend-All of 1469). The Yorkshire rebels of 1489 summoned support 'in the name of Master Hobbe Hyrste, Robin Goodfellow's brother he is, as I trow'.

Sources

1. King's Bench Roll, 1441.
2. Lordship and Learning: studies in memory of Tevor Aston, edited by Ralph Evans. (Boydell Press, 2004, p. 175)
3. Collections For a History of Staffordshire (William Salt Archaeological Society, new ser., x. part I, 1907), pp. 80-1.
4. Sir Ralph Winwood, Memorials of Affairs of State (London 1725), ii, pp. 172-3.
5. For the references used in this paragraph see: Holt, Robin Hood, p. 58; A.J. Pollard,1990, North- Eastern England During the Wars of the Roses, Lay Society, War,and Politics 1450-1500, pp. 304-305; John Gillingham, 1981, The Wars of the Roses, Peace and Conflict in Fifteenth-Century England, pp. 160-161; Anthony Goodman, 1981, The War of the Roses, Military Activity and English Society,1452-97, p. 205.
6. E. L. G.Stones, 'The Folvilles of Ashby Folville, Leicestershire and Their Associates in Crime 1326-41', Transactions of the Royal Historical Society, 5 ser., vii(1957), pp. 134-5.

Sir John Conyers,
Hedgecote Field, married to Alice de Neville, born 1437,Roxborough Castle, Ireland. Sir John was the sheriff at Yorkshire at the time of the War of the Roses and was one of the Warwick's Captains, looking after Warwick's lands and interests in Yorkshire.

Sir John Conyers' first son Christopher is buried under an alabaster tomb in South Cowton

Church built by Sir Richard Conyers. His second son William became the first Baron Conyers and inherited Hornby Castle. His daughter Margery St. Quentin married yet another Sir John Conyers who subsequently inherited the Castle. Christopher was attorney to Ralph de Neville 1st Earl of Westmoreland, the most powerful man in North England in the late 14th century (the character Westmoreland in Shakespeare's plays Henry IV and Henry V is based on Neville).

His second wife was Joan Beaufort, a Princess of Blood Royal.

Christopher Conyers is buried in Hornby Church which is located next to Hornby Castle. It is believed that he was responsible for building the North Wing of the Castle. It is uncertain where Sir John Conyers (KG) is buried.

The current owner of Hornby has set money aside for Sir John Conyers' grave to be properly marked if it can be found. Because of his great wealth and status, British archeologists contacted by Paul Redfern believe that he is buried in one of the major monasteries connected with the family – Fountains Abbey, Easby Abbey, Marrick Priory or Holy Trinity Priory York.

Sir John Conyers, husband of Margery Conyers,
daughter of Sir John Conyers (KG) is buried at
at the Church of Hornby under an alabaster effigy.

The Church of Hornby in North Yorkshire, also known as St. Mary's, was rebuilt on the site of an earlier Saxon church. It began about 14 years after the Norman Conquest, around 1080. The oldest parts are the tower. The lower stages of the tower show a combination of Saxon and Norman styles. The Saxon influence is most notable in the third stage of the tower, the original belfry which contains four bells, the oldest of which was originally provided by William, Lord Conyers (1468-1524).

Many fine monuments decorate the church. Stone and alabaster figures and brass images of Crusader knights and their families lie in the chapels.Medieval paintings of birds and foliage decorate the chantry chapel screen. The north aisle's east window contains original medieval glass from the 14th century.

Paul Redfern has been in contact with the leader of the Council of British Archaeology for York shore excavation team, who reported in July 2011 that the surviving Hornby Castle building was undertaken by Sir John Conyers KG "who played a major role in regional and national politics and had tastes to match!" The British archeological team has found evidence that the North Wing of the Castle was built by an earlier Sir John Conyers who acquired Hornby in the right of his wife in the 1390s.

The 2010 excavation of the Banqueting House of Hornby Castle, built in the 1760s for then owner Robert Conyers-Dracy 4th Earl of Holdnerness, led by Erik Matthews of the Architectural & Archaeological Society of Durham and Northumberland, also found evidence in the form of a stone revetted flower bed, a sand lined path and an open sided motor and tile floored building, of a detached garden of Medieval date. This was securely identified by stratified pottery from the Saintonge region of Western France (center of the French Huguenots where our family originated from) dating to the late 14th Century.

Surviving section of Hornby Castle (south wing and tower)constructed by John Conyers KG in the late 1440s and modernized by John Carr(prolific architect and Lord Mayor of York) for the 4th Earl of Holderness in 1760. The plan is to reopen it hopefully in 2016 or so. Archeologists are actively digging there.

In 2011, an 18th Century gravel path associated with the land scaping works of Lancelot "Capability" Brown, (considered England's greatest gardener who designed over 170 parks, many of which still endure), for the 4th Earl of Holderness was uncovered.

Very quickly, beneath, they uncovered the remains of a substantial well-built stone complex yielding significant quantities of high status Medieval pottery, drinking glass, food bones including venison and boar as well as a range of small finds including a spur used on boots for horseback riding and family dice made out of whale bone dated mid 15th Century.

They also discovered in 2011 that the castle had a very rare conduit fed piped fresh water supply system using a mix of elm timer and earthen ware pipes which in view of the archeologist "places the building amongst the very highest status in England in view of the shear expense to undertake and maintain this work that dates at the very latest to the mid 15th century."
The manor house that the John Conyers family lived in existed on the Sockburn estate until at least 1682. There is a large farmhouse on the estate now where English Romantic poet William Wordsworth courted Mary Hutchinson while staying at the farm in 1799. Wordsworth's friend Samuel Taylor Coleridge also stayed at the farm in 1799 and fell in love with Mary's sister, Sara, although he was married at the time. It was the Sockburn estate where our family lived that Coleridge wrote his ballad-poem "Love," dedicated to Sara, which mentions a knight, based on a figure on the Sir John Conyers tomb in the ruined All Saints Sockburn Church.

"Love" by Samuel Coleridge (partial, written at Sockburn estate)
All thoughts, all passions, all delights,
Whatever stirs this mortal frame,
All are but ministers of Love,
 And feed his sacred flame.
Oft in my waking dreams do I
Live o'er again that happy hour,
When midway on the mount I lay,
 Beside the ruined tower.
The moonshine, stealing o'er the scene
Had blended with the lights of eve;
And she was there, my hope, my joy,
 My own dear Genevieve!

Hornby Castle woodblock print published in Hornby Castle door at the
Morris's "County Seats" in 1880 Burrell Collection,Glasgow
The knight in Coleridge's ballad-poem "Love" is based on Sir John Conyer's
tomb (left) which is located in the ruins of All Saints Church in Sockburn (right).
Beneath Conyer's boot (with spur identical to the spur in the photo from the
archeological dig above) is the dead serpent which the family dog is confronting.

William Conyers left the family's Sockburn estate where Coleridge's poem was written to his daughter Anne. She conveyed it by marriage to Francis Talbot, by whom it was sold to Sir William Blacket, whom it has descended to the present proprietor. Sockburn Hall built in 1834 is currently on the Sockburn estate as is the farm house. There is a current project to save it.

NEVILLE - (KNIGHT O THE GARTER) # 155:Sir William (b. 1401)
FAUCONBERG:Joan (b. 1406) NEVILLE:Alice (b. 1437) England **Alice Neville**, daughter of Sir William Neville - (KNIGHT O THE GARTER) # 155 and Joan Fauconberg, was born in 1437 in England.England She died on 21 Apr 1491 at the age of 54 in England. Alice Neville

F, #15068, b. circa 1437, d. before 21 April 1491
Father   Sir William Neville, Earl of Kent, 6th Baron Fauconberg, Admiral of England, Ireland, & Aquitaine 3,4,8,6,9 b. a 1401, d. 9 Jan 1463
Mother Joan Fauconberg 3,4,8,6,9 b. 18 Oct 1406, d. 11 Dec 1490

   Alice Neville was born circa 1437; Age 26 in 1463. 10,4,6 She married Sir John Conyers, son of Sir John Conyers, Sheriff of Yorkshire, Constable of Middleham, Bailiff &Steward of Richmond Liberty, Steward of the lordship of Middleham and Margery Darcy, circa 1460; They had 2 sons (John; & Sir William, 1st Lord Conyers)and 2 daughters (Margery, wife of Sir William Bulmer; & Anne, wife of Richard, 4th Lord Lumley).10,3,4,5,7 Alice Neville died before 21 April 1491.10,4,6
Family
Sir John Conyers b. c 1432, d. 26 Jul 1469
Children
Anne Conyers 11,10
Reginald Converse (Conyers)+ d. 1514
John Conyers 12,13 b. c 1461, d. a 1472
Sir William Conyers, 1st Lord Conyers, Constable of Richmond & Middleton Castles, Bailiff of the Liberty of Richmond+2,4,6 b.21 Dec 1468, d. c 14 Apr 1524
Margery Conyers+10 b. c 1469, d. 10 May 1524

SOURCES:

[S3945] Unknown author, The Complete Peerage, by Cokayne,Vol. V, p. 286/7; Burke's Peerage, 1938, p. 738, 2639; Plantagenet Ancestry of 17th Century Colonists, by David Faris, p. 70.
[S5] Douglas Richardson, Plantagenet Ancestry, p.227-228.
[S5] Douglas Richardson, Plantagenet Ancestry, p. 304.
[S16] Douglas Richardson, Magna Carta Ancestry, 2nd Edition, Vol. I, p. 531.
[S16] Douglas Richardson, Magna Carta Ancestry, 2nd Edition, Vol. II, p. 145.
[S4] Douglas Richardson, Royal Ancestry, Vol. II, p.288-289.
[S4] Douglas Richardson, Royal Ancestry, Vol. II, p. 552.
[S16] Douglas Richardson, Magna Carta Ancestry, 2nd Edition, Vol. II, p. 144-145.
[S4] Douglas Richardson, Royal Ancestry, Vol. II, p.551-552.
[S5] Douglas Richardson, Plantagenet Ancestry, p. 227.
[S11568] The Complete Peerage of England, Scotland,Ireland, Great Britain, and the United Kingdom, by George Edward Cokayne, Vol.VIII, p. 274-5.
[S16] Douglas Richardson, Magna Carta Ancestry, 2nd Edition, Vol. I, p. 532.
[S4] Douglas Richardson, Royal Ancestry, Vol. II, p. 289.

Sir John Conyers V and Alice Neville had the following child:

CONYERS I:Reginald (b. 1468)   +14   i.   **Reginald Conyers I**, born 1468, Hornby, Yorkshire, EnglandEngland:Yorkshire:Hornby ; married Anna Norwich, 1525, Hornby, Yorkshire, EnglandEngland:Yorkshire:Hornby ; died 1535, Hornby, Yorkshire, EnglandEngland:Yorkshire:Hornby .

Fourteenth Generation

14. CONYERS I:Reginald (b. 1468) England:Yorkshire:Hornby **Reginald Conyers I** (Sir John-13, Sir John-12, Sir Christopher-11, Sir John-10, Robert-9, Sir John-8, Sir Roger-7, Sir John-6, Sir Humphrey-5, Sir Geoffery-4, Roger-3, Roger-2, Roger-1) was born in 1468 in Hornby, Yorkshire, England.England:Yorkshire:Hornby He died in 1535 at the age of 67 in Hornby, Yorkshire, England. Reginald Conyers, died at Wakerly, Northampton, 1535.Married Anna Norwich in 1525. Through Reginald mother's tree, the current generation are granddaughters and grandsons of 5 Kings of England:

King Henry II (1133-1189) – 24
th great grandfather of the current generation
King John (1166-1216) – 23
rd great grandfather
King Henry III (1207-1272) – 22
nd great grandfather
King Edward I Longshanks (1239-1307) – 21
st great grandfather
King Edward III (1312-1377) – 19
th great grandfather

The current generation are also cousins of 6 other Kings of England and 1 Queen:
King Henry IV (1366-1413)
King Henry V (1386-1422)
King Henry VI (1421-1471)
King Henry VII (1457-1509)
King Henry VIII (1491-1547)
King Edward VI (1537-1553)
Queen Mary I (1553-1558)

Here is the line from King Edward III to Reginald Conyers:
King Edward III
John of Gaunt, 1st Duke of Lancaster (1340-1399)
Son of Edward
Joan Beaufort, Countess of Westmorland (1375-1445)
King Edward III Four
other Kings of England are
great grandfathers.
Henry VIII is a cousin of
our current generation
as is 3 other Henry's,
King Edward IV, and
Queen Mary I.
Elizabeth II's 13th great
grandmother was Margaret
Tudor, sister of Henry VIII,
father of Elizabeth I. Through
Elizabeth I, we are distant
cousins of Elizabeth II.
Daughter of John of Gaunt
William Neville, 1st Earl of Kent (1410-1463)
Son of Joan Beaufort

Alice Neville (~1437-1470)
Daughter of William
Reginald Conyers
Son of Alice

Separately, there is a direct family line from Reginald Conyers through his father Sir John
Conyers to King Edward I Longshanks as follows:

King Edward I Longshanks (1239-1307)
Elizabeth of Rhuddlan (1282-1316)
Daughter of Edward I Longshanks
Eleanor de Bohun, Countess of Ormond (1304-1363)
Daughter of Elizabeth o
Petronilla Butler, Baroness Talbot (-1387)
Daughter of Eleanor
Elizabeth Talbot (1388-)
Daughter of Petronilla
Margaret Grey (1381-1454)
Daughter of Elizabeth
Phillip Darcy, 6th Baron Darcy (1398-1418)
Son of Margaret
Margaret Darcy (1418-1469)
Daughter of Phillip
Sir John Conyers (1458-1520)
Son of Margaret
Sir John V. Conyers, Knight (KG)
Son of Sir John
Reginald Conyers
Son of Sir John

The following is reprinted from Genealogical Gleanings in England by Henry F. Waters, A.M., Boston, 1901, published in
two volumes by The New England Historic Genealogical Society

Baron of the bishopric of Durham and Lord of Bishopton.

Geoffery "Galfrid" Conyers, Lord of Sockburn and Bishopton, 1213-1238. ,
John Conyers, Sockburn, England.
Sir Humphrey' Conyers, Sockburn, England.
Sir John' Conyers, Sockburn, England.
Roger Conyers, Sockburn, England.
Sir John' Conyers, Sockburn, England; died 1395.
Robert Conyers, Sockburn, England; born 1371; died 1433.
John" Conyers, Hornby, England.
Sir Christopher" Conyers, Hornby, England.
Sir John Conyers, of Hornby Castle; sheriff of the shire; governor of the castle at York; in 1460 joined Richard, Duke of
York, against the King.
Sir John" Conyers, of Hornby, England; Knight of the Order of the Garter; died 1490.
Reginald" Conyers, Wakerly, England; died 1514.
Richard" Conyers, Wakerly, England.
Christopher" Conyers, Wakerly, England, baptized 1552.

Sources:
Plantagenet Ancestry, p. 227.

Sources:

1. 'Parishes: Sockburn', A History of the County of York North Riding:
Volume 1 (1914), pp. 449-454
2. Harleian Society, Vol 80, Knights of Edward I , Vol I (London:
1929) p 234
3. Calendar of Fine Rolls, Vol 1, p 403
4. Calendar of Fine Rolls, Vol 1, p 424
5. Chancery: Certificates of Statute Merchant and Statute Staple, C
241/68/74
6. Calendar of Fine Rolls, Vol 1, p 432
7. 'Parishes: Long Newton', A History of the County of Durham: Volume
3 (1928), pp. 299-304
8. Archaeologica Aeliana, Third Series, Vol 6 (Newcastle:1910) p 45
9. John Hodgson, A History of Northumberland, Vol V (Vol 3, Part 1)
(London: 1820) p 53 & 104
10. Archaeologica Aeliana, Third Series, Vol 6 (Newcastle: 1910) p 48
11. 45th Annual Report of the Deputy Keeper of the Public Records
(London: 1885) p 175
12. 'Parishes: Ormesby', A History of the County of York North Riding:
Volume 2 (1923), pp. 276-283
13. 45th Annual Report of the Deputy Keeper of the Public Records
(London: 1885) p 183
14. Archaeologica Aeliana, Third Series, Vol 7(Newcastle: 1910) p 59
15. Surtees Society, Vol 30, Testamenta Eboracensia, Part II (Durham:
1855) p 64n
16. Calendar of Patent Rolls, Henry 6, Vol 1, p 28
17. Complete Peerage, Vol 5, p 277
18. Lincolnshire Archives, Yarborough [YARB 16/1/1]

Title: VCH-Yorkshire North Riding, available inwww.british-history.ac.uk
Repository:
Media: Book
Page: see notes under Robert Conyers, d. 1431

England:Yorkshire:Hornby
Reginald Conyers I and Anna Norwich were married in 1525 in Hornby, Yorkshire, England.NORWICH:Simon
TYRELL:Margaret NORWICH:Anna **Anna Norwich**, daughter of Simon Norwich and Margaret Tyrell, was born (date
unknown). Sources:
Plantagenet Ancestry, p. 227.

Sources:

1. 'Parishes: Sockburn', A History of the County of York North Riding:
Volume 1 (1914), pp. 449-454
2. Harleian Society, Vol 80, Knights of Edward I , Vol I (London:
1929) p 234
3. Calendar of Fine Rolls, Vol 1, p 403
4. Calendar of Fine Rolls, Vol 1, p 424

5. Chancery: Certificates of Statute Merchant and Statute Staple, C 241/68/74

6. Calendar of Fine Rolls, Vol 1, p 432

7. 'Parishes: Long Newton', A History of the County of Durham: Volume 3 (1928), pp. 299-304

8. Archaeologica Aeliana, Third Series, Vol 6 (Newcastle:1910) p 45

9. John Hodgson, A History of Northumberland, Vol V (Vol 3, Part 1) (London: 1820) p 53 & 104

10. Archaeologica Aeliana, Third Series, Vol 6(Newcastle: 1910) p 48

11. 45th Annual Report of the Deputy Keeper of the Public Records (London: 1885) p 175

12. 'Parishes: Ormesby', A History of the County of York North Riding: Volume 2 (1923), pp. 276-283

13. 45th Annual Report of the Deputy Keeper of the Public Records (London: 1885) p 183

14. Archaeologica Aeliana, Third Series, Vol 7(Newcastle: 1910) p 59

15. Surtees Society, Vol 30, Testamenta Eboracensia, Part II (Durham: 1855) p 64n

16. Calendar of Patent Rolls, Henry 6, Vol 1, p 28

17. Complete Peerage, Vol 5, p 277

18. Lincolnshire Archives, Yarborough [YARB 16/1/1]

Title: VCH-Yorkshire North Riding, available inwww.british-history.ac.uk
Repository:
Media: Book
Page: see notes under Robert Conyers, d. 1431

Reginald Conyers I and Anna Norwich had the following child:

CONYERS I:Richard (b. 1525)   +15   i.   **Richard Conyers I**, born 1525, Wakerly, North Hampton, EnglandEngland:North Hampton:Wakerly ; died 1552, Wakerly, North Hampton, EnglandEngland:North Hampton:Wakerly .

Fifteenth Generation

15. CONYERS I:Richard (b. 1525) England:North Hampton:Wakerly **Richard Conyers I** (Reginald-14, Sir John-13, Sir John-12, Sir Christopher-11, Sir John-10, Robert-9, Sir John-8, Sir Roger-7, Sir John-6, Sir Humphrey-5, Sir Geoffery-4, Roger-3, Roger-2, Roger-1) was born in 1525 in Wakerly, North Hampton, England.England:North Hampton:Wakerly He died in 1552 at the age of 27 in Wakerly, North Hampton, England. The following is reprinted from Genealogical Gleanings in England by Henry F. Waters, A.M., Boston, 1901, published in two volumes by The New England Historic Genealogical Society

Baron of the bishopric of Durham and Lord of Bishopton.

Geoffery "Galfrid" Conyers, Lord of Sockburn and Bishopton, 1213-1238. ,
John Conyers, Sockburn, England.
Sir Humphrey' Conyers, Sockburn, England.
Sir John' Conyers, Sockburn, England.

Roger Conyers, Sockburn, England.
Sir John' Conyers, Sockburn, England; died 1395.
Robert Conyers, Sockburn, England; born 1371; died 1433.
John" Conyers, Hornby, England.
Sir Christopher" Conyers, Hornby, England.
Sir John Conyers, of Hornby Castle; sheriff of the shire; governor of the castle at York; in 1460 joined Richard, Duke of York, against the King.
Sir John" Conyers, of Hornby, England; Knight of the Order of the Garter; died 1490.
Reginald" Conyers, Wakerly, England; died 1514.
Richard" Conyers, Wakerly, England.
Christopher" Conyers, Wakerly, England, baptized 1552.

Sources:
Plantagenet Ancestry, p. 227.

Sources:

1. 'Parishes: Sockburn', A History of the County of York North Riding: Volume 1 (1914), pp. 449-454
2. Harleian Society, Vol 80, Knights of Edward I , Vol I (London: 1929) p 234
3. Calendar of Fine Rolls, Vol 1, p 403
4. Calendar of Fine Rolls, Vol 1, p 424
5. Chancery: Certificates of Statute Merchant and Statute Staple, C 241/68/74
6. Calendar of Fine Rolls, Vol 1, p 432
7. 'Parishes: Long Newton', A History of the County of Durham: Volume 3 (1928), pp. 299-304
8. Archaeologica Aeliana, Third Series, Vol 6 (Newcastle:1910) p 45
9. John Hodgson, A History of Northumberland, Vol V (Vol 3, Part 1) (London: 1820) p 53 & 104
10. Archaeologica Aeliana, Third Series, Vol 6 (Newcastle: 1910) p 48
11. 45th Annual Report of the Deputy Keeper of the Public Records (London: 1885) p 175
12. 'Parishes: Ormesby', A History of the County of York North Riding: Volume 2 (1923), pp. 276-283
13. 45th Annual Report of the Deputy Keeper of the Public Records (London: 1885) p 183
14. Archaeologica Aeliana, Third Series, Vol 7(Newcastle: 1910) p 59
15. Surtees Society, Vol 30, Testamenta Eboracensia, Part II (Durham: 1855) p 64n
16. Calendar of Patent Rolls, Henry 6, Vol 1, p 28
17. Complete Peerage, Vol 5, p 277
18. Lincolnshire Archives, Yarborough [YARB 16/1/1]

Title: VCH-Yorkshire North Riding, available inwww.british-history.ac.uk
Repository:
Media: Book
Page: see notes under Robert Conyers, d. 1431

BLOUNT:William

BLOUNT:Mary (b. 1530) England:Devon:Holcomb Bicton **Mary Blount**, daughter of William Blount, was born in 1530 in Holcomb Bicton, Devon, England. Sources:

1. 'Parishes: Sockburn', A History of the County of York North Riding:
Volume 1 (1914), pp. 449-454
2. Harleian Society, Vol 80, Knights of Edward I , Vol I(London:
1929) p 234
3. Calendar of Fine Rolls, Vol 1, p 403
4. Calendar of Fine Rolls, Vol 1, p 424
5. Chancery: Certificates of Statute Merchant and Statute Staple, C
241/68/74
6. Calendar of Fine Rolls, Vol 1, p 432
7. 'Parishes: Long Newton', A History of the County of Durham: Volume
3 (1928), pp. 299-304
8. Archaeologica Aeliana, Third Series, Vol 6 (Newcastle:1910) p 45
9. John Hodgson, A History of Northumberland, Vol V (Vol 3, Part 1)
(London: 1820) p 53 & 104
10. Archaeologica Aeliana, Third Series, Vol 6 (Newcastle: 1910) p 48
11. 45th Annual Report of the Deputy Keeper of the Public Records
(London: 1885) p 175
12. 'Parishes: Ormesby', A History of the County of York North Riding:
Volume 2 (1923), pp. 276-283
13. 45th Annual Report of the Deputy Keeper of the Public Records
(London: 1885) p 183
14. Archaeologica Aeliana, Third Series, Vol 7(Newcastle: 1910) p 59
15. Surtees Society, Vol 30, Testamenta Eboracensia, Part II (Durham:
1855) p 64n
16. Calendar of Patent Rolls, Henry 6, Vol 1, p 28
17. Complete Peerage, Vol 5, p 277
18. Lincolnshire Archives, Yarborough [YARB 16/1/1]

Title: VCH-Yorkshire North Riding, available in www.british-history.ac.uk
Repository:
Media: Book
Page: see notes under Robert Conyers, d. 1431

Richard Conyers I and Mary Blount had the following child:

CONYERS II:Christopher (b. 1552) +16 i. **Christopher Conyers II**, born 6 Mar 1552, Wakerly, North Hampton, EnglandEngland:North Hampton:Wakerly ; died 28 Jun 1639, Wakerly, North Hampton, EnglandEngland:North Hampton:Wakerly .

Sixteenth Generation

16. CONYERS II:Christopher (b. 1552) England:North Hampton:Wakerly **Christopher Conyers II** (Richard-15, Reginald-14, Sir John-13, Sir John-12, Sir Christopher-11, Sir John-10, Robert-9, Sir John-8, Sir Roger-7, Sir John-6, Sir Humphrey-5, Sir Geoffery-4, Roger-3, Roger-2, Roger-1) was born on 6 Mar 1552 in Wakerly, North Hampton, England.England:North Hampton:Wakerly He died on 28 Jun 1639 at the age of 87 in Wakerly, North Hampton, England. The following is reprinted from Genealogical Gleanings in England by Henry F. Waters, A.M., Boston, 1901, published in two volumes by The New

England Historic Genealogical Society

Baron of the bishopric of Durham and Lord of Bishopton.

Geoffery "Galfrid" Conyers, Lord of Sockburn and Bishopton, 1213-1238. ,
John Conyers, Sockburn, England.
Sir Humphrey' Conyers, Sockburn, England.
Sir John' Conyers, Sockburn, England.
Roger Conyers, Sockburn, England.
Sir John' Conyers, Sockburn, England; died 1395.
Robert Conyers, Sockburn, England; born 1371; died 1433.
John" Conyers, Hornby, England.
Sir Christopher" Conyers, Hornby, England.
Sir John Conyers, of Hornby Castle; sheriff of the shire;governor of the castle at York; in 1460 joined Richard, Duke of York, against the King.
Sir John" Conyers, of Hornby, England; Knight of the Order of the Garter; died 1490.
Reginald" Conyers, Wakerly, England; died 1514.
Richard" Conyers, Wakerly, England.
Christopher" Conyers, Wakerly, England, baptized 1552.

Sources:

1. 'Parishes: Sockburn', A History of the County of York North Riding:
Volume 1 (1914), pp. 449-454
2. Harleian Society, Vol 80, Knights of Edward I , Vol I (London:
1929) p 234
3. Calendar of Fine Rolls, Vol 1, p 403
4. Calendar of Fine Rolls, Vol 1, p 424
5. Chancery: Certificates of Statute Merchant and Statute Staple, C 241/68/74
6. Calendar of Fine Rolls, Vol 1, p 432
7. 'Parishes: Long Newton', A History of the County of Durham: Volume 3 (1928), pp. 299-304
8. Archaeologica Aeliana, Third Series, Vol 6 (Newcastle:1910) p 45
9. John Hodgson, A History of Northumberland, Vol V (Vol 3, Part 1) (London: 1820) p 53 & 104
10. Archaeologica Aeliana, Third Series, Vol 6(Newcastle: 1910) p 48
11. 45th Annual Report of the Deputy Keeper of the Public Records (London: 1885) p 175
12. 'Parishes: Ormesby', A History of the County of York North Riding: Volume 2 (1923), pp. 276-283
13. 45th Annual Report of the Deputy Keeper of the Public Records (London: 1885) p 183
14. Archaeologica Aeliana, Third Series, Vol 7(Newcastle: 1910) p 59
15. Surtees Society, Vol 30, Testamenta Eboracensia, Part II (Durham: 1855) p 64n
16. Calendar of Patent Rolls, Henry 6, Vol 1, p 28
17. Complete Peerage, Vol 5, p 277
18. Lincolnshire Archives, Yarborough [YARB 16/1/1]

Title: VCH-Yorkshire North Riding, available inwww.british-history.ac.uk
Repository:
Media: Book
Page: see notes under Robert Conyers, d. 1431

HALFORD:Margaret (b. 1560)

England:North Hampton:Wakerly **Margaret Halford** was born in 1560 in Wakerly, North Hampton, England.England:North Hampton:Wakerly She died on 22 Jun 1602 at the age of 42 in Wakerly, North Hampton, England. Sources:

1. 'Parishes: Sockburn', A History of the County of YorkNorth Riding:
Volume 1 (1914), pp. 449-454
2. Harleian Society, Vol 80, Knights of Edward I , Vol I(London:
1929) p 234
3. Calendar of Fine Rolls, Vol 1, p 403
4. Calendar of Fine Rolls, Vol 1, p 424
5. Chancery: Certificates of Statute Merchant and StatuteStaple, C
241/68/74
6. Calendar of Fine Rolls, Vol 1, p 432
7. 'Parishes: Long Newton', A History of the County ofDurham: Volume
3 (1928), pp. 299-304
8. Archaeologica Aeliana, Third Series, Vol 6 (Newcastle:1910) p 45
9. John Hodgson, A History of Northumberland, Vol V (Vol3, Part 1)
(London: 1820) p 53 & 104
10. Archaeologica Aeliana, Third Series, Vol 6(Newcastle: 1910) p 48
11. 45th Annual Report of the Deputy Keeper of the PublicRecords
(London: 1885) p 175
12. 'Parishes: Ormesby', A History of the County of YorkNorth Riding:
Volume 2 (1923), pp. 276-283
13. 45th Annual Report of the Deputy Keeper of the PublicRecords
(London: 1885) p 183
14. Archaeologica Aeliana, Third Series, Vol 7(Newcastle: 1910) p 59
15. Surtees Society, Vol 30, Testamenta Eboracensia, PartII (Durham:
1855) p 64n
16. Calendar of Patent Rolls, Henry 6, Vol 1, p 28
17. Complete Peerage, Vol 5, p 277
18. Lincolnshire Archives, Yarborough [YARB 16/1/1]

Title: VCH-Yorkshire North Riding, available inwww.british-history.ac.uk
Repository:
Media: Book
Page: see notes under Robert Conyers, d. 1431

Christopher Conyers II and Margaret Halford had the following child:

CONYERS I:Joshua (b. 1596)   +17   i.   **Joshua Conyers I**, born 1596, EnglandEngland ; died 1646,
                  EnglandEngland .

Seventeenth Generation

17. CONYERS I:Joshua (b. 1596) England **Joshua Conyers I** (Christopher-16, Richard-15, Reginald-14, Sir John-13, Sir
John-12, Sir Christopher-11, Sir John-10, Robert-9, Sir John-8, Sir Roger-7, Sir John-6, Sir Humphrey-5, Sir Geoffery-4,

Roger-3, Roger-2, Roger-1) was born in 1596 in England.England He died in 1646 at the age of 50 in England. Sources:

1. 'Parishes: Sockburn', A History of the County of York North Riding:
Volume 1 (1914), pp. 449-454
2. Harleian Society, Vol 80, Knights of Edward I , Vol I(London:
1929) p 234
3. Calendar of Fine Rolls, Vol 1, p 403
4. Calendar of Fine Rolls, Vol 1, p 424
5. Chancery: Certificates of Statute Merchant and Statute Staple, C
241/68/74
6. Calendar of Fine Rolls, Vol 1, p 432
7. 'Parishes: Long Newton', A History of the County of Durham: Volume
3 (1928), pp. 299-304
8. Archaeologica Aeliana, Third Series, Vol 6 (Newcastle:1910) p 45
9. John Hodgson, A History of Northumberland, Vol V (Vol 3, Part 1)
(London: 1820) p 53 & 104
10. Archaeologica Aeliana, Third Series, Vol 6(Newcastle: 1910) p 48
11. 45th Annual Report of the Deputy Keeper of the Public Records
(London: 1885) p 175
12. 'Parishes: Ormesby', A History of the County of York North Riding:
Volume 2 (1923), pp. 276-283
13. 45th Annual Report of the Deputy Keeper of the Public Records
(London: 1885) p 183
14. Archaeologica Aeliana, Third Series, Vol 7(Newcastle: 1910) p 59
15. Surtees Society, Vol 30, Testamenta Eboracensia, Part II (Durham:
1855) p 64n
16. Calendar of Patent Rolls, Henry 6, Vol 1, p 28
17. Complete Peerage, Vol 5, p 277
18. Lincolnshire Archives, Yarborough [YARB 16/1/1]

Title: VCH-Yorkshire North Riding, available inwww.british-history.ac.uk
Repository:
Media: Book
Page: see notes under Robert Conyers, d. 1431

RICHARDS:Susanna (b. 1603)
Susanna Richards was born on 3 Oct 1603. Sources:

1. 'Parishes: Sockburn', A History of the County of York North Riding:
Volume 1 (1914), pp. 449-454
2. Harleian Society, Vol 80, Knights of Edward I , Vol I (London:
1929) p 234
3. Calendar of Fine Rolls, Vol 1, p 403
4. Calendar of Fine Rolls, Vol 1, p 424
5. Chancery: Certificates of Statute Merchant and Statute Staple, C
241/68/74
6. Calendar of Fine Rolls, Vol 1, p 432
7. 'Parishes: Long Newton', A History of the County of Durham: Volume
3 (1928), pp. 299-304
8. Archaeologica Aeliana, Third Series, Vol 6 (Newcastle:1910) p 45
9. John Hodgson, A History of Northumberland, Vol V (Vol 3, Part 1)
(London: 1820) p 53 & 104
10. Archaeologica Aeliana, Third Series, Vol 6(Newcastle: 1910) p 48

11. 45th Annual Report of the Deputy Keeper of the Public Records
(London: 1885) p 175
12. 'Parishes: Ormesby', A History of the County of York North Riding:
Volume 2 (1923), pp. 276-283
13. 45th Annual Report of the Deputy Keeper of the Public Records
(London: 1885) p 183
14. Archaeologica Aeliana, Third Series, Vol 7(Newcastle: 1910) p 59
15. Surtees Society, Vol 30, Testamenta Eboracensia, Part II (Durham:
1855) p 64n
16. Calendar of Patent Rolls, Henry 6, Vol 1, p 28
17. Complete Peerage, Vol 5, p 277
18. Lincolnshire Archives, Yarborough [YARB 16/1/1]

Title: VCH-Yorkshire North Riding, available inwww.british-history.ac.uk
Repository:
Media: Book
Page: see notes under Robert Conyers, d. 1431

Joshua Conyers I and Susanna Richards had the following child:

CONYERS I:Thomas (b. 1634)   +18   i.   **Thomas Conyers I**, born bef 1634, Wakerly, North Hampton,
    EnglandEngland:North Hampton:Wakerly ; died 1726, Westmoreland, VirginiaVirginia:Westmoreland .

Eighteenth Generation

18. CONYERS I:Thomas (b. 1634) Virginia:Westmoreland **Thomas Conyers I** (Joshua-17, Christopher-16, Richard-15,
Reginald-14, Sir John-13, Sir John-12, Sir Christopher-11, Sir John-10, Robert-9, Sir John-8, Sir Roger-7, Sir John-6, Sir
Humphrey-5, Sir Geoffery-4, Roger-3, Roger-2, Roger-1) died in 1726 at the age of 92 in Westmoreland,
Virginia.England:North Hampton:Wakerly He was born before 1634 in Wakerly, North Hampton, England. Sources:

1. 'Parishes: Sockburn', A History of the County of York North Riding:
Volume 1 (1914), pp. 449-454
2. Harleian Society, Vol 80, Knights of Edward I , Vol I (London:
1929) p 234
3. Calendar of Fine Rolls, Vol 1, p 403
4. Calendar of Fine Rolls, Vol 1, p 424
5. Chancery: Certificates of Statute Merchant and Statute Staple, C
241/68/74
6. Calendar of Fine Rolls, Vol 1, p 432
7. 'Parishes: Long Newton', A History of the County of Durham: Volume
3 (1928), pp. 299-304
8. Archaeologica Aeliana, Third Series, Vol 6 (Newcastle:1910) p 45
9. John Hodgson, A History of Northumberland, Vol V (Vol 3, Part 1)
(London: 1820) p 53 & 104
10. Archaeologica Aeliana, Third Series, Vol 6(Newcastle: 1910) p 48
11. 45th Annual Report of the Deputy Keeper of the Public Records
(London: 1885) p 175
12. 'Parishes: Ormesby', A History of the County of York North Riding:
Volume 2 (1923), pp. 276-283

13. 45th Annual Report of the Deputy Keeper of the Public Records (London: 1885) p 183

14. Archaeologica Aeliana, Third Series, Vol 7 (Newcastle: 1910) p 59

15. Surtees Society, Vol 30, Testamenta Eboracensia, Part II (Durham: 1855) p 64n

16. Calendar of Patent Rolls, Henry 6, Vol 1, p 28

17. Complete Peerage, Vol 5, p 277

18. Lincolnshire Archives, Yarborough [YARB 16/1/1]

Title: VCH-Yorkshire North Riding, available inwww.british-history.ac.uk
Repository:
Media: Book
Page: see notes under Robert Conyers, d. 1431

<NO SURNAME>:Elizabeth

Elizabeth was born (date unknown). Sources:

1. 'Parishes: Sockburn', A History of the County of York North Riding: Volume 1 (1914), pp. 449-454

2. Harleian Society, Vol 80, Knights of Edward I , Vol I (London: 1929) p 234

3. Calendar of Fine Rolls, Vol 1, p 403

4. Calendar of Fine Rolls, Vol 1, p 424

5. Chancery: Certificates of Statute Merchant and Statute Staple, C 241/68/74

6. Calendar of Fine Rolls, Vol 1, p 432

7. 'Parishes: Long Newton', A History of the County of Durham: Volume 3 (1928), pp. 299-304

8. Archaeologica Aeliana, Third Series, Vol 6 (Newcastle:1910) p 45

9. John Hodgson, A History of Northumberland, Vol V (Vol 3, Part 1) (London: 1820) p 53 & 104

10. Archaeologica Aeliana, Third Series, Vol 6(Newcastle: 1910) p 48

11. 45th Annual Report of the Deputy Keeper of the Public Records (London: 1885) p 175

12. 'Parishes: Ormesby', A History of the County of York North Riding: Volume 2 (1923), pp. 276-283

13. 45th Annual Report of the Deputy Keeper of the Public Records (London: 1885) p 183

14. Archaeologica Aeliana, Third Series, Vol 7 (Newcastle: 1910) p 59

15. Surtees Society, Vol 30, Testamenta Eboracensia, Part II (Durham: 1855) p 64n

16. Calendar of Patent Rolls, Henry 6, Vol 1, p 28

17. Complete Peerage, Vol 5, p 277

18. Lincolnshire Archives, Yarborough [YARB 16/1/1]

Title: VCH-Yorkshire North Riding, available inwww.british-history.ac.uk
Repository:
Media: Book
Page: see notes under Robert Conyers, d. 1431

Thomas Conyers I and Elizabeth had the following child:

CONYERS:Henry (b. 1660)   +19   i.   **Henry Conyers**, born 1660; married Elizabeth Foote; died 13 Jun 1733, Stafford, VirginiaVirginia:Stafford .

Nineteenth Generation

19. CONYERS:Henry (b. 1660) **Henry Conyers** (Thomas-18, Joshua-17, Christopher-16, Richard-15, Reginald-14, Sir John-13, Sir John-12, Sir Christopher-11, Sir John-10, Robert-9, Sir John-8, Sir Roger-7, Sir John-6, Sir Humphrey-5, Sir Geoffery-4, Roger-3, Roger-2, Roger-1) was born in 1660.Virginia:Stafford He died on 13 Jun 1733 at the age of 73 in Stafford, Virginia. Sources:

1. 'Parishes: Sockburn', A History of the County of York North Riding:
Volume 1 (1914), pp. 449-454
2. Harleian Society, Vol 80, Knights of Edward I , Vol I(London:
1929) p 234
3. Calendar of Fine Rolls, Vol 1, p 403
4. Calendar of Fine Rolls, Vol 1, p 424
5. Chancery: Certificates of Statute Merchant and Statute Staple, C
241/68/74
6. Calendar of Fine Rolls, Vol 1, p 432
7. 'Parishes: Long Newton', A History of the County of Durham: Volume
3 (1928), pp. 299-304
8. Archaeologica Aeliana, Third Series, Vol 6 (Newcastle:1910) p 45
9. John Hodgson, A History of Northumberland, Vol V (Vol3, Part 1)
(London: 1820) p 53 & 104
10. Archaeologica Aeliana, Third Series, Vol 6(Newcastle: 1910) p 48
11. 45th Annual Report of the Deputy Keeper of the Public Records
(London: 1885) p 175
12. 'Parishes: Ormesby', A History of the County of York North Riding:
Volume 2 (1923), pp. 276-283
13. 45th Annual Report of the Deputy Keeper of the Public Records
(London: 1885) p 183
14. Archaeologica Aeliana, Third Series, Vol 7(Newcastle: 1910) p 59
15. Surtees Society, Vol 30, Testamenta Eboracensia, Part II (Durham:
1855) p 64n
16. Calendar of Patent Rolls, Henry 6, Vol 1, p 28
17. Complete Peerage, Vol 5, p 277
18. Lincolnshire Archives, Yarborough [YARB 16/1/1]

Title: VCH-Yorkshire North Riding, available inwww.british-history.ac.uk
Repository:
Media: Book
Page: see notes under Robert Conyers, d. 1431

Henry Conyers and Elizabeth Foote were married.FOOTE:Elizabeth (b. 1668) England:London **Elizabeth Foote** was born on 27 Oct 1668 in London, England. She died in 1715 at the age of 47. Sources:

1. 'Parishes: Sockburn', A History of the County of YorkNorth Riding:

Volume 1 (1914), pp. 449-454

2. Harleian Society, Vol 80, Knights of Edward I , Vol I(London: 1929) p 234

3. Calendar of Fine Rolls, Vol 1, p 403

4. Calendar of Fine Rolls, Vol 1, p 424

5. Chancery: Certificates of Statute Merchant and StatuteStaple, C 241/68/74

6. Calendar of Fine Rolls, Vol 1, p 432

7. 'Parishes: Long Newton', A History of the County ofDurham: Volume 3 (1928), pp. 299-304

8. Archaeologica Aeliana, Third Series, Vol 6 (Newcastle:1910) p 45

9. John Hodgson, A History of Northumberland, Vol V (Vol3, Part 1) (London: 1820) p 53 & 104

10. Archaeologica Aeliana, Third Series, Vol 6(Newcastle: 1910) p 48

11. 45th Annual Report of the Deputy Keeper of the PublicRecords (London: 1885) p 175

12. 'Parishes: Ormesby', A History of the County of YorkNorth Riding: Volume 2 (1923), pp. 276-283

13. 45th Annual Report of the Deputy Keeper of the PublicRecords (London: 1885) p 183

14. Archaeologica Aeliana, Third Series, Vol 7(Newcastle: 1910) p 59

15. Surtees Society, Vol 30, Testamenta Eboracensia, PartII (Durham: 1855) p 64n

16. Calendar of Patent Rolls, Henry 6, Vol 1, p 28

17. Complete Peerage, Vol 5, p 277

18. Lincolnshire Archives, Yarborough [YARB 16/1/1]

Title: VCH-Yorkshire North Riding, available inwww.british-history.ac.uk
Repository:
Media: Book
Page: see notes under Robert Conyers, d. 1431

Henry Conyers and Elizabeth Foote had the following child:

CONYERS:Dennis (b. 1685)   +20   i.   **Dennis Conyers**, born 1685; died 1755, Prince William County, VirginiaVirginia:Prince William County .

20th Generation

20. CONYERS:Dennis (b. 1685) **Dennis Conyers** (Henry-19, Thomas-18, Joshua-17, Christopher-16, Richard-15, Reginald-14, Sir John-13, Sir John-12, Sir Christopher-11, Sir John-10, Robert-9, Sir John-8, Sir Roger-7, Sir John-6, Sir Humphrey-5, Sir Geoffery-4, Roger-3, Roger-2, Roger-1) was born in 1685.Virginia:Prince William County He died in 1755 at the age of 70 in Prince William County, Virginia. Notes for DENNIS CONYERS:

1715 Dennis Conyers August 16, 1715 - Grant to John Baylor, land in St. Stephen's Parish, King and Queen County, for transportation of 27 persons, including Dennis Conyers.

1723 April 9, 1723 - Grant to Dennis Conyers of Stafford Co., 840 acres on

Licking Run.

1724-1726 Dennis Conyers, owner on Occoquan, Turkey Run and Licking Run, Stafford Co.

1728 October 10, 1728 Grant to Dennis Conyers of Stafford Co. 605 acres in Stafford Co. on Pignut Ridge.

1738 Dennis Connyers on Northumberland Co. rent roll.

1739 November 29, 1939 - Prince William Co. Land of Dennis Connyers from Richard Thornbury, for whom surveyed 298 acres on south side of Carter's Run; Marker: Samuel Conyers. Richard Thornbury being dead, deed was made out in name of his father in law Dennis Conner with the widow's consent.

1740 Dennis deeds land; Margaret relinquishes dower 3/19/1740, 8/23/1740 Prince William County.
Dennis Conniers & Margaret his wife granted land to their son and kinsman Richard Thornburry 9/26/1741 Deed BKE p.476 Prince Wm County. Film 7862

1740-1741 March 18/19, 1740/1741 Dennis Connyers of Prince William Co, planter, sells to John Folly, Sr. of Stafford Co. and James Folly of Prince William Co.,........605 acre tract on Pignut Ridge (Prince William Co. deeds, E: 180-5).

1742 Grant to Dennis Conyers of Prince William Co. 298 acres in said county on Carters Run.

1743 February 17, 1743 - Land patent to Rice Duncan, 189 acres in Prince William Co., adj. Dennis Connyers.

1747 August 3, 1747 - Land patent to William Fairfax, 488 acres in Prince William Co., adj. Richard Thornberry's now Dennis Conyers.

1752 Land patent to William Duling, 218 acres in Prince William Co., adj. Dennis Conners (2:20)

1755 Record in Prince William Co. that he married Margaret Thornhill, widow of Richard Thornbury.

1755 Dennis Conyers and Sarah his wife acknowledge a deed of gift to their sons Samuel and John Conyers 1/27/1755 Prince Wm County / Film 7866. Last will of Dennis Conyers to court by Samuel and John Conyers named executors 3/24/1755. Prince Wm order BK p 187.

1755 Sarah Conyers, widow of Dennis waives rights under will 4/28/1755. Order BK pg 220

1770 Land document which was recorded November 27, 1770. It reads: "......which sd. land was divided to sd. Alice Conyers wife of John Conyers, dec'd, John and William Conyers by their Grandfather Denis Conyers, dec'd......ack. by grantors."

1770 August 23, 1770 - Grant to James Folly Sr. of Fauquier Co. 117 acres on Broad Run in Fauquier Co., adj. Dennis Conyers.

1780 April 4, 1780 - Grant to Capt. William Pickett, 420 acres in Fauquier Co., adj. land of Dennis Conyers deceased.

Marriage Notes for DENNIS CONYERS and MARGARET THORNHILL:
MSSI M3587 a119 - Platt that reads: "Settle bought of Siclin (sp), W. Dulirn(sp) bought of McLanahan. McLanahan married the daughter and grandaughter to D. Conyers. Richard Thornbury was the former proprietor of ____ and now D. Conyers. Platt is not dated.

Dennis and Margaret may have had a daughter who married a man named McLanahan and there may have been a dispute over some land. I think the above mentioned document (Platt) is that land.

If Margaret was married to Richard Thornbury, then Dennis may have been married to someone else named Margaret. So far the oldest document I have where Margaret is mentioned by name, as his wife, is 1739. Since Samuel was born about 1719 and John in 1725 this may mean Dennis had three wives, Margaret being the 2nd and Sarah being the 3rd.

From the information I have seen it almost appears Richard Thornbury Sr. was still alive in the early 1730's.

Now there is another notation in parish (SPR, pg. 33) records that show "...baptized John, Son of Dennis and Margaret Conyers 6 June 1925." Did Dennis have two wives named Margaret?

1755 record in Prince William Co. that Dennis married Margaret Thornhill, widow of Richard Thornbury.

We need to find out when Richard Thornbury Sr. died to determine the above.

Children of DENNIS CONYERS and MARGARET THORNHILL are:

3.i. SAMUEL3 CONYERS, b. Abt. 1719, Stafford County, VA; d. 1815, Ford Mill, Wyoming Valley, Bath County, KY.

4.ii. JOHN CONYERS, b. June 1725, Stafford County, VA; d. Abt. 1770, Fauquier County, VA.

From the Loess Hills of Iowa with the Descendants of Dennis Conyers
By Terri Napoli, Arden Iva Sleadd
Pages 105 & 106

THORNHILL:Margaret (b. 1700)
Virginia:Stafford **Margaret Thornhill** was born in 1700 in Stafford, Virginia.Virginia:Stafford She died on 26 Sep 1741 at the age of 41 in Stafford, Virginia. Notes for MARGARET THORNHILL:

MSSI M3587 a119 - Platt that reads: "Settle bought of Siclin(sp), W. Dulirn(sp) bought of McLanahan. McLanahan married the daughter and grandaughter to D. Conyers. Richard Thornbury was the former proprietor of _____ and now D. Conyers. Platt is not dated.

1739 November 29, 1939 - Prince William Co. Land of Dennis Connyers from Richard Thornbury, for whom surveyed 298 acres on south side of Carter's Run; Marker: Samuel Conyers. Richard Thornbury being dead, deed was made out in name of his father in law Dennis Conner with the widow's consent.
Richard Thornbury and the said petitioner entered land in Thornbury's name only and he sold his part to Connyers. Thornbury died suddenly and deed not transferred.

1740 Dennis deeds land; Margaret relinquishes dower 3/19/1740, 8/23/1740 Prince William County.
Dennis Conniers & Margaret his wife granted land to their son and kinsman Richard Thornburry 9/26/1741 Deed BKE p.476 Prince Wm County. Film 7862

1755 Record in Prince William Co. that he married Margaret Thornhill, widow of Richard Thornbury.

Marriage Notes for DENNIS CONYERS and MARGARET THORNHILL:
MSSI M3587 a119 - Platt that reads: "Settle bought of Siclin(sp), W. Dulirn(sp) bought of McLanahan. McLanahan married the daughter and grandaughter to D. Conyers. Richard Thornbury was the former proprietor of _____ and now D. Conyers. Platt is not dated.

Dennis and Margaret may have had a daughter who married a man named McLanahan and there may have been a dispute over some land. I think the above mentioned document (Platt) is that land.

If Margaret was married to Richard Thornbury, then Dennis may have been married to someone else named Margaret. So far the oldest document I have where Margaret is mentioned by name, as his wife, is 1739. Since Samuel was born about 1719 and John in 1725 this may mean Dennis had three wives, Margaret being the 2nd and Sarah being the 3rd.

From the information I have seen it almost appears Richard Thornbury Sr. was still alive in the early 1730's.

Now there is another notation in parish (SPR, pg. 33) records that show "...baptized John, Son of Dennis and Margaret Conyers 6 June 1925." Did Dennis have two wives named Margaret?

1755 record in Prince William Co. that Dennis married Margaret Thornhill, widow of Richard Thornbury.

We need to find out when Richard Thornbury Sr. died to determine the above.

Children of DENNIS CONYERS and MARGARET THORNHILL are:

3.i. SAMUEL3 CONYERS, b. Abt. 1719, Stafford County, VA; d. 1815, Ford Mill, Wyoming Valley, Bath County, KY.

4.ii. JOHN CONYERS, b. June 1725, Stafford County, VA; d. Abt. 1770,
Fauquier County, VA.

From the Loess Hills of Iowa with the Descendants of Dennis Conyers
By Terri Napoli, Arden Iva Sleadd
Pages 105 & 106

Dennis Conyers and Margaret Thornhill had the following child:

CONYERS:Samuel (b. 1719)   +21   i.   **Samuel Conyers**, born 1719, Stafford County,
        VirginiaVirginia:Stafford County ; married Keisha Sparks; died 1815, Bath County, Kentucky, United
        StatesUnited States:Kentucky:Bath County .

21st Generation

21. CONYERS:Samuel (b. 1719) Virginia:Stafford County **Samuel Conyers** (Dennis-20, Henry-19, Thomas-18, Joshua-17,
Christopher-16, Richard-15, Reginald-14, Sir John-13, Sir John-12, Sir Christopher-11, Sir John-10, Robert-9, Sir John-8, Sir
Roger-7, Sir John-6, Sir Humphrey-5, Sir Geoffery-4, Roger-3, Roger-2, Roger-1) was born in 1719 in Stafford County,
Virginia.United States:Kentucky:Bath County He died in 1815 at the age of 96 in Bath County, Kentucky, United States.
Sources:

Lived in Fauquer County until the Revolution, then hemoved to Fayette County, PA and neighboring Westmoreland Co., (per
Paul Giffordnotes) where he is listed in 1796.
According to pension file of Benjamin Conyers, Samuel settled along the Monogahela River at the beginning of 1778.

1739 November 29, 1739 - Prince William Co.Land of Dennis Connyers from Richard Thornbury, for whom surveyed 298
acres on south side of Carter's Run; Marker: Samuel Conyers.Richard Thornbury being dead, deed was made out in name of
his father in law Dennis Conner with the widow's consent.

1755 Dennis Conyers and Sarah his wife acknowledge a deed of gift to their sons Samuel and John Conyers 1/27/1755 Prince
Wm County / Film 7866.

1755 Last will of Dennis Conyers to court by Samuel and John Conyers named executors 3/24/1755. Prince Wm order BK p
187.

1774 Indenture Conyers to Pickett"...Samuel Conyers of the County of Fauquier..."

1777 Indenture Conyers to Ball"...between Samuel Conyers of the County of Fauquier and Keziah his wife..."

1778 Fayette/Westmoreland Co, PA tax list

1783 Tax list of Franklin township, Westmoreland Co., PA

1786 Westmoreland Co., PA tax list

Rent Rolls: 1777, Fauquier Co., VA
Residence: Bet. 1779 - 1796, Westmoreland County, PA

From the Loess Hills of Iowa with the Descendants of Dennis Conyers
By Terri Napoli, Arden Iva Sleadd
Pages 105 & 106

Samuel Conyers and Keisha Sparks were married. Notes for SAMUEL CONYERS:
Lived in Fauquer County until the Revolution, then he moved to Fayette County,
PA and neighboring Westmoreland Co., (per Paul Gifford notes) where he is listed
in 1796.

According to pension file of Benjamin Conyers, Samuel settled along the
Monogahela River at the beginning of 1778.

1739 November 29, 1739 - Prince William Co. Land of Dennis Connyers from Richard
Thornbury, for whom surveyed 298 acres on south side of Carter's Run; Marker:
Samuel Conyers. Richard Thornbury being dead, deed was made out in name of his
father in law Dennis Conner with the widow's consent.

1755 Dennis Conyers and Sarah his wife acknowledge a deed of gift to their sons
Samuel and John Conyers 1/27/1755 Prince Wm County / Film 7866.

1755 Last will of Dennis Conyers to court by Samuel and John Conyers named
executors 3/24/1755. Prince Wm order BK p 187.

1774 Indenture Conyers to Pickett "...Samuel Conyers of the County of
Fauquier..."

1777 Indenture Conyers to Ball "...between Samuel Conyers of the County of
Fauquier and Keziah his wife..."

1783 Tax list of Franklin township, Westmoreland Co., PA

1763
1770
1777
1788
1786
1786
1793
SPARKS:Keisha (b. 1730) Virginia:Prince William County **Keisha Sparks** was born in 1730 in Prince William County,
Virginia. She died. sources:

From the Loess Hills of Iowa with the Descendants of Dennis Conyers
By Terri Napoli, Arden Iva Sleadd
Pages 105 & 106

More About KESIAH SPARKS:
Fact 6: Abt. 1793, went to KY

Children of SAMUEL CONYERS and KESIAH SPARKS are:

5.i. DAVID4 CONYERS, b. Abt. 1750.

6.ii. MARGARET CONYERS, b. December 30, 1755; d. October 1836, Barren

County, KY.

iii. JOHN CONYERS, b. 1757; d. May 21, 1832, Stafford County, VA.

7.iv. BENJAMIN CONYERS, b. July 12, 1759, Fauquier Co., VA.

v. ANNE CONYERS, b. 1762.

8.vi. ISAAC NEWTON CONYERS, b. March 14, 1763, Hampshire County, VA; d. February 13, 1845, Bath County, KY.

9.vii. ISHMAEL CONYERS, b. February 15, 1767; d. July 02, 1835, Washington County, PA.

viii. SETH CONYERS, b. June 02, 1769.

10.ix. DENNIS CONYERS, b. November 02, 1771; d. Abt. 1826.

11.x. LEATHA CONYERS, b. 1773.

xi. ENOCH CONYERS, b. January 09, 1774; m. POLLY W. WEST, September 20, 1821.

xii. NANCY CONYERS, b. 1777.

Sources:

Census: Abt. 1793, Bourbon Co., KY

Samuel Conyers and Keisha Sparks had the following child:

CONYERS:David (b. 1750)   +22   i.   **David Conyers**, born 1750, VirginiaVirginia ; married Nancy Scatterfiled; married Ann ; died 1819.

22nd Generation

22. CONYERS:David (b. 1750) Virginia **David Conyers** (Samuel-21, Dennis-20, Henry-19, Thomas-18, Joshua-17, Christopher-16, Richard-15, Reginald-14, Sir John-13, Sir John-12, Sir Christopher-11, Sir John-10, Robert-9, Sir John-8, Sir Roger-7, Sir John-6, Sir Humphrey-5, Sir Geoffery-4, Roger-3, Roger-2, Roger-1) was born in 1750 in Virginia. He died in 1819 at the age of 69. sources:

From the Loess Hills of Iowa with the Descendants of Dennis Conyers
By Terri Napoli, Arden Iva Sleadd
Pages 165 & 166

Living in Fayette Co., KY in 1787 per Tax List .
Was living in Barren Co., KY as late as 1811.
Census: went to PA
Land Grant: 1799, grant in Barren Co., KY
Tax List: 1790, Fayette Co., KY tax list

David Conyers and Nancy Scatterfiled were married. DAVID4 CONYERS was born Abt. 1750. He married
(2) NANCY SATTERFIELD 1811 in Barren Co., KY (now Metcalfe).
Notes for DAVID CONYERS:
Was living in Barren Co., KY as late as 1811.
More About DAVID CONYERS:
Fact 6: went to PA
Fact 7: 1790, Fayette Co., KY tax list
Fact 8: 1792, Bourbon Co., KY tax list
Fact 9: 1793, Bourbon Co., KY tax list
Fact 10: 1799, grant in Barren Co., KY
Fact 11: 1800, Barren Co., KY tax list
Fact 12: 1810, Barren Co., KY censusSCATTERFILED:Nancy (b. 1748) **Nancy Scatterfiled** was born in 1748.Virginia
She died in 1813 at the age of 65 in Virginia. sources:

From the Loess Hills of Iowa with the Descendants of Dennis Conyers
By Terri Napoli, Arden Iva Sleadd
Pages 165 & 166

David Conyers and Nancy Scatterfiled had the following child:

CONYERS:James Mordecai (b. 1782)   +23   i.   **James Mordecai Conyers**, born 7 Jul 1782,
KentuckyKentucky ; married Elizabeth Turk, 1810, KentuckyKentucky ; died 22 Oct 1858, Henry,
Tennessee, United StatesUnited States:Tennessee:Henry .

David Conyers and Ann were married.<NO SURNAME>:Ann **Ann** was born (date unknown). sources:

From the Loess Hills of Iowa with the Descendants of Dennis Conyers
By Terri Napoli, Arden Iva Sleadd
Pages 165 & 166

David Conyers and Ann had the following child:

CONYERS:William (b. 1783)   +24   i.   **William Conyers**, born 1783; married Susannah Price, 2 Aug 1802;
died 1840.

23rd Generation

23. CONYERS:James Mordecai (b. 1782) Kentucky **James Mordecai Conyers** (David-22, Samuel-21, Dennis-20, Henry-
19, Thomas-18, Joshua-17, Christopher-16, Richard-15, Reginald-14, Sir John-13, Sir John-12, Sir Christopher-11, Sir John-
10, Robert-9, Sir John-8, Sir Roger-7, Sir John-6, Sir Humphrey-5, Sir Geoffery-4, Roger-3, Roger-2, Roger-1) was born on
7 Jul 1782 in Kentucky.United States:Tennessee:Henry He died on 22 Oct 1858 at the age of 76 in Henry, Tennessee, United
States. Sources:

Mordecai Conyers
Birth: Jul. 7,1782
North Carolina, USA
Death: Oct. 22,1858
Tennessee, USA

Burial:

Potts Cemetery

Henry County, Tennessee, USA

GPS (lat/lon): 36.44875, -88.29272

http://www.findagrave.com/cgi-bin/fg.cgi?page=gr&GSln=Conyers&GSiman=1&GScid=17381&GRid=23887008&

1830 Barren Co, KY, Pg. 433 & 434: Mordica Conyers:Males: 1 age 20-30; 1 age 40-50; Females: 1 age 10-15; 1 age 20-30; 1 age 40-50

1840 Henry Co TN: Mordaica Conyers: Males: 1 age 15-20; 1 age 50-60; Females: 1 age 50-60

1850 Henry Co TN, 14th Dist, pg. 366, HH 18/18: Mordecai Conyers, 69, Farmer, NC; Elizabeth, 69, KY

1860 Henry Co, TN, P.O. Conyersville, Pg. 242, HH1660/1690:

Elizabeth Conyers, 77, F, Farmer, $2400, $3350, KY

Malinda C. Holland, 25, F, PA

William H. Booth, 29, M, Blacksmith, $275, $75, PA

Mary E. Booth, 4, F, PA

If Elizabeth is buried in the same cemetery as her husband, the stone was illegible as it is not cited in the transcription which is posted on the Henry Co TN website. Mordecai Conyers, b. 7 July 1782, N.C.;died 22 Oct 1858, Henry County TN. Burial Newport Cemetery, Henry Co TN.

This may be daughter of Mordecai and Elizabeth: Conyers, Phebey; Newport, Abraham Reed, 05 Feb 1818, Kentucky, Barren Co. Also Conyers, Phebe; Newport, Abraham Reed, 26 Jan 1818, Kentucky, Warren County.

1850 United States Federal Census

Name   James Conyers

Age   68

Birth Year   abt 1782

Birthplace   Kentucky

Home in 1850   District 4, Henry, Tennessee

Gender Male

Family Number 41

Household Members

Name   Age

James Conyers 68

Elizabeth Conyers   69

John Conyers   28

Emily Conyers   27

Mordecai F Conyers   23

Masel Conyers 24

Vaste Boyd   27

Willis Bonner   22

1850 Census: a Baptist minister

Kentucky

James Mordecai Conyers and Elizabeth Turk were married in 1810 in Kentucky.TURK:Thomas GLEAVES:Mary TURK:Elizabeth (b. 1790) **Elizabeth Turk**, daughter of Thomas Turk and Mary Gleaves, was born in 1790. sources:

1830 Barren Co, KY, Pg. 433 & 434: Mordica Conyers:Males: 1 age 20-30; 1 age 40-50; Females: 1 age 10-15; 1 age 20-30; 1 age 40-50

1840 Henry Co TN: Mordaica Conyers: Males: 1 age 15-20; 1 age 50-60; Females: 1 age 50-60

1850 Henry Co TN, 14th Dist, pg. 366, HH 18/18: Mordecai Conyers, 69, Farmer, NC; Elizabeth, 69, KY

1860 Henry Co, TN, P.O. Conyersville, Pg. 242, HH1660/1690:

Elizabeth Conyers, 77, F, Farmer, $2400, $3350, KY

Malinda C. Holland, 25, F, PA

William H. Booth, 29, M, Blacksmith, $275, $75, PA

Mary E. Booth, 4, F, PA

If Elizabeth is buried in the same cemetery as her husband, the stone was illegible as it is not cited in the transcription which is posted on the Henry Co TN website. Mordecai Conyers, b. 7 July 1782, N.C.;died 22 Oct 1858, Henry County TN. Burial Newport Cemetery, Henry Co TN.

This may be daughter of Mordecai and Elizabeth: Conyers, Phebey; Newport, Abraham Reed, 05 Feb 1818, Kentucky, Barren Co. Also Conyers, Phebe; Newport, Abraham Reed, 26 Jan 1818, Kentucky, Warren County.

1850 United States Federal Census

Name   Elizabeth Conyers
Age   69
Birth Year   abt 1781
Birthplace   North Carolina
Home in 1850   District 4, Henry, Tennessee
Gender Female
Family Number 41
Household Members
Name   Age
James Conyers 68
Elizabeth Conyers   69
John Conyers   28
Emily Conyers   27
Mordecai F Conyers   23
Masel Conyers 24
Vaste Boyd   27
Willis Bonner   22

James Mordecai Conyers and Elizabeth Turk had the following child:

CONYERS:James Monroe (b. 1823)   +25   i.   **James Monroe Conyers**, born 2 Mar 1823, Barren County, Kentucky, United StatesUnited States:Kentucky:Barren County ; married Martha Ann Johnson; died 28 Oct 1862, Benton, St. Louis, Missouri, United StatesUnited States:Missouri:St. Louis:Benton .

24. CONYERS:William (b. 1783) **William Conyers** (David-22, Samuel-21, Dennis-20, Henry-19, Thomas-18, Joshua-17, Christopher-16, Richard-15, Reginald-14, Sir John-13, Sir John-12, Sir Christopher-11, Sir John-10, Robert-9, Sir John-8, Sir Roger-7, Sir John-6, Sir Humphrey-5, Sir Geoffery-4, Roger-3, Roger-2, Roger-1) was born in 1783. He died in 1840 at the age of 57. sources:

From the Loess Hills of Iowa with the Descendants of Dennis Conyers
By Terri Napoli, Arden Iva Sleadd
Pages 165 & 166

Census: 1820, living in Hart Co., KY
Tax List: 1819, Hart Co., KY - 2 entries, both Barren Co.
Residence: 1850, Henry Co., TN

William Conyers and Susannah Price were married on 2 Aug 1802. They were married.PRICE:Susannah (b. 1766)
Susannah Price was born in 1766–1784. sources:

From the Loess Hills of Iowa with the Descendants of Dennis Conyers
By Terri Napoli, Arden Iva Sleadd
Pages 165 & 166

Residence: 1850, Henry Co., TN

William Conyers and Susannah Price had the following child:

CONYERS:Pascal Cerdic (b. 1809)   +26   i.   **Pascal Cerdic Conyers**, born 31 Mar 1809; died 2 Mar 1865.

24th Generation

25. CONYERS:James Monroe (b. 1823) United States:Kentucky:Barren County **James Monroe Conyers** (James Mordecai-23, David-22, Samuel-21, Dennis-20, Henry-19, Thomas-18, Joshua-17, Christopher-16, Richard-15, Reginald-14, Sir John-13, Sir John-12, Sir Christopher-11, Sir John-10, Robert-9, Sir John-8, Sir Roger-7, Sir John-6, Sir Humphrey-5, Sir Geoffery-4, Roger-3, Roger-2, Roger-1) was born on 2 Mar 1823 in Barren County, Kentucky, United States.United States:Missouri:St. Louis:Benton He died on 28 Oct 1862 at the age of 39 in Benton, St. Louis, Missouri, United States.
James Monroe "Jim" Conyers   -   Civil War Soldier
Birth: 1823
Barren County
Kentucky, USA
Death: Oct. 28,1862
Benton
St. Louis County
Missouri, USA

Jim married Martha Ann Johnson, 2 Oct 1843 in Henry County, Tennessee. During the Civil War on 20 July 1862 at age 39, Jim enlisted in the Union Army in Helena, Arkansas, Pvt, Co D, 1 Batt'n Arkansas Infantry, M 383 roll 1. He died in a military hospital at Benton Barracks in St. Louis,Missouri.

Burial:
Conyers Cemetery
Mount Pleasant
Izard County
Arkansas, USA

http://www.findagrave.com/cgi-bin/fg.cgi?page=gr&GSln=conyers&GSfn=james&GSmn=monroe&GSbyrel=all&GSdyrel=all&GSob=n&GRid=34790985&df=all&

Sources:

1850 United States Federal Census

Name   James M Conyers
Age   27
Birth Year   abt 1823

Birthplace   Kentucky
Home in 1850   District 14, Henry, Tennessee
Gender Male
Family Number 33
Household Members
Name   Age
James M Conyers   27
Martha Ann Conyers   25
William Z Conyers   3
Louisianna A Conyers   1
Marian Coleman   23
Martha Coleman   16

1860 United States Federal Census

Name   James M Conyers
Age   37
Birth Year   abt 1823
Gender Male
Birth Place   Kentucky
Home in 1860   Jefferson, Independence, Arkansas
Post Office   Polk Bayou
Family Number 440
Household Members
Name   Age
James M Conyers   37
Martha A Conyers   34
William G Conyers   13
L A Conyers   11
Alice A Conyers   9
Sarah E Conyers   5
William R Johnson   27
Rebecca Johnson   63

Tennessee State Marriages, 1780-2002

Name   Martha Johnson
Gender Female
Marriage Date   10 Oct 1843
Marriage Place Henry
Household Members
Name   Age
James M Conyers
Martha Johnson

U.S., Civil War Soldier Records and Profiles, 1861-1865

Name   James M Conyers
Residence   Jacksonport, Arkansas
Age at enlistment   39
Enlistment Date   1 Jul 1862
Rank at enlistment   Private
Enlistment Place   Jacksonport, Arkansas
State Served   Arkansas

Survived the War?   No
Birth Date   abt 1823

James Monroe Conyers and Martha Ann Johnson were married.JOHNSTON:James B. PEARCE:Rebecca JOHNSON:Martha Ann (b. 1823) United States:Tennessee:Henry **Martha Ann Johnson**, daughter of James B. Johnston and Rebecca Pearce, was born on 2 Oct 1823 in Henry, Tennessee, United States. Sources:

1850 United States Federal Census

Name   Martha AnnConyers
Age   25
Birth Year   abt1825
Birthplace   Tennessee
Home in 1850   District14, Henry, Tennessee
Gender Female
Family Number 33
Household Members
Name   Age
James M Conyers   27
Martha Ann Conyers   25
William Z Conyers   3
Louisianna A Conyers   1
Marian Coleman   23
Martha Coleman   16

1860 United States Federal Census

Name   Martha AConyers
Age   34
Birth Year   abt1826
Gender Female
Birth Place   Tennessee
Home in 1860   Jefferson,Independence, Arkansas
Post Office   PolkBayou
Family Number 440
Household Members
Name   Age
James M Conyers   37
Martha A Conyers   34
William G Conyers   13
L A Conyers   11
Alice A Conyers 9
Sarah E Conyers   5
William R Johnson   27
Rebecca Johnson   63

Tennessee State Marriages, 1780-2002

Name   MarthaJohnson
Gender Female
Marriage Date   10Oct 1843
Marriage Place Henry
Household Members
Name   Age
James M Conyers

Martha Johnson

James Monroe Conyers and Martha Ann Johnson had the following child:

CONYERS:William Zachariah (b. 1847)   +27   i.   **William Zachariah Conyers**, born 1847,
TennesseeTennessee ; died 14 Feb 1922.

26. CONYERS:Pascal Cerdic (b. 1809) **Pascal Cerdic Conyers** (William-23, David-22, Samuel-21, Dennis-20, Henry-19, Thomas-18, Joshua-17, Christopher-16, Richard-15, Reginald-14, Sir John-13, Sir John-12, Sir Christopher-11, Sir John-10, Robert-9, Sir John-8, Sir Roger-7, Sir John-6, Sir Humphrey-5, Sir Geoffery-4, Roger-3, Roger-2, Roger-1) was born on 31 Mar 1809. He died on 2 Mar 1865 at the age of 55. Paschal Craddic Conyers
Birth: Mar. 31,1809
Hart County
Kentucky, USA
Death: Mar. 2, 1865
Mount Pleasant
Izard County
Arkansas, USA

Son of William Conyers & Susannah Price
Married Elizabeth Ann Ralston, Dec 4 1832, Hart Co., KY
Married Tabitha Arthur Gooch, 16 Mar 1841, Barren Co., KY

Family links:
 Spouses:
  Tabitha Arthur Gooch Conyers (1819 - 1902)
  Elizabeth Ann Ralston Conyers (1812 - 1838)*

 Children:
  John Milton Jeptha Conyers (1835 - 1922)*
  Thomas A Conyers (1836 - 1874)*
  William Alfred Conyers (1838 - 1895)*
  Malissa F.Conyers Morrow (1844 - 1926)*
  Margaret A. Bone (1845 - 1905)*
  Abner Lewis Conyers (1847 - 1926)*
  Martha Susan Conyers Wiles (1850 - 1908)*

Burial:
Barren Fork Cemetery
Mount Pleasant
Izard County
Arkansas, USA

http://www.findagrave.com/cgi-bin/fg.cgi?page=gr&GRid=21786874

sources:

From the Loess Hills of Iowa with the Descendants of Dennis Conyers

By Terri Napoli, Arden Iva Sleadd
Pages 165 & 168
RALSTON:Elizabeth
Elizabeth Ralston died on 13 Feb 1838. Elizabeth Ann "Eliza" Ralston Conyers
Birth: Nov. 2,1812
Bear Wallow
Barren County
Kentucky, USA
Death: Feb. 13,1838
Three Springs
Hart County
Kentucky, USA

Eliza married Paschal G. Conyers 4 December 1832 in Glasgow, Barren Co., Kentucky.

Paschal was b. 31 March 1809, Bear Wallow, Hart/ Barren Co., Kentucky; d. 2 March 1865, Mt. Pleasant, Izard Co., Arkansas. He later m. Tabitha Arthur Gooch 16 March 1841.

They had 3 children:
1. John Milton Jeptha Conyers, b. 6 Mar. 1835; d. 15 May 1922; he m. Nancy America Billington in 1865; they are buried in Barren Fork Cemetery, Mount Pleasant, Izard Co.,
Arkansas. They had 12 children.

2. Thomas A. Conyers, b. 1 Feb. 1836; d. 16 Oct. 1874; hem. Mildred Frances Morris in 1865, KY; they are buried in Sandidge-Morris Cemetery, Metcalfe Co., Kentucky. They had 4 children.

3. William Alfred Conyers, b. 4 Feb. 1838; d. 9 July 1895, Monroe, Hart Co.; he m. Mary Bell Wilcoxson 6 September 1865 in Center, Metcalfe Co., Kentucky; they are buried in Bearwallow Baptist Cemetery, Horse Cave, Hart Co., Kentucky. They had 5 children.

All the boys were born in Bear Wallow, Barren Co., KY. There is no Bear Wallow in Hart Co., KY.

Family links:
 Parents:
  Andrew Ralston (1786 - 1867)
  Rodia Atkinson Ralston (1791 - 1839)

 Spouse:
  Paschal Craddic Conyers (1809 - 1865)

 Children:
  John Milton Jeptha Conyers (1835 - 1922)*
  Thomas A Conyers (1836 - 1874)*
  William Alfred Conyers (1838 - 1895)*
  Margaret A. Bone (1845 - 1905)*

Burial:
Three Springs Baptist Church Cemetery
Three Springs
Hart County
Kentucky, USA

http://www.findagrave.com/cgi-bin/fg.cgi?page=gr&GRid=63827937

sources:

From the Loess Hills of Iowa with the Descendants of Dennis Conyers
By Terri Napoli, Arden Iva Sleadd
Pages 165 & 168

Pascal Cerdic Conyers and Elizabeth Ralston had the following child:

CONYERS:John Milton Jepha (b. 1835)   +28   i.   **John Milton Jepha Conyers**, born 6 Mar 1835; died 15 May
1922.

25th Generation

27. CONYERS:William Zachariah (b. 1847) Tennessee **William Zachariah Conyers** (James Monroe-24, James Mordecai-23, David-22, Samuel-21, Dennis-20, Henry-19, Thomas-18, Joshua-17, Christopher-16, Richard-15, Reginald-14, Sir John-13, Sir John-12, Sir Christopher-11, Sir John-10, Robert-9, Sir John-8, Sir Roger-7, Sir John-6, Sir Humphrey-5, Sir Geoffery-4, Roger-3, Roger-2, Roger-1) was born in 1847 in Tennessee. He died on 14 Feb 1922 at the age of 75. William Z Conyers
Birth: 1847
Tennessee, USA
Death: Feb. 14,1923
Cushman
Independence County
Arkansas, USA

 Family links:
 Parents:
  James Monroe Conyers (1823 - 1862)
  Spouses:
  Martha Carter Conyers (1861 - ____)*
  Mary E Brown Conyers (1861 - 1920)*
 Children:
  Charles Mordica Conyers (1871 - 1953)*
  Robert Frank Conyers (1885 - 1960)*

Burial:
Conyers Cemetery
Mount Pleasant
Izard County
Arkansas, USA

http://www.findagrave.com/cgi-bin/fg.cgi?page=gr&GRid=37402069

sources:

1900 United States Federal Census

Name   William Z Conyers
Age   53
Birth Date   Nov 1846

Birthplace   Tennessee
Home in 1900   Barren Fork, Izard, Arkansas
Race   White
Gender Male
Relation to Head of House   Head
Marital Status   Married
Spouse's Name Mary E Conyers
Marriage Year   1881
Years Married   19
Father's Birthplace   Kentucky
Mother's Birthplace   Tennessee
Household Members
Name   Age
William Z Conyers   53
Mary E Conyers 39
Mary E Conyers 16
Robert F Conyers   14
Isaac F Conyers 11
Lucy F Neighbors   16
Carrie B Neighbors   13
Cora E Neighbors   11
Lona E Neighbors   8
Daniel W Brown   62

1910 United States Federal Census

Name   William Z Conyers
Age in 1910   63
Birth Year   abt 1847
Birthplace   Tennessee
Home in 1910   Johnson,Sharp, Arkansas
Street   Sidney And Cushman Road
Race   White
Gender Male
Relation to Head of House   Head
Marital Status   Married
Spouse's Name Mary E Conyers
Father's Birthplace   Kentucky
Mother's Birthplace   Tennessee
Native Tongue English
Occupation   Farmer
Industry   General Farm
Employer, Employee or Other   Employer
Home Owned or Rented   Own
Home Free or Mortgaged   Mortgaged
Farm or House Farm
Able to read   Yes
Able to Write   Yes
Years Married   13
Household Members
Name   Age
William Z Conyers   63
Mary E Conyers 49
Robert F Conyers   24

Arkansas Death Index, 1914-1950

Name   William Z Conyers
Death Day   15
Death Month   Feb
Death Year   1923
County Independence
Volume Number   11
Roll number   19141923
Certificate Number   581

U.S., Civil War Soldier Records and Profiles, 1861-1865

Name   William Z Conyers
Residence   Jacksonport, Arkansas
Age at enlistment   18
Enlistment Date   1 Jul 1862
Rank at enlistment   Sergeant
Enlistment Place   Jacksonport, Arkansas
State Served   Arkansas
Survived the War?   Yes
Birth Date   abt 1844
Death Date   14 Feb 1923
Death Place   Cushman, Arkansas

BROWN:Daniel W.
HARREL:Sarah Amanda BROWN:Mary E. (b. 1861) United States:Arkansas:Fulton County **Mary E. Brown**, daughter of Daniel W. Brown and Sarah Amanda Harrel, was born on 11 Mar 1861 in Fulton County, Arkansas, United States.United States:Texas:Red River:Madras She died on 1 Jan 1920 at the age of 58 in Madras, Red River, Texas, United States. Martha Carter Conyers
Birth: 1861
Death: unknown

 Family links:
 Spouse:
  William Z Conyers(1847 - 1923)
 Children:
  Charles Mordica Conyers (1871 - 1953)*
  Robert Frank Conyers (1885 - 1960)*

Burial:
Conyers Cemetery
Mount Pleasant
Izard County
Arkansas, USA

http://www.findagrave.com/cgi-bin/fg.cgi?page=gr&GRid=37431184

Sources:

1870 United States Federal Census

Name   Mary Brown
Age in 1870   10
Birth Year   abt 1860
Birthplace   Arkansas
Home in 1870   Jefferson, Independence, Arkansas
Race   White
Gender Female
Post Office   Polk Bayon
Household Members
Name   Age
Daniel Brown   33
Amanda Brown 35
John Brown   14
Rebecca Brown 12
Mary Brown   10
William Brown 8
Newton Brown 2
Simpson Brown 4

1880 United States Federal Census

Name   Mary E.Brown
Age   19
Birth Year   abt 1861
Birthplace   Arkansas
Home in 1880   Ashley, Independence, Arkansas
Race   White
Gender Female
Relation to Head of House   Daughter
Marital Status   Single
Father's Name D. W.Brown
Father's Birthplace   Georgia
Mother's Name   Sarah A. Brown
Mother's Birthplace   Georgia
Household Members
Name   Age
D. W. Brown   43
Sarah A. Brown 41
Mary E. Brown 19
Joseph S. Brown   13
Jasper N. Brown   11
Mariuh G. Brown   8
Kivial J. Brown 4
Robert F. Brown   2

1900 United States Federal Census
Name   Mary E Conyers
Age   39
Birth Date   Mar 1861
Birthplace   Arkansas
Home in 1900   Barren Fork, Izard, Arkansas
Race   White

Gender Female
Relation to Head of House   Wife
Marital Status   Married
Spouse's Name William Z Conyers
Marriage Year   1881
Years Married   19
Father's Birthplace   Georgia
Mother's Birthplace   Georgia
Mother: number of living children   5
Mother: How many children   5
Household Members
Name   Age
William Z Conyers   53
Mary E Conyers 39
Mary E Conyers 16
Robert F Conyers   14
Isaac F Conyers 11
Lucy F Neighbors   16
Carrie B Neighbors   13
Cora E Neighbors   11
Lona E Neighbors   8
Daniel W Brown   62

1910 United States Federal Census

Name   Mary E Conyers
Age in 1910   49
Birth Year   abt 1861
Birthplace   Arkansas
Home in 1910   Johnson, Sharp, Arkansas
Street   Sidney And Cushman Road
Race   White
Gender Female
Relation to Head of House   Wife
Marital Status   Married
Spouse's Name William Z Conyers
Father's Birthplace   Georgia
Mother's Birthplace   Georgia
Native Tongue English
Able to read   Yes
Able to Write   Yes
Years Married   13
Number of Children Born   5
Number of Children Living   4
Household Members
Name   Age
William Z Conyers   63
Mary E Conyers 49
Robert F Conyers   24

Arkansas, County Marriages Index, 1837-1957

Name   Mary Brown
Gender Female
Age   19

Birth Year   abt 1861
Residence   Independence,Arkansas
Spouse's Name Demarcus L Neighbors
Spouse's Gender   Male
Spouse's Age   20
Spouse's Residence   Independence,Arkansas
Marriage Date   27 Jun 1880
Marriage License Date   15 Jun 1880
Marriage County   Independence
Event Type   Marriage
FHL Film Number   1288647
Household Members
Name   Age
Mary Brown
Demarcus L Neighbors
Texas Death Index, 1903-2000

Name   Mary E. Conyers
Death Date   1 Jan 1920
Death County   Red River
Certificate   2895

William Zachariah Conyers and Mary E. Brown had the following child:

CONYERS:Robert (b. 1885)   +29   i.   **Robert Conyers**, born 25 Dec 1885, Sidney, Sharp, Arkansas, United
StatesUnited States:Arkansas:Sharp:Sidney ; died 25 Jul 1960, Izard Co., Arkansas, United StatesUnited
States:Arkansas:Izard Co. .

28. CONYERS:John Milton Jepha (b. 1835) **John Milton Jepha Conyers** (Pascal Cerdic-24, William-23, David-22, Samuel-21, Dennis-20, Henry-19, Thomas-18, Joshua-17, Christopher-16, Richard-15, Reginald-14, Sir John-13, Sir John-12, Sir Christopher-11, Sir John-10, Robert-9, Sir John-8, Sir Roger-7, Sir John-6, Sir Humphrey-5, Sir Geoffery-4, Roger-3, Roger-2, Roger-1) was born on 6 Mar 1835. He died on 15 May 1922 at the age of 87. John Milton Jeptha Conyers - Civil War Soldier
Birth: Mar. 6,1835
Bear Wallow
Barren County
Kentucky, USA
Death: May 15, 1922

John Milton Jeptha Conyers. "Uncle Mitt"

A son of P. C. and Eliza (Ralston) Conyers.

Married to Nany Billington on February 6, 1867 in Lacrosse, Izard County, Arkansas.

Children:

William P.
Thomas A.
Franklin M.
James A.
Newton A.
Nathaniel E.
Dora A.
Nancy A.
Mary E.
Jeptha A.
Sarah J.

Family links:
 Parents:
  Paschal Craddic Conyers (1809 - 1865)
  Elizabeth Ann Ralston Conyers (1812 - 1838)

 Spouse:
  Nancy America Billington Conyers (1848 - 1916)*

 Children:
  William P Conyers (1867 - 1907)*
  Thomas A Conyers (1870 - 1940)*
  James A Conyers (1873 - 1881)*
  Dora A. Conyers (1879 - 1885)*
  Mary Emma Conyers Hodge (1884 - 1941)*
  Sarah J. Conyers (1888 - 1888)*
  Charles Ewing Conyers (1894 - 1926)*

 Siblings:
  John Milton Jeptha Conyers (1835 - 1922)
  Thomas A Conyers (1836 - 1874)*
  William Alfred Conyers (1838 - 1895)*
  Malissa F.Conyers Morrow (1844 - 1926)**
  Margaret A. Bone(1845 - 1905)*
  Abner Lewis Conyers (1847 - 1926)**
  Martha Susan Conyers Wiles (1850 - 1908)**

Inscription:
Husband of Nany A. Conyers

Burial:
Barren Fork Cemetery
Mount Pleasant
Izard County
Arkansas, USA

http://www.findagrave.com/cgi-bin/fg.cgi?page=gr&GRid=70044409

sources:

From the Loess Hills of Iowa with the Descendants of Dennis Conyers
By Terri Napoli, Arden Iva Sleadd
Pages 165 - 171

1910 United States Federal Census

Name   John M Conyers
Age in 1910   75
Birth Year   abt 1835
Birthplace   Tennessee
Home in 1910   Barren Fork, Izard, Arkansas
Street   Baccus Forst and Sieting Road
Race   White
Gender Male
Relation to Head of House   Head
Marital Status   Married
Spouse's Name Nancy A Conyers
Father's Birthplace   United States
Mother's Birthplace   United States
Native Tongue English
Occupation   Farmer
Industry   General Farm
Employer, Employee or Other   Employer
Home Owned or Rented   Own
Home Free or Mortgaged   Free
Farm or House Farm
Able to read   Yes
Able to Write   Yes
Years Married   43
Household Members
Name   Age
John M Conyers   75
Nancy A Conyers   62
Mary E Conyers 25
Charley E Conyers   18

Sources: JOHN MILTON JEPTHA CONYERS:

He was owner of 307 acres of land, all located in Dry Town Township. Educated in Henry Co., TN. In 1867 he moved to Arkansas. Held office of Junior Deacon in the Masonic order and deputy sheriff of the county. also held the position of constable of his township.Worshipped in the Cumberland Presbyterian Church.He was a member of this church since 1853.

 John M. J. Conyers
Age: 27
Civil War (Confederate)
Branch:
Confederate Army
Enlistment Date:
1861
Military Unit:
Eighth Infantry, Bu-C
State:

Arkansas

BILLINGTON:Nancy America (b. 1848)
United States:Tennessee:Williamson County **Nancy America Billington** was born on 3 Mar 1848 in Williamson County, Tennessee, United States.United States:Arkansas She died on 7 Feb 1916 at the age of 67 in Arkansas, United States. Nancy America "Nany" Billington Conyers
Birth: Mar. 3,1848
Williamson County
Tennessee, USA
Death: Feb. 7, 1916
Arkansas, USA

Nancy America Billington Conyers.

A daughter of William and Permelia (Gilliam) Billington.

Married to J. M. J. Conyers on February 6, 1867 in Lacrosse, Izard County, Arkansas.

Family links:
 Spouse:
  John Milton Jeptha Conyers (1835 - 1922)

 Children:
  William P Conyers (1867 - 1907)*
  Thomas A Conyers (1870 - 1940)*
  James A Conyers (1873 - 1881)*
  Dora A. Conyers (1879 - 1885)*
  Mary Emma Conyers Hodge (1884 - 1941)*
  Sarah J. Conyers (1888 - 1888)*
  Charles Ewing Conyers (1894 - 1926)*

Inscription:
Nany A. Conyers

Wife of J. M. J. Conyers

Gone but not forgotten.

Burial:
Barren Fork Cemetery
Mount Pleasant
Izard County
Arkansas, USA

http://www.findagrave.com/cgi-bin/fg.cgi?page=gr&GRid=70044518

 sources:

From the Loess Hills of Iowa with the Descendants of Dennis Conyers
By Terri Napoli, Arden Iva Sleadd
Pages 165 - 171

1910 United States Federal Census

Name   John M Conyers
Age in 1910   75
Birth Year   abt 1835
Birthplace   Tennessee
Home in 1910   Barren Fork, Izard, Arkansas
Street   Baccus Forst and Sieting Road
Race   White
Gender Male
Relation to Head of House   Head
Marital Status   Married
Spouse's Name Nancy A Conyers
Father's Birthplace   United States
Mother's Birthplace   United States
Native Tongue English
Occupation   Farmer
Industry   General Farm
Employer, Employee or Other   Employer
Home Owned or Rented   Own
Home Free or Mortgaged   Free
Farm or House Farm
Able to read   Yes
Able to Write   Yes
Years Married   43
Household Members
Name   Age
John M Conyers   75
Nancy A Conyers   62
Mary E Conyers 25
Charley E Conyers   18

John Milton Jepha Conyers and Nancy America Billington had the following child:

CONYERS:Charles Ewing (b. 1894)   +30   i.   **Charles Ewing Conyers**, born 29 Jul 1894; died 21 Jan 1926.

26th Generation

29. CONYERS:Robert (b. 1885) United States:Arkansas:Sharp:Sidney **Robert Conyers** (William Zachariah-25, James Monroe-24, James Mordecai-23, David-22, Samuel-21, Dennis-20, Henry-19, Thomas-18, Joshua-17, Christopher-16, Richard-15, Reginald-14, Sir John-13, Sir John-12, Sir Christopher-11, Sir John-10, Robert-9, Sir John-8, Sir Roger-7, Sir John-6, Sir Humphrey-5, Sir Geoffery-4, Roger-3, Roger-2, Roger-1) was born on 25 Dec 1885 in Sidney, Sharp, Arkansas, United States.United States:Arkansas:Izard Co. He died on 25 Jul 1960 at the age of 74 in Izard Co., Arkansas, United States. Robert Frank "Bob" Conyers
Birth: Dec. 25,1885

Sidney
Sharp County
Arkansas, USA
Death: Jul. 25,1960
Izard County
Arkansas, USA

Son of William Z and Martha (Carter) Conyers.
Family links:
 Parents:
  William Z Conyers (1847 - 1923)
  Martha Carter Conyers (1861 - ____)
  Spouse:
  Estella Shaw Conyers (1887 - 1979)

Burial:
Barren Fork Cemetery
Mount Pleasant
Izard County
Arkansas, USA

http://www.findagrave.com/cgi-bin/fg.cgi?page=gr&GRid=70044553

Sources:

1900 United States Federal Census

Name   Robert F Conyers
Age   14
Birth Date   Dec 1885
Birthplace   Arkansas
Home in 1900   Barren Fork, Izard, Arkansas
Race   White
Gender Male
Relation to Head of House   Son
Marital Status   Single
Father's Name William Z Conyers
Father's Birthplace   Tennessee
Mother's Name   Mary E Conyers
Mother's Birthplace   Tennessee
Household Members
Name   Age
William Z Conyers   53
Mary E Conyers 39
Mary E Conyers 16
Robert F Conyers   14
Isaac F Conyers 11
Lucy F Neighbors   16
Carrie B Neighbors   13
Cora E Neighbors   11
Lona E Neighbors   8
Daniel W Brown   62

1910 United States Federal Census

Name   Robert F Conyers
Age in 1910   24
Birth Year   abt 1886
Birthplace   Arkansas
Home in 1910   Johnson,Sharp, Arkansas
Street   Sidney And Cushman Road
Race   White
Gender Male
Relation to Head of House   Son
Marital Status   Single
Father's Birthplace   Tennessee
Mother's Name   Mary E Conyers
Mother's Birthplace   Tennessee
Native Tongue English
Occupation   Farmer
Industry   General Farm
Employer, Employee or Other   Employer
Home Owned or Rented   Rent
Farm or House Farm
Able to read   Yes
Able to Write   Yes
Out of Work   N
Household Members
Name   Age
William Z Conyers   63
Mary E Conyers 49
Robert F Conyers   24

1920 United States Federal Census

Name   Robert F Conyers
Age   34
Birth Year   abt 1886
Birthplace   Arkansas
Home in 1920   Johnson,Sharp, Arkansas
House Number Farm
Race   White
Gender Male
Relation to Head of House   Head
Marital Status   Married
Spouse's Name Margarette E Conyers
Father's Birthplace   Tennessee
Mother's Birthplace   Tennessee
Able to Speak English   Yes
Occupation   Farmer
Industry   General Farm
Employment Field   Own Account
Home Owned or Rented   Rent
Able to read   Yes
Able to Write   Yes
Household Members
Name   Age
Robert F Conyers   34
Margarette E Conyers   32

Ray T Conyers   8
Edwin F Conyers   6
Nola E Conyers 4
Melba C Conyers   0

1930 United States Federal Census

Name   Robert F Conyers
Age in 1930   48
Birth Year   abt 1882
Gender Male
Race   White
Birthplace   Arkansas
Marital Status   Married
Relation to Head of House   Head
Home in 1930   Johnson,Sharp, Arkansas
House Number in Cities or Towns   Apr 5
Dwelling Number   16
Family Number 16
Home Owned or Rented   Owned
Home Value   800
Radio Set   No
Lives on Farm   Yes
Age at First Marriage   24
Attended School   No
Able to Read and Write Yes
Father's Birthplace   Tennessee
Mother's Birthplace   Tennessee
Able to Speak English   Yes
Occupation   Farmer
Industry   General Farm
Class of Worker Working on own account
Employment   Yes
Household Members
Name   Age
Robert F Conyers   48
Stella Conyers 42
Ray Conyers   18
Edwin Conyers 16
Nala Conyers   14
Melba Conyers 10
Veona Conyers 10
Porter Conyers 4

U.S., World War I Draft Registration Cards, 1917-1918
Name   Robert Frank Conyers
County Sharp
State   Arkansas
Birth Date   25 Dec 1885

U.S., World War II Draft Registration Cards, 1942
Name   Robert Frank Conyers
Birth Date   23 Dec 1885
Birth Place   Arkansas,Arkansas, USA
Residence   Izard, Arkansas, USA

Race   White

SHAW:Margarite Estella (b. 1887)
United States:Arkansas:Izard Co. **Margarite Estella Shaw** was born on 20 Oct 1887 in Izard Co., Arkansas, United States.United States:Arkansas:Izard Co. She died on 12 Oct 1979 at the age of 91 in Izard Co., Arkansas, United States.
Estella Shaw Conyers
Birth: Oct. 20,1887
Death: Oct. 12,1979

Family links:
 Spouse:
  Robert Frank Conyers (1885 - 1960)*

Burial:
Barren Fork Cemetery
Mount Pleasant
Izard County
Arkansas, USA

http://www.findagrave.com/cgi-bin/fg.cgi?page=gr&GRid=70044347

Sources:

1920 United States Federal Census

Name   Robert F Conyers
Age   34
Birth Year   abt 1886
Birthplace   Arkansas
Home in 1920   Johnson,Sharp, Arkansas
House Number Farm
Race   White
Gender Male
Relation to Head of House   Head
Marital Status   Married
Spouse's Name Margarette E Conyers
Father's Birthplace   Tennessee
Mother's Birthplace   Tennessee
Able to Speak English   Yes
Occupation   Farmer
Industry   General Farm
Employment Field   Own Account
Home Owned or Rented   Rent
Able to read   Yes
Able to Write   Yes
Household Members
Name   Age
Robert F Conyers   34
Margarette E Conyers   32
Ray T Conyers   8
Edwin F Conyers   6

Nola E Conyers 4
Melba C Conyers   0

1930 United States Federal Census

Name   Robert F Conyers
Age in 1930   48
Birth Year   abt 1882
Gender Male
Race   White
Birthplace   Arkansas
Marital Status   Married
Relation to Head of House   Head
Home in 1930   Johnson,Sharp, Arkansas
House Number in Cities or Towns   Apr 5
Dwelling Number   16
Family Number 16
Home Owned or Rented   Owned
Home Value   800
Radio Set   No
Lives on Farm   Yes
Age at First Marriage   24
Attended School   No
Able to Read and Write Yes
Father's Birthplace   Tennessee
Mother's Birthplace   Tennessee
Able to Speak English   Yes
Occupation   Farmer
Industry   General Farm
Class of Worker Working on own account
Employment   Yes
Household Members
Name   Age
Robert F Conyers   48
Stella Conyers 42
Ray Conyers   18
Edwin Conyers 16
Nala Conyers   14
Melba Conyers 10
Veona Conyers 10
Porter Conyers 4

Robert Conyers and Margarite Estella Shaw had the following child:

CONYERS:Truman Ray (b. 1911) +31   i.   **Truman Ray Conyers**, born 2 Oct 1911; died 16 Dec 1996.

30. CONYERS:Charles Ewing (b. 1894) **Charles Ewing Conyers** (John Milton Jepha-25, Pascal Cerdic-24, William-23, David-22, Samuel-21, Dennis-20, Henry-19, Thomas-18, Joshua-17, Christopher-16, Richard-15, Reginald-14, Sir John-13, Sir John-12, Sir Christopher-11, Sir John-10, Robert-9, Sir John-8, Sir Roger-7, Sir John-6, Sir Humphrey-5, Sir Geoffery-4, Roger-3, Roger-2, Roger-1) was born on 29 Jul 1894. He died on 21 Jan 1926 at the age of 31.
Charles Ewing Conyers

Birth: Jul. 30,1894
Death: Jan. 21,1926

Family links:
 Parents:
  John Milton Jeptha Conyers (1835 - 1922)
  Nancy America Billington Conyers (1848 - 1916)
 Spouse:
  Euna Blanche McSpadden Conyers (1894 - 1971)
  Children:
  Beulah Irene Conyers (1917 - 2012)*
 Siblings:
  William P Conyers (1867 - 1907)*
  Thomas A Conyers (1870 - 1940)*
  James A Conyers (1873 - 1881)*
  Dora A. Conyers (1879 - 1885)*
  Mary Emma Conyers Hodge (1884 - 1941)*
  Sarah J. Conyers (1888 - 1888)*
  Charles Ewing Conyers (1894 - 1926)

Burial:
Barren Fork Cemetery
Mount Pleasant
Izard County
Arkansas, USA

http://www.findagrave.com/cgi-bin/fg.cgi?page=gr&GRid=70044377

sources:

From the Loess Hills of Iowa with the Descendants of Dennis Conyers
By Terri Napoli, Arden Iva Sleadd
Pages 165 - 176

 1900 United States Federal Census

Name   Charley E Conyers
Age   9
Birth Date   Jul 1891
Birthplace   Arkansas
Home in 1900   Barren Fork, Izard, Arkansas
Race   White
Gender Male
Relation to Head of House   Son
Marital Status   Single
Father's Name John J Conyers
Father's Birthplace   Kentucky
Mother's Birthplace   Tennessee
Household Members
Name   Age
John J Conyers 63
Nancy M Conyers   52

Jebtha A Conyers   14
Charley E Conyers   9
Mary E Conyers 16
William Y Billingtin   20

1910 United States Federal Census

Name   Charley E Conyers
Age in 1910   18
Birth Year   abt 1892
Birthplace   Arkansas
Home in 1910   Barren Fork, Izard, Arkansas
Street   Baccus Forst and Sieting Road
Race   White
Gender Male
Relation to Head of House   Son
Marital Status   Single
Father's Birthplace   Tennessee
Mother's Name   Nancy A Conyers
Mother's Birthplace   Tennessee
Native Tongue English
Occupation   Farm Laborer
Industry   Home Farm
Employer, Employee or Other   Wage Earner
Able to read   Yes
Able to Write   Yes
Out of Work   N
Number of Weeks Out of Work 12
Household Members
Name   Age
John M Conyers   75
Nancy A Conyers   62
Mary E Conyers 25
Charley E Conyers   18

1920 United States Federal Census

Name   Charlie E Conyers
Age   28
Birth Year   abt 1892
Birthplace   Arkansas
Home in 1920   Barren Fork, Izard, Arkansas
House Number Farm
Race   White
Gender Male
Relation to Head of House   Head
Marital Status   Married
Spouse's Name Emma B Conyers
Father's Name John M J Conyers
Father's Birthplace   Kentucky
Mother's Birthplace   Tennessee
Able to Speak English   Yes
Occupation   Farmer
Industry   General Farm
Employment Field   Own Account

Home Owned or Rented   Own
Home Free or Mortgaged   Free
Able to read   Yes
Able to Write   Yes
Household Members
Name   Age
Charlie E Conyers   28
John M J Conyers   84
Emma B Conyers   25
Beulah J Conyers   2

Arkansas Death Index, 1914-1950

Name   Charley Ewi Conyers
Death Day   21
Death Month   Jan
Death Year   1926
County Izard
Roll number   19241933

Arkansas, County Marriages Index, 1837-1957

Name   Ewin Conyers
Gender Male
Age   23
Birth Year   abt 1891
Residence   Independence,Arkansas
Spouse's Name Euna McSpadden
Spouse's Gender   Female
Spouse's Age   20
Spouse's Residence   Independence,Arkansas
Marriage Date   23 Dec 1914
Marriage License Date   19 Dec 1914
Marriage County   Independence
Event Type   Marriage
FHL Film Number   1288742
Household Members
Name   Age
Euna McSpadden
Ewin Conyers

U.S., World War I Draft Registration Cards, 1917-1918

Name   Charley Erving Conyers
County Izard
State   Arkansas
Birthplace   Arkansas,United States of America
Birth Date   29 Jul 1891
Race   Caucasian

MCSPADDEN:Lucius
EVANS:Kate MCSPADDEN:Euna Blanche (b. 1894) **Euna Blanche McSpadden**, daughter of Lucius McSpadden and Kate Evans, was born on 30 Jul 1894. She died on 4 Mar 1971 at the age of 76. Euna Blanche McSpadden Conyers Birth: Jul. 30,1894

Death: Mar. 4, 1971

Family links:
 Spouse:
  Charles EwingConyers (1894 - 1926)*

 Children:
  Beulah IreneConyers (1917 - 2012)*

Burial:
Barren Fork Cemetery
Mount Pleasant
Izard County
Arkansas, USA

http://www.findagrave.com/cgi-bin/fg.cgi?page=gr&GRid=70044363

sources:

From the Loess Hills of Iowa with the Descendants of Dennis Conyers
By Terri Napoli, Arden Iva Sleadd
Pages 165 - 176

1910 United States Federal Census

Name   Una BMcspadden
Age in 1910   15
Birth Year   abt1895
Birthplace   Arkansas
Home in 1910   BarrenFork, Izard, Arkansas
Race   White
Gender Female
Relation to Head of House   Daughter
Marital Status   Single
Father's Birthplace   Arkansas
Mother's Name   LizzieS Mcspadden
Mother's Birthplace   Arkansas
Native Tongue English
Occupation   FarmLaborer
Industry   HomeFarm
Employer, Employee or Other   Wage Earner
Attended School   Yes
Able to read   Yes
Able to Write   Yes
Out of Work   N
Number of Weeks Out of Work 40
Household Members
Name   Age
Loraine E Mcspadden   39
Elizabeth J Mcspadden 65
Lizzie S Mcspadden   43
Una B Mcspadden   15

Lando L Mcspadden	13
Vera E Mcspadden	10
Roy B Mcspadden	4
Mabel R Mcspadden	3

1920 United States Federal Census

Name   Emma BConyers
Age   25
Birth Year   abt1895
Birthplace   Arkansas
Home in 1920   BarrenFork, Izard, Arkansas
Race   White
Gender Female
Relation to Head of House   Wife
Marital Status   Married
Spouse's Name CharlieE Conyers
Father's Birthplace   Arkansas
Mother's Birthplace   Arkansas
Able to Speak English   Yes
Occupation   None
Able to read   Yes
Able to Write   Yes
Household Members

Name	Age
Charlie E Conyers	28
John M J Conyers	84
Emma B Conyers	25
Beulah J Conyers	2

1930 United States Federal Census

Name   Erma BConyers
Age in 1930   35
Birth Year   abt1895
Gender Female
Race   White
Birthplace   Arkansas
Marital Status   Widowed
Relation to Head of House   Head
Homemaker?   Yes
Home in 1930   BarrenFork, Izard, Arkansas
Dwelling Number   88
Family Number 88
Home Owned or Rented   Owned
Radio Set   No
Lives on Farm   Yes
Age at First Marriage   19
Attended School   No
Able to Read and Write Yes
Father's Birthplace   Arkansas
Mother's Birthplace   Arkansas
Able to Speak English   Yes
Occupation   Farmer
Industry   Generalfarm

Class of Worker Workingon own account
Employment   Yes
Household Members
Name   Age
Erma B Conyers 35
Eulah I Conyers 13
Donna R Conyers   9
Clyde R Conyers   23

Arkansas, County Marriages Index, 1837-1957

Name   EunaMcSpadden
Gender Female
Age   20
Birth Year   abt1894
Residence   Independence,Arkansas
Spouse's Name EwinConyers
Spouse's Gender   Male
Spouse's Age   23
Spouse's Residence   Independence,Arkansas
Marriage Date   23Dec 1914
Marriage License Date   19Dec 1914
Marriage County   Independence
Event Type   Marriage
FHL Film Number   1288742
Household Members
Name   Age
Euna McSpadden
Ewin Conyers

U.S. City Directories, 1822-1995

Name   Mrs EunaMcSpadden
Gender Female
Residence Year 1935
Street Address 309Woodrow apt 2
Residence Place   LittleRock, Arkansas, USA
Occupation   TelephoneOperator
Publication Title   LittleRock, Arkansas, City Directory, 1935
Household Members
Name   Age
Mrs Euna McSpadden

U.S., Social Security Death Index, 1935-2014

Name   Euna Conyers
SSN   431-58-7204
Born   30 Jul1894
Died   Mar 1971
State (Year) SSN issued Arkansas - Before 1951

Charles Ewing Conyers and Euna Blanche McSpadden had the following child:

CONYERS:Beulah Irene (b. 1917) +32   i.   **Beulah Irene Conyers**, born 18 Feb 1917; died 17 Dec 2012.

27th Generation

31. CONYERS:Truman Ray (b. 1911) **Truman Ray Conyers** (Robert-26, William Zachariah-25, James Monroe-24, James Mordecai-23, David-22, Samuel-21, Dennis-20, Henry-19, Thomas-18, Joshua-17, Christopher-16, Richard-15, Reginald-14, Sir John-13, Sir John-12, Sir Christopher-11, Sir John-10, Robert-9, Sir John-8, Sir Roger-7, Sir John-6, Sir Humphrey-5, Sir Geoffery-4, Roger-3, Roger-2, Roger-1) was born on 2 Oct 1911. He died on 16 Dec 1996 at the age of 85. sources:

Ray Conyers
Birth: Oct. 2,1911
Death: Dec. 16,1996

Family links:
 Spouse:
  Beulah Irene Conyers (1917 - 2012)

 Children:
  Darrell Ewing Conyers (____ - 1946)*
  Douglas Ray Conyers (1937 - 1998)*
 Burial:
Barren Fork Cemetery
Mount Pleasant
Izard County
Arkansas, USA

http://www.findagrave.com/cgi-bin/fg.cgi?page=gr&GRid=70044538

1920 United States Federal Census
Name   Ray T Conyers
Age   8
Birth Year   abt 1912
Birthplace   Arkansas
Home in 1920   Johnson,Sharp, Arkansas
Race   White
Gender Male
Relation to Head of House   Son
Marital Status   Single
Father's Name Robert F Conyers
Father's Birthplace   Arkansas
Mother's Name   Margarette E Conyers
Mother's Birthplace   Arkansas
Occupation   None
Attended School   Yes
Household Members
Name   Age
Robert F Conyers   34
Margarette E Conyers   32
Ray T Conyers   8
Edwin F Conyers   6
Nola E Conyers 4

Melba C Conyers   0

1930 United States Federal Census
Name   Ray Conyers
Age in 1930   18
Birth Year   abt 1912
Gender Male
Race   White
Birthplace   Arkansas
Marital Status   Single
Relation to Head of House   Son
Home in 1930   Johnson, Sharp, Arkansas
House Number in Cities or Towns   Apr 5
Dwelling Number   16
Family Number 16
Attended School   Yes
Able to Read and Write Yes
Father's Birthplace   Arkansas
Mother's Birthplace   Arkansas
Able to Speak English   Yes
Occupation   NP
Class of Worker Unpaid worker, member of the family
Employment   Yes
Household Members
Name   Age
Robert F Conyers   48
Stella Conyers   42
Ray Conyers   18
Edwin Conyers   16
Nala Conyers   14
Melba Conyers 10
Veona Conyers 10
Porter Conyers 4

1940 United States Federal Census
Name   Ray Conyers
Respondent   Yes
Age   28
Estimated Birth Year   abt 1912
Gender Male
Race   White
Birthplace   Arkansas
Marital Status   Married
Relation to Head of House   Head
Home in 1940   Barren Fork, Izard, Arkansas
Farm   Yes
Inferred Residence in 1935   Barren Fork, Izard, Arkansas
Residence in 1935   Same House
Sheet Number 1B
Number of Household in Order of Visitation   16
Occupation   Farmer
House Owned or Rented   Rented
Value of Home or Monthly Rental if Rented   5
Attended School or College   No
Highest Grade Completed   Elementary school, 8th grade

Hours Worked Week Prior to Census 48
Class of Worker Working on own account
Weeks Worked in 1939 52
Income 0
Income Other Sources Yes
Household Members
Name Age
Ray Conyers 28
Beulah Conyers 23
Douglas Conyers 2
Charlotte Ruth Conyers 4/12

Arkansas Marriage Index, 1933-1939
Name Ray Conyers
Gender Male
County Independence
Spouse Beulah Conyers
License Date 23 Dec 1935
Certificate Number 11069
Volume Number 0001
Household Members
Name Age
Ray Conyers
Beulah Conyers

U.S., Social Security Death Index, 1935-2014
Name T. R.Conyers
SSN 429-14-0190
Born 2 Oct 1911
Died 16 Dec 1996
State (Year) SSN issued Arkansas- Before 1951

CONYERS:Charles Ewing (b. 1894)
MCSPADDEN:Euna Blanche (b. 1894) CONYERS:Beulah Irene (b. 1917) **Beulah Irene Conyers**, daughter of Charles Ewing Conyers and Euna Blanche McSpadden, was born on 18 Feb 1917. She died on 17 Dec 2012 at the age of 95. Beulah Irene Conyers, daughter of Charlie Ewing and Euna Blanche McSpadden Conyers, was born of February 18, 1917 in Mount Pleasant, Arkansas. She departed this life on December 17, 2012 at the age of 95 years and 10 months.
She was a member of the Barren Fork Cumberland Presbyterian Church where she was an active member until the last few years of her life.
She was preceded in death by her parents, her husband of 62 years, Truman Ray Conyers, two sons, Douglas Ray Conyers and infant son, Darrell Ewing Conyers, two grandchildren, Kendra Leigh Tiner and David Lynn Conyers.
She spent most of her life as a wife, homemaker, and mother. She worked outside the home as a bookkeeper for the C R Anthony Co. in Roswell, NM and the Marbax shirt factory in Melbourne, AR.
She is survived by two daughters and sons-in-law, Charlotte and Benny Dean of Mount Pleasant, AR and Donna and Kenneth Tiner of Sebring, FL; one daughter-in-law, Gwendolyn Conyers of Mount Pleasant, AR; one sister and brother-in-law, Dorma and Jim Lamb of Union, MO; seven grandchildren: Ronnie Conyers (Teresa), Steve Conyers, Mike Conyers (Janice), Madelyn Milligan (Steve), Darren Dean (Julie), Tracy Jansen (Patrick), Kim Tiner, and one granddaughter-in-law, Pattie Conyers; sixteen great-grandchildren; and twelve great-great grandchildren, and many special nieces, nephews, and cousins.
Pallbearers are Paul Bray, J. T. Evans, Harold Crafton, Barry Bray, Ronnie Bray, and Curtis Mynatt. Honorary pallbearers are members of Barren Fork Cumberland Presbyterian Church.
The funeral will be at 2:00 p.m. Friday at the Barren Fork Cumberland Presbyterian Church with Mike Conyers and Steve Shauf officiating. Burial will follow at the Barren Fork Cemetery in Mount Pleasant under the direction of Roller-Crouch Funeral Home of Melbourne.
Visitation will be from 5:00 to 7:00 p.m Thursday at the funeral home.

Beulah Irene Conyers

Birth: Feb. 18,1917
Izard County
Arkansas, USA
Death: Dec. 17,2012
The funeral will be at 2:00 p.m. Friday at the Barren Fork Cumberland Presbyterian Church with Mike Conyers and Steve Shauf officiating.
Burial will follow at the Barren Fork Cemetery in Mount Pleasant under the direction of Roller-Crouch Funeral Home of Melbourne.
Visitation will be from 5:00 to 7:00 p.m Thursday at the funeral home.

Family links:
 Parents:
  Charles Ewing Conyers (1894 - 1926)
  Euna Blanche McSpadden Conyers (1894 - 1971)
  Spouse:
  Ray Conyers (1911- 1996)*
  Children:
  Darrell Ewing Conyers (____ - 1946)*
  Douglas Ray Conyers (1937 - 1998)*

Burial:
Barren Fork Cemetery
Mount Pleasant
Izard County
Arkansas, USA

1920 United States Federal Census
Name   Beulah J Conyers
Age   2
Birth Year   abt 1918
Birthplace   Arkansas
Home in 1920   BarrenFork, Izard, Arkansas
Race   White
Gender Female
Relation to Head of House   Daughter
Marital Status   Single
Father's Name Charlie E Conyers
Father's Birthplace   Arkansas
Mother's Name   Emma B Conyers
Mother's Birthplace   Arkansas
Occupation   None
Household Members
Name   Age
Charlie E Conyers   28
John M J Conyers   84
Emma B Conyers   25
Beulah J Conyers   2

1930 United States Federal Census
Name   Eulah I Conyers

Age in 1930   13
Birth Year   abt 1917
Gender Female
Race   White
Birthplace   Arkansas
Marital Status   Single
Relation to Head of House   Daughter
Home in 1930   Barren Fork, Izard, Arkansas
Dwelling Number   88
Family Number 88
Attended School   Yes
Able to Read and Write Yes
Father's Birthplace   Arkansas
Mother's Birthplace   Arkansas
Able to Speak English   Yes
Occupation   Farm laborer
Industry   Farm
Class of Worker Unpaid worker, member of the family
Employment   Yes
Household Members
Name   Age
Erma B Conyers   35
Eulah I Conyers   13
Donna R Conyers   9
Clyde R Conyers   23

1940 United States Federal Census
Name   Beulah Conyers
Age   23
Estimated Birth Year   abt 1917
Gender Female
Race   White
Birthplace   Arkansas
Marital Status   Married
Relation to Head of House   Wife
Home in 1940   Barren Fork, Izard, Arkansas
Inferred Residence in 1935   Barren Fork, Izard, Arkansas
Residence in 1935   Same Place Izard Arkansas
Resident on farm in 1935   Yes
Sheet Number 1B
Attended School or College   No
Highest Grade Completed   High School, 4th year
Weeks Worked in 1939 0
Income 0
Income Other Sources No
Household Members
Name   Age
Ray Conyers   28
Beulah Conyers 23
Douglas Conyers   2
Charlotte Ruth Conyers 4/12

Arkansas Marriage Index, 1933-1939
Name   Beulah Conyers
Gender Female

County Independence
Spouse Ray Conyers
License Date   23 Dec 1935
Certificate Number   11069
Volume Number   0001
Household Members
Name   Age
Ray Conyers
Beulah Conyers

U.S., Social Security Death Index, 1935-2014
Name   Beulah I Conyers
Born   18 Feb 1917
Died   17 Dec 2012
State (Year) SSN issued Arkansas- Before 1951

sources:

From the Loess Hills of Iowa with the Descendants of Dennis Conyers
By Terri Napoli, Arden Iva Sleadd
Pages 165 - 176

Truman Ray Conyers and Beulah Irene Conyers had the following child:

CONYERS:Douglas Ray (b. 1937) +33   i.   **Douglas Ray Conyers**, born 6 Sep 1937, Izard Co., Arkansas, United
StatesUnited States:Arkansas:Izard Co. ; married Gwendolyn Laverne Melton, 21 Jun 1958, Cumberland
Presbyterian Church, Calico Rock, ArkansasArkansas:Calico Rock:Cumberland Presbyterian Church ;
died 10 Aug 1998, Mt Pleasant, Izard, Arkansas, United StatesUnited States:Arkansas:Izard:Mt Pleasant .

32. CONYERS:Beulah Irene (b. 1917) **Beulah Irene Conyers** (Charles Ewing-26, John Milton Jepha-25, Pascal Cerdic-24,
William-23, David-22, Samuel-21, Dennis-20, Henry-19, Thomas-18, Joshua-17, Christopher-16, Richard-15, Reginald-14,
Sir John-13, Sir John-12, Sir Christopher-11, Sir John-10, Robert-9, Sir John-8, Sir Roger-7, Sir John-6, Sir Humphrey-5, Sir
Geoffery-4, Roger-3, Roger-2, Roger-1) was born on 18 Feb 1917. She died on 17 Dec 2012 at the age of 95. Beulah Irene
Conyers, daughter of Charlie Ewing and Euna Blanche McSpadden Conyers, was born of February 18, 1917 in Mount
Pleasant, Arkansas. She departed this life on December 17, 2012 at the age of 95 years and 10 months.
She was a member of the Barren Fork Cumberland Presbyterian Church where she was an active member until the last few
years of her life.
She was preceded in death by her parents, her husband of 62 years, Truman Ray Conyers, two sons, Douglas Ray Conyers
and infant son, Darrell Ewing Conyers, two grandchildren, Kendra Leigh Tiner and David Lynn Conyers.
She spent most of her life as a wife, homemaker, and mother. She worked outside the home as a bookkeeper for the C R
Anthony Co. in Roswell, NM and the Marbax shirt factory in Melbourne, AR.
She is survived by two daughters and sons-in-law, Charlotte and Benny Dean of Mount Pleasant, AR and Donna and
Kenneth Tiner of Sebring, FL; one daughter-in-law, Gwendolyn Conyers of Mount Pleasant, AR; one sister and brother-in-
law, Dorma and Jim Lamb of Union, MO; seven grandchildren: Ronnie Conyers (Teresa), Steve Conyers, Mike Conyers
(Janice), Madelyn Milligan (Steve), Darren Dean (Julie), Tracy Jansen (Patrick), Kim Tiner, and one granddaughter-in-law,
Pattie Conyers; sixteen great-grandchildren; and twelve great-great grandchildren, and many special nieces, nephews, and
cousins.

Pallbearers are Paul Bray, J. T. Evans, Harold Crafton, Barry Bray, Ronnie Bray, and Curtis Mynatt. Honorary pallbearers are members of Barren Fork Cumberland Presbyterian Church.

The funeral will be at 2:00 p.m. Friday at the Barren Fork Cumberland Presbyterian Church with Mike Conyers and Steve Shauf officiating. Burial will follow at the Barren Fork Cemetery in Mount Pleasant under the direction of Roller-Crouch Funeral Home of Melbourne.

Visitation will be from 5:00 to 7:00 p.m Thursday at the funeral home.

Beulah Irene Conyers

Birth: Feb. 18,1917
Izard County
Arkansas, USA
Death: Dec. 17,2012
The funeral will be at 2:00 p.m. Friday at the Barren Fork Cumberland Presbyterian Church with Mike Conyers and Steve Shauf officiating.
Burial will follow at the Barren Fork Cemetery in Mount Pleasant under the direction of Roller-Crouch Funeral Home of Melbourne.
Visitation will be from 5:00 to 7:00 p.m Thursday at the funeral home.

Family links:
 Parents:
  Charles Ewing Conyers (1894 - 1926)
  Euna Blanche McSpadden Conyers (1894 - 1971)
  Spouse:
  Ray Conyers (1911- 1996)*
  Children:
  Darrell Ewing Conyers (____ - 1946)*
  Douglas Ray Conyers (1937 - 1998)*

Burial:
Barren Fork Cemetery
Mount Pleasant
Izard County
Arkansas, USA

1920 United States Federal Census
Name   Beulah J Conyers
Age   2
Birth Year   abt 1918
Birthplace   Arkansas
Home in 1920   BarrenFork, Izard, Arkansas
Race   White
Gender Female
Relation to Head of House   Daughter
Marital Status   Single
Father's Name Charlie E Conyers
Father's Birthplace   Arkansas
Mother's Name   Emma B Conyers
Mother's Birthplace   Arkansas
Occupation   None
Household Members
Name   Age
Charlie E Conyers   28

John M J Conyers   84
Emma B Conyers   25
Beulah J Conyers   2

1930 United States Federal Census
Name   Eulah I Conyers
Age in 1930   13
Birth Year   abt 1917
Gender Female
Race   White
Birthplace   Arkansas
Marital Status   Single
Relation to Head of House   Daughter
Home in 1930   Barren Fork, Izard, Arkansas
Dwelling Number   88
Family Number 88
Attended School   Yes
Able to Read and Write Yes
Father's Birthplace   Arkansas
Mother's Birthplace   Arkansas
Able to Speak English   Yes
Occupation   Farm laborer
Industry   Farm
Class of Worker Unpaid worker, member of the family
Employment   Yes
Household Members
Name   Age
Erma B Conyers   35
Eulah I Conyers   13
Donna R Conyers   9
Clyde R Conyers   23

1940 United States Federal Census
Name   Beulah Conyers
Age   23
Estimated Birth Year   abt 1917
Gender Female
Race   White
Birthplace   Arkansas
Marital Status   Married
Relation to Head of House   Wife
Home in 1940   Barren Fork, Izard, Arkansas
Inferred Residence in 1935   Barren Fork, Izard, Arkansas
Residence in 1935   Same Place Izard Arkansas
Resident on farm in 1935   Yes
Sheet Number 1B
Attended School or College   No
Highest Grade Completed   High School, 4th year
Weeks Worked in 1939 0
Income 0
Income Other Sources   No
Household Members
Name   Age
Ray Conyers   28
Beulah Conyers 23

Douglas Conyers   2
Charlotte Ruth Conyers 4/12

Arkansas Marriage Index, 1933-1939
Name   Beulah Conyers
Gender Female
County Independence
Spouse Ray Conyers
License Date   23 Dec 1935
Certificate Number   11069
Volume Number   0001
Household Members
Name   Age
Ray Conyers
Beulah Conyers

U.S., Social Security Death Index, 1935-2014
Name   Beulah I Conyers
Born   18 Feb 1917
Died   17 Dec 2012
State (Year) SSN issued Arkansas- Before 1951

sources:

From the Loess Hills of Iowa with the Descendants of Dennis Conyers
By Terri Napoli, Arden Iva Sleadd
Pages 165 - 176

CONYERS:Robert (b. 1885)
SHAW:Margarite Estella (b. 1887) CONYERS:Truman Ray (b. 1911) **Truman Ray Conyers**, son of Robert Conyers and Margarite Estella Shaw, was born on 2 Oct 1911. He died on 16 Dec 1996 at the age of 85. sources:

Ray Conyers
Birth: Oct. 2,1911
Death: Dec. 16,1996

Family links:
 Spouse:
  Beulah Irene Conyers (1917 - 2012)

 Children:
  Darrell Ewing Conyers (____ - 1946)*
  Douglas Ray Conyers (1937 - 1998)*
 Burial:
Barren Fork Cemetery
Mount Pleasant
Izard County
Arkansas, USA

http://www.findagrave.com/cgi-bin/fg.cgi?page=gr&GRid=70044538

1920 United States Federal Census
Name   Ray T Conyers
Age   8
Birth Year   abt 1912
Birthplace   Arkansas
Home in 1920   Johnson,Sharp, Arkansas
Race   White
Gender Male
Relation to Head of House   Son
Marital Status   Single
Father's Name Robert F Conyers
Father's Birthplace   Arkansas
Mother's Name   Margarette E Conyers
Mother's Birthplace   Arkansas
Occupation   None
Attended School   Yes
Household Members
Name   Age
Robert F Conyers   34
Margarette E Conyers   32
Ray T Conyers 8
Edwin F Conyers   6
Nola E Conyers 4
Melba C Conyers   0

1930 United States Federal Census
Name   Ray Conyers
Age in 1930   18
Birth Year   abt 1912
Gender Male
Race   White
Birthplace   Arkansas
Marital Status   Single
Relation to Head of House   Son
Home in 1930   Johnson, Sharp, Arkansas
House Number in Cities or Towns   Apr 5
Dwelling Number   16
Family Number 16
Attended School   Yes
Able to Read and Write Yes
Father's Birthplace   Arkansas
Mother's Birthplace   Arkansas
Able to Speak English   Yes
Occupation   NP
Class of Worker Unpaid worker, member of the family
Employment   Yes
Household Members
Name   Age
Robert F Conyers   48
Stella Conyers 42
Ray Conyers   18
Edwin Conyers 16
Nala Conyers   14
Melba Conyers 10

Veona Conyers 10
Porter Conyers 4

1940 United States Federal Census
Name   Ray Conyers
Respondent   Yes
Age   28
Estimated Birth Year   abt 1912
Gender Male
Race   White
Birthplace   Arkansas
Marital Status   Married
Relation to Head of House   Head
Home in 1940   Barren Fork, Izard, Arkansas
Farm   Yes
Inferred Residence in 1935   Barren Fork, Izard, Arkansas
Residence in 1935   Same House
Sheet Number 1B
Number of Household in Order of Visitation   16
Occupation   Farmer
House Owned or Rented   Rented
Value of Home or Monthly Rental if Rented   5
Attended School or College   No
Highest Grade Completed   Elementary school, 8th grade
Hours Worked Week Prior to Census   48
Class of Worker Working on own account
Weeks Worked in 1939 52
Income 0
Income Other Sources   Yes
Household Members
Name   Age
Ray Conyers   28
Beulah Conyers 23
Douglas Conyers   2
Charlotte Ruth Conyers 4/12

Arkansas Marriage Index, 1933-1939
Name   Ray Conyers
Gender Male
County Independence
Spouse Beulah Conyers
License Date   23 Dec 1935
Certificate Number   11069
Volume Number   0001
Household Members
Name   Age
Ray Conyers
Beulah Conyers

U.S., Social Security Death Index, 1935-2014
Name   T. R.Conyers
SSN   429-14-0190
Born   2 Oct 1911
Died   16 Dec 1996

State (Year) SSN issued Arkansas- Before 1951

Truman Ray Conyers and Beulah Irene Conyers had the following child:

CONYERS:Douglas Ray (b. 1937) +33   i.   **Douglas Ray Conyers**, born 6 Sep 1937, Izard Co., Arkansas, United StatesUnited States:Arkansas:Izard Co. ; married Gwendolyn Laverne Melton, 21 Jun 1958, Cumberland Presbyterian Church, Calico Rock, ArkansasArkansas:Calico Rock:Cumberland Presbyterian Church ; died 10 Aug 1998, Mt Pleasant, Izard, Arkansas, United StatesUnited States:Arkansas:Izard:Mt Pleasant .

28th Generation

33. CONYERS:Douglas Ray (b. 1937) United States:Arkansas:Izard Co. **Douglas Ray Conyers** (Truman Ray-27, Robert-26, William Zachariah-25, James Monroe-24, James Mordecai-23, David-22, Samuel-21, Dennis-20, Henry-19, Thomas-18, Joshua-17, Christopher-16, Richard-15, Reginald-14, Sir John-13, Sir John-12, Sir Christopher-11, Sir John-10, Robert-9, Sir John-8, Sir Roger-7, Sir John-6, Sir Humphrey-5, Sir Geoffery-4, Roger-3, Roger-2, Roger-1) was born on 6 Sep 1937 in Izard Co., Arkansas, United States.United States:Arkansas:Izard:Mt Pleasant He died on 10 Aug 1998 at the age of 60 in Mt Pleasant, Izard, Arkansas, United States. sources:

U.S., Social Security Death Index, 1935-2014

Name **Douglas R. Conyers**
SSN **430-64-1830**
Born **6 Sep 1937**
Died **10 Aug 1998**
State (Year) SSN issued **Arkansas - 1953**

1940 United States Federal Census
Name **Douglas Conyers**

Age **2**
Estimated Birth Year **abt 1938**
Gender **Male**
Race **White**
Birthplace **Arkansas**
Marital Status **Single**
Relation to Head of House **Son**
Home in 1940 **Barren Fork, Izard, Arkansas**
Sheet Number **1B**
Attended School or College **No**
Highest Grade Completed **None**
Household Members Name Age
Ray Conyers 28
Beulah Conyers 23
Douglas Conyers 2
Charlotte Ruth Conyers 4/12

U.S., Department of Veterans Affairs BIRLS Death File, 1850-2010
Name **Douglas Conyers**
Gender **Male**
Birth Date **6 Sep 1937**
Death Date **10 Aug 1998**

Cause of Death **Natural**
SSN **430641830**
Branch 1 **A**
Enlistment Date 1 **5 Mar 1956**
Release Date 1 **21 Aug 1958**
Branch 2 **ARMY**
Enlistment Date 2 **1 Dec 1965**
Release Date 2 **31 Mar 1976**

Douglas Ray Conyers
Birth: Sep. 6,1937
Death: Aug. 10,1998
Husband of Gwen (Melton) Conyers
 Family links:
 Parents:
  Ray Conyers (1911- 1996)
  Beulah Irene Conyers (1917 - 2012)
 Sibling:
  Darrell Ewing Conyers (____ - 1946)*
  Douglas Ray Conyers (1937 - 1998)

Burial:
Barren Fork Cemetery
Mount Pleasant
Izard County
Arkansas, USA

http://www.findagrave.com/cgi-
bin/fg.cgi?page=gr&GSln=CON&GSpartial=1&GSbyrel=all&GSst=4&GScntry=4&GSsr=3081&GRid=70044310&

Arkansas:Calico Rock:Cumberland Presbyterian Church
Douglas Ray Conyers and Gwendolyn Laverne Melton were married on 21 Jun 1958 in Cumberland Presbyterian Church,
Calico Rock, Arkansas.MELTON:Gwendolyn Laverne (b. 1940) **Gwendolyn Laverne Melton** was born on 9 May 1940.

Douglas Ray Conyers and Gwendolyn Laverne Melton had the following children:

CONYERS:Ronald Douglas (b. 1959)   +34   i.   **Ronald Douglas Conyers**, born 2 Aug 1959; married Teresa
                 LaRae Brooks, 12 Mar 1982.
CONYERS:Madelyn (b. 1961)   +35   ii.   **Madelyn Conyers**, born 11 Jan 1961.
CONYERS:David Lynn (b. 1963) +36   iii.   **David Lynn Conyers**, born 12 Jan 1963, Calico Rock, Izard,
                 Arkansas, United StatesUnited States:Arkansas:Izard:Calico Rock ; married Patty Burgess, 28 Oct 1983;
                 died 27 Jun 2009, Calico Rock, Izard, Arkansas, United StatesUnited States:Arkansas:Izard:Calico Rock .
CONYERS:Steven (b. 1968)   +37   iv.   **Steven Conyers**, born 12 Apr 1968; married Debbie Phipps.
CONYERS:Michael (b. 1970)   +38   v.   **Michael Conyers**, born 16 Sep 1970; married Janice Mitchell.

29th Generation

34. CONYERS:Ronald Douglas (b. 1959) **Ronald Douglas Conyers** (Douglas Ray-28, Truman Ray-27, Robert-26, William Zachariah-25, James Monroe-24, James Mordecai-23, David-22, Samuel-21, Dennis-20, Henry-19, Thomas-18, Joshua-17, Christopher-16, Richard-15, Reginald-14, Sir John-13, Sir John-12, Sir Christopher-11, Sir John-10, Robert-9, Sir John-8, Sir Roger-7, Sir John-6, Sir Humphrey-5, Sir Geoffery-4, Roger-3, Roger-2, Roger-1) was born on 2 Aug 1959.
BROOKS:Teresa LaRae (b. 1964)
Teresa LaRae Brooks was born on 19 Jan 1964.

Ronald Douglas Conyers and Teresa LaRae Brooks had the following children:

CONYERS:Ronicia LaRae (b. 1982)   +39   i.   **Ronicia LaRae Conyers**, born 2 Oct 1982; married Christopher Lee Smith, 15 Jul 2006.
CONYERS:Ryan Douglas (b. 1985)   +40   ii.   **Ryan Douglas Conyers**, born 27 Mar 1985; married Kendra Isreal.

Ronald Douglas Conyers and Teresa LaRae Brooks were married on 12 Mar 1982.BROOKS:Teresa LaRae (b. 1964) **Teresa LaRae Brooks** was born on 19 Jan 1964.

35. CONYERS:Madelyn (b. 1961) **Madelyn Conyers** (Douglas Ray-28, Truman Ray-27, Robert-26, William Zachariah-25, James Monroe-24, James Mordecai-23, David-22, Samuel-21, Dennis-20, Henry-19, Thomas-18, Joshua-17, Christopher-16, Richard-15, Reginald-14, Sir John-13, Sir John-12, Sir Christopher-11, Sir John-10, Robert-9, Sir John-8, Sir Roger-7, Sir John-6, Sir Humphrey-5, Sir Geoffery-4, Roger-3, Roger-2, Roger-1) was born on 11 Jan 1961.

Madelyn Conyers was married.

Madelyn Conyers had the following children:

PICKREN:Sarah (b. 1985)   +41   i.   **Sarah Pickren**, born 14 Oct 1985.
CONYER:Cori (b. 1987) +42   ii.   **Cori Conyer**, born 12 Apr 1987; married Robby Perkey.

36. CONYERS:David Lynn (b. 1963) United States:Arkansas:Izard:Calico Rock **David Lynn Conyers** (Douglas Ray-28, Truman Ray-27, Robert-26, William Zachariah-25, James Monroe-24, James Mordecai-23, David-22, Samuel-21, Dennis-20, Henry-19, Thomas-18, Joshua-17, Christopher-16, Richard-15, Reginald-14, Sir John-13, Sir John-12, Sir Christopher-11, Sir John-10, Robert-9, Sir John-8, Sir Roger-7, Sir John-6, Sir Humphrey-5, Sir Geoffery-4, Roger-3, Roger-2, Roger-1) was born on 12 Jan 1963 in Calico Rock, Izard, Arkansas, United States.United States:Arkansas:Izard:Calico Rock He died on 27 Jun 2009 at the age of 46 in Calico Rock, Izard, Arkansas, United States. **David Lynn CONYERS**
Roselawn (at Calico Rock) Cemetery

Izard County, Arkansas

Born January 12, 1963, Calico Rock, Izard County, Arkansas.
Died June 27, 2009, Calico Rock, Izard County, Arkansas.
Son of Douglas Ray Conyers & Gwendolyn L. Melton Conyers.
Married Patricia Burgess, October 28, 1983, Gid, Izard County, Arkansas.

David Lynn Conyers and Patty Burgess were married on 28 Oct 1983.BURGESS:Patty (b. 1964) **Patty Burgess** was born on 10 Oct 1964.

David Lynn Conyers and Patty Burgess had the following children:

CONYERS:Daniel (b. 1987)	43	i.	**Daniel Conyers** was born on 11 Jun 1987.
CONYERS:Adam Clayton (b. 1989)	+44	ii.	**Adam Clayton Conyers**, born 8 Apr 1989.
CONYERS:Jessie (b. 1990)	+45	iii.	**Jessie Conyers**, born 28 Dec 1990; married Devin Hicks, 23 Apr 2011.

37. CONYERS:Steven (b. 1968) **Steven Conyers** (Douglas Ray-28, Truman Ray-27, Robert-26, William Zachariah-25, James Monroe-24, James Mordecai-23, David-22, Samuel-21, Dennis-20, Henry-19, Thomas-18, Joshua-17, Christopher-16, Richard-15, Reginald-14, Sir John-13, Sir John-12, Sir Christopher-11, Sir John-10, Robert-9, Sir John-8, Sir Roger-7, Sir John-6, Sir Humphrey-5, Sir Geoffery-4, Roger-3, Roger-2, Roger-1) was born on 12 Apr 1968.

Steven Conyers and Debbie Phipps were married.PHIPPS:Debbie (b. 1965) **Debbie Phipps** was born on 3 Dec 1965.

Steven Conyers and Debbie Phipps had the following children:

CONYERS:Justin (b. 1986)	+46	i.	**Justin Conyers**, born 31 Aug 1986; married Cassey Rozyle.
CONYERS:Haley Nicole (b. 1987)	+47	ii.	**Haley Nicole Conyers**, born 7 Dec 1987; married Jason Derrick McCandlis, 11 Sep 2006.
CONYERS:Kasey (b. 1989)	+48	iii.	**Kasey Conyers**, born 17 Jun 1989; married Neil Campbell, 27 May 2012.
CONYERS:Brady (b. 1990)	49	iv.	**Brady Conyers** was born on 26 Apr 1990.

38. CONYERS:Michael (b. 1970) **Michael Conyers** (Douglas Ray-28, Truman Ray-27, Robert-26, William Zachariah-25, James Monroe-24, James Mordecai-23, David-22, Samuel-21, Dennis-20, Henry-19, Thomas-18, Joshua-17, Christopher-16, Richard-15, Reginald-14, Sir John-13, Sir John-12, Sir Christopher-11, Sir John-10, Robert-9, Sir John-8, Sir Roger-7, Sir John-6, Sir Humphrey-5, Sir Geoffery-4, Roger-3, Roger-2, Roger-1) was born on 16 Sep 1970.

Michael Conyers and Janice Mitchell were married.MITCHELL:Janice (b. 1970) **Janice Mitchell** was born on 1 Aug 1970.

Michael Conyers and Janice Mitchell had the following children:

CONYERS:Blake (b. 1992)	+50	i.	**Blake Conyers**, born 30 Sep 1992; married Tera Goodman, 10 Oct 2014.
CONYERS:Hannah (b. 1995)	51	ii.	**Hannah Conyers** was born on 19 Dec 1995.

30th Generation

39. CONYERS:Ronicia LaRae (b. 1982) **Ronicia LaRae Conyers** (Ronald Douglas-29, Douglas Ray-28, Truman Ray-27, Robert-26, William Zachariah-25, James Monroe-24, James Mordecai-23, David-22, Samuel-21, Dennis-20, Henry-19, Thomas-18, Joshua-17, Christopher-16, Richard-15, Reginald-14, Sir John-13, Sir John-12, Sir Christopher-11, Sir John-10, Robert-9, Sir John-8, Sir Roger-7, Sir John-6, Sir Humphrey-5, Sir Geoffery-4, Roger-3, Roger-2, Roger-1) was born on 2 Oct 1982.

1. William I of England
2. Henry I of England
3. Empress Matilda
4. Henry II of England
5. John of England
6. Henry III of England
7. Edward I of England
8. Edward II of England
9. Edward III of England

10. Lionel of Antwerp, 1st Duke of Clarence	10. Sir John "of Gaunt" Plantagenet
11. Philippa Plantagenet, 5th Countess of Ulster	11. Joan Beaufort
12. Roger de Mortimer, 4th Earl of March	12. Sir William Neville
13. Anne de Mortimer	13. Alice Neville
14. Richard Plantagenet, 3rd Duke of York	14. Reginald Conyers I
15. Edward IV of England	15. Richard Conyers I
16. Elizabeth of York	16. Christopher Conyers II
17. Margaret Tudor	17. Joshua Conyers I
18. James V of Scotland	18. Thomas Conyers I
19. Mary, Queen of Scots'	19. Henry Conyers
20. James VI of Scotland and I of England	20. Dennis Conyers
21. Elizabeth of Bohemia	21. Samuel Conyers
22. Sophia of Hanover	22. David Conyers
23. George I of Great Britain	23. James Mordecai Conyers
24. George II of Great Britain	24. James Monroe Conyers
25. Frederick, Prince of Wales	25. William Zachariah Conyers
26. George III of the United Kingdom	26. Robert Conyers
27. Prince Edward, Duke of Kent and Strathearn	27. Truman Ray Conyers
28. Victoria of the United Kingdom	28. Douglas Ray Conyers
29. Edward VII of the United Kingdom	29. Ronald Douglas Conyers
30. George V of the United Kingdom	30. Ronicia LaRae Conyers
31. George VI of the United Kingdom	
32. Elizabeth II of the United Kingdom	

Ronicia Larue Conyers & Queen Elizabeth II are 20th cousins, 2 times removed.

Ronicia LaRae Conyers and Christopher Lee Smith were married on 15 Jul 2006.SMITH:Christopher Lee (b. 1968) **Christopher Lee Smith** was born on 22 Jun 1968.

Christopher Lee Smith and Ronicia LaRae Conyers had the following child:

SMITH:Caris Leigh (b. 2006)   52   i.   **Caris Leigh Smith** was born on 17 Jul 2006.

40. CONYERS:Ryan Douglas (b. 1985) **Ryan Douglas Conyers** (Ronald Douglas-29, Douglas Ray-28, Truman Ray-27, Robert-26, William Zachariah-25, James Monroe-24, James Mordecai-23, David-22, Samuel-21, Dennis-20, Henry-19, Thomas-18, Joshua-17, Christopher-16, Richard-15, Reginald-14, Sir John-13, Sir John-12, Sir Christopher-11, Sir John-10, Robert-9, Sir John-8, Sir Roger-7, Sir John-6, Sir Humphrey-5, Sir Geoffery-4, Roger-3, Roger-2, Roger-1) was born on 27 Mar 1985.

Ryan Douglas Conyers and Kendra Isreal were married.ISREAL:Kendra (b. 1987) **Kendra Isreal** was born on 28 May 1987.

Ryan Douglas Conyers and Kendra Isreal had the following child:

CONYERS:Karson Douglas (b. 2014)   53   i.   **Karson Douglas Conyers** was born on 22 Oct 2014.

41. PICKREN:Sarah (b. 1985) **Sarah Pickren** (Madelyn Conyers-29, Douglas Ray-28, Truman Ray-27, Robert-26, William Zachariah-25, James Monroe-24, James Mordecai-23, David-22, Samuel-21, Dennis-20, Henry-19, Thomas-18, Joshua-17, Christopher-16, Richard-15, Reginald-14, Sir John-13, Sir John-12, Sir Christopher-11, Sir John-10, Robert-9, Sir John-8, Sir Roger-7, Sir John-6, Sir Humphrey-5, Sir Geoffery-4, Roger-3, Roger-2, Roger-1) was born on 14 Oct 1985.

Sarah Pickren was married.

Sarah Pickren had the following children:

PICKREN:Jaxon (b. 2006)   54   i.   **Jaxon Pickren** was born on 21 Nov 2006.
PICKREN:Lauren Claire (b. 2011) 55   ii.   **Lauren Claire Pickren** was born on 7 Sep 2011.

42. CONYER:Cori (b. 1987) **Cori Conyer** (Madelyn Conyers-29, Douglas Ray-28, Truman Ray-27, Robert-26, William Zachariah-25, James Monroe-24, James Mordecai-23, David-22, Samuel-21, Dennis-20, Henry-19, Thomas-18, Joshua-17, Christopher-16, Richard-15, Reginald-14, Sir John-13, Sir John-12, Sir Christopher-11, Sir John-10, Robert-9, Sir John-8, Sir Roger-7, Sir John-6, Sir Humphrey-5, Sir Geoffery-4, Roger-3, Roger-2, Roger-1) was born on 12 Apr 1987.

Cori Conyer and Robby Perkey were married on 23 Jun 2007. They were married.PERKEY:Robby (b. 1984) **Robby Perkey** was born on 31 Oct 1984.

Robby Perkey and Cori Conyer had the following children:

PERKEY:Andrew (b. 2008)   56   i.   **Andrew Perkey** was born on 1 Jan 2008.
PERKEY:Alley Mae (b. 2011)   57   ii.   **Alley Mae Perkey** was born on 10 Aug 2011.

44. CONYERS:Adam Clayton (b. 1989) **Adam Clayton Conyers** (David Lynn-29, Douglas Ray-28, Truman Ray-27, Robert-26, William Zachariah-25, James Monroe-24, James Mordecai-23, David-22, Samuel-21, Dennis-20, Henry-19, Thomas-18, Joshua-17, Christopher-16, Richard-15, Reginald-14, Sir John-13, Sir John-12, Sir Christopher-11, Sir John-10, Robert-9, Sir John-8, Sir Roger-7, Sir John-6, Sir Humphrey-5, Sir Geoffery-4, Roger-3, Roger-2, Roger-1) was born on 8 Apr 1989.

Adam Clayton Conyers was married.

Adam Clayton Conyers had the following child:

CONYERS:Hayden (b. 2011)   58   i.   **Hayden Conyers** was born on 13 Sep 2011.

45. CONYERS:Jessie (b. 1990) **Jessie Conyers** (David Lynn-29, Douglas Ray-28, Truman Ray-27, Robert-26, William Zachariah-25, James Monroe-24, James Mordecai-23, David-22, Samuel-21, Dennis-20, Henry-19, Thomas-18, Joshua-17, Christopher-16, Richard-15, Reginald-14, Sir John-13, Sir John-12, Sir Christopher-11, Sir John-10, Robert-9, Sir John-8, Sir Roger-7, Sir John-6, Sir Humphrey-5, Sir Geoffery-4, Roger-3, Roger-2, Roger-1) was born on 28 Dec 1990.

Jessie Conyers and Devin Hicks were married on 23 Apr 2011.HICKS:Devin (b. 1984) **Devin Hicks** was born on 30 Jan 1984.

Devin Hicks and Jessie Conyers had the following children:

HICKS:Gracie Ann (b. 2010)	59	i.	**Gracie Ann Hicks** was born on 13 Sep 2010.
HICKS:Jase David - Michael (b. 2014)	60	ii.	**Jase David - Michael Hicks** was born on 20 Feb 2014.

46. CONYERS:Justin (b. 1986) **Justin Conyers** (Steven-29, Douglas Ray-28, Truman Ray-27, Robert-26, William Zachariah-25, James Monroe-24, James Mordecai-23, David-22, Samuel-21, Dennis-20, Henry-19, Thomas-18, Joshua-17, Christopher-16, Richard-15, Reginald-14, Sir John-13, Sir John-12, Sir Christopher-11, Sir John-10, Robert-9, Sir John-8, Sir Roger-7, Sir John-6, Sir Humphrey-5, Sir Geoffery-4, Roger-3, Roger-2, Roger-1) was born on 31 Aug 1986.

Justin Conyers and Cassey Rozyle were married on 13 May 2010. They were married.ROZYLE:Cassey (b. 1990) **Cassey Rozyle** was born on 13 Mar 1990.

Justin Conyers and Cassey Rozyle had the following children:

CONYERS:Nathan (b. 2010)	61	i.	**Nathan Conyers** was born on 31 Jul 2010.
CONYERS:Waylon (b. 2011)	62	ii.	**Waylon Conyers** was born on 24 Jul 2011.
CONYERS:Keaton (b. 2013)	63	iii.	**Keaton Conyers** was born on 28 Jun 2013.
CONYERS:Keeley (b. 2015)	64	iv.	**Keeley Conyers** was born on 28 May 2015.

47. CONYERS:Haley Nicole (b. 1987) **Haley Nicole Conyers** (Steven-29, Douglas Ray-28, Truman Ray-27, Robert-26, William Zachariah-25, James Monroe-24, James Mordecai-23, David-22, Samuel-21, Dennis-20, Henry-19, Thomas-18, Joshua-17, Christopher-16, Richard-15, Reginald-14, Sir John-13, Sir John-12, Sir Christopher-11, Sir John-10, Robert-9, Sir John-8, Sir Roger-7, Sir John-6, Sir Humphrey-5, Sir Geoffery-4, Roger-3, Roger-2, Roger-1) was born on 7 Dec 1987.

Haley Nicole Conyers and Jason Derrick McCandlis were married on 11 Sep 2006.MCCANDLIS:Jason Derrick (b. 1985) **Jason Derrick McCandlis** was born on 21 Jun 1985.

Jason Derrick McCandlis and Haley Nicole Conyers had the following children:

MCCANDLIS:Michael Alexander (b. 2006)	65	i.	**Michael Alexander McCandlis** was born on 9 Oct 2006.
MCCANDLIS:Steven Braxton (b. 2008)	66	ii.	**Steven Braxton McCandlis** was born on 22 Oct 2008.
MCCANDLIS:Ella Danielle (b. 2013)	67	iii.	**Ella Danielle McCandlis** was born on 18 Apr 2013.

48. CONYERS:Kasey (b. 1989) **Kasey Conyers** (Steven-29, Douglas Ray-28, Truman Ray-27, Robert-26, William Zachariah-25, James Monroe-24, James Mordecai-23, David-22, Samuel-21, Dennis-20, Henry-19, Thomas-18, Joshua-17, Christopher-16, Richard-15, Reginald-14, Sir John-13, Sir John-12, Sir Christopher-11, Sir John-10, Robert-9, Sir John-8, Sir Roger-7, Sir John-6, Sir Humphrey-5, Sir Geoffery-4, Roger-3, Roger-2, Roger-1) was born on 17 Jun 1989.

Kasey Conyers and Neil Campbell were married on 27 May 2012.CAMPBELL:Neil (b. 1988) **Neil Campbell** was born on 2 Jun 1988.

Neil Campbell and Kasey Conyers had the following children:

CAMPBELL:Nash (b. 2012)	68	i.	**Nash Campbell** was born on 19 Nov 2012.
CAMPBELL:Barrett (b. 2015)	69	ii.	**Barrett Campbell** was born on 23 Feb 2015.

50. CONYERS:Blake (b. 1992) **Blake Conyers** (Michael-29, Douglas Ray-28, Truman Ray-27, Robert-26, William Zachariah-25, James Monroe-24, James Mordecai-23, David-22, Samuel-21, Dennis-20, Henry-19, Thomas-18, Joshua-17, Christopher-16, Richard-15, Reginald-14, Sir John-13, Sir John-12, Sir Christopher-11, Sir John-10, Robert-9, Sir John-8, Sir Roger-7, Sir John-6, Sir Humphrey-5, Sir Geoffery-4, Roger-3, Roger-2, Roger-1) was born on 30 Sep 1992.

Blake Conyers and Tera Goodman were married on 10 Oct 2014.GOODMAN:Tera (b. 1993) **Tera Goodman** was born on 13 Sep 1993.

Blake Conyers and Tera Goodman had the following child:

CONYERS:Haddie (b. 2015)	70	i.	**Haddie Conyers** was born on 12 Apr 2015.

Preparer:

Printed in Great Britain
by Amazon